Music,
Lakes
&
Blue
Corduroy

Cindy Housh Glovinsky

THUNDER BAY
P R E S S

Music, Lakes & Blue Corduroy
by Cindy Housh Glovinsky

Copyright © 2021 Cindy Housh Glovinsky

Published March 2021
Thunder Bay Press
West Branch, Michigan 48661

All photos, except those attributed to the author, are under Photo copyright ARTICA - Archives of the Interlochen Center for the Arts - and are used by their permission.

Grateful acknowledgment is made to the following for permission to reprint previously published material:

Baker Publishing Group: "Prayer of a Camper" from *The New Hymnal for American Youth* by H. Augustine Smith, copyright © 1930 Fleming H. Revell Company. Reprinted by permission of Baker Publishing Group.

SOUND THE CALL (INTERLOCHEN BOWL MARCH)
Music by Edwin Franko Goldman
Words by T. Henry Francis
Copyright © 1934 (Renewed) by G. Schirmer, Inc.
International Copyright Secured. All Rights Reserved.
Reprinted by Permission

Cover Design: Diane Kolak, Page 9 Design

ISBN 13: 978-1-933-27268-9

Printed in the United States of America

To Joseph E. Maddy, Thor Johnson, and all the Interlochen faculty, staff, and trustees who helped to make a bunch of struggling Sixties teenagers into loving, giving artists

Contents

Note to the Reader: This memoir covers a period of over two years, from June 1964 through August 1966, during which, both summer and winter, I was a student and camper at what is now called the Interlochen Center for the Arts. It also extends back to my years on the road to Interlochen and forward to my many returns, both mental and physical, to a place around which I have somehow always felt my whole life's story revolved.

The act of remembering is not the same as constructing a history. There is, to be sure, a historical aspect. But, as we all know, memory tends to distort, and in a memoir, one's duty to create a readable narrative may sometimes conflict with one's duty to stick to the facts. For that reason and because of gaps I needed to fill, I can't say that every word in this book is factually true, though I can say that the important things are, and that the story, from my unique perspective, is emotionally true, which is what I think matters most. Furthermore, as I've allowed Cindy at ages eight, fifteen, thirty-five, or whatever, to tell her story in her own voice, I've sometimes used pre-PC language that I would not think of using in the twenty-first century and say things I wouldn't dream of saying now. Furthermore, Joseph E. Maddy, Thor Johnson, and other major "characters" in my story are not presented as I necessarily see them now, nor as my classmates may remember them, but only as Cindy Housh the teenager experienced them, neither as idealized saints nor as historical phenomena but as sometimes difficult but ultimately lovable human beings.

One issue over which I agonized was whether to change people's names. In the end, I compromised and changed the names of most former students but not those of faculty or staff, as Interlochen with Dr. Maddy or Van Cliburn or Thor Johnson called something else would not feel like the same place my fellow alums and I knew and loved.

Prelude

The girl is walking towards me along the road. Face blurred out, like those of anonymous speakers on a TV talk show, but clothes clearly visible: the light-blue shirt, the madras jacket, and the regulation navy blue corduroy "knickers," pants that gather and button just below the knees, relics of the 1930s. Zeroing in, I can see the light blue knee-socks slipping down the girl's calves, the penny loafers with crushed-in arches, and the soft puff of ash-blond hair religiously set on big brush rollers every night and blasted with hairspray every morning. I can see the round, navy blue Academy badge pinned to one hip, and the girl's name and hometown typed in its little window: Cynthia Housh, Des Moines, Iowa. And I can see what she carries—a blue canvas bookbag, a brown, canvas-covered violin case, and a square, black folder of orchestra music.

The girl is walking towards me along the road, silently calling me back into herself, back to Interlochen, a camp and school between two lakes in the Michigan woods, where dreamers still pinch themselves and wonder if they'll wake up back in Iowa or New Jersey, Finland or Japan, far from this magic land where they can play or sing or dance or act or paint or write to their hearts' content.

For just a little while, I want to slip back into this girl's skin. I want to see what she sees, hear what she hears, and feel what she feels. Most of all, I want to recapture her belief that she can make absolutely any dream come true if only she works hard enough. I can't do this, of course, not in my seventies, with a lifetime of efforts behind me, most of which paid off only in part or not at all. But what I can do is take out a certain old LP, settle it onto a turntable, and set the needle down at just the right spot. Then I can sit back in my wooden rocker with my cat in my lap, close my eyes, and listen. And as I sit listening, somewhere between the music and the scratches, I can make out a little girl's voice, starting to tell her story.

Part I:
The Road to Interlochen

1. The Silvery Voice

"SHALL . . . WE . . . DONCE?" dum, dum, dum. The silvery voice with the English accent soars up out of my little suitcase record player and carries me around and around the room, barefoot in my blue shorts and white sleeveless blouse. My blond pigtails bounce and flop against the sides of my head as I dance. It's early evening and still light out. Soon it will be dark and there will be lightning bugs to catch, but I don't care. All I care about is the music.

I'm eight years old and about to start fourth grade at Hanawalt School in Des Moines. I saw *The King and I* twice at the Paramount this summer, once at a matinee with Mom and another time at a double feature with Mom and Dad. It was the best movie I ever saw, so good it made me sad that I couldn't just stay in it forever instead of coming back out to plain old everyday life.

The record album from the movie cost five whole dollars at Dahl's supermarket. I had to give up three weeks of allowances and spend an hour digging dandelions before Dad felt sorry for me and let me have the rest of the money. Now the record's all mine, and I can play it as much as I want, the first long-play I ever owned.

The record is big and black and shiny, with little rings that show where each new song starts. If you set the needle down just right, you can start it on any song you want. The ring for the song I'm playing is the next-to-the-last one on Side 2. I play the song over and over. Already, I've played it so many times that even when I'm not playing it, when I'm riding my bike or playing jacks or drying the dishes while my big brother Davy washes, the music is still inside me, playing away on the record player in my head whether I want it to or not.

The song is a river of shining water that flows and flows as I fly around the room. It's the same feeling as when you race down a hill on your bike with your hair streaming out behind you or when the big swings at Riverview swoop out and carry you up towards the stars and you wish the ride would never end. I try to sing along with it as I dance, but my voice is weak and full of air, not silvery like the voice on the record, and the words come out all wrong. Finally, I stop trying to sing and just dance.

I have no idea what my feet are doing, and I don't care. All I care about is the music, flowing on until I'm the red-haired lady whirling across the golden ballroom with the bald, barefoot king, my huge lavender satin skirt billowing and bobbing.

2. Can I Take Violin?

It's Friday afternoon, the first week of school, and I take the shortcut home between Gruen's and Levage's, across the cracked squares of the patio, and onto the screened back porch of our green ranch house, letting the door slam behind me. Mom is sitting at the picnic table on the porch, snapping green beans into a pot. Even though school started the day after Labor Day, the weather is still hot, and the pile of papers in my hand is damp and wrinkly.

I lay the papers on the table in front of Mom, and she moves the pot over and looks down at them. There's a list of spelling words from Mrs. Webster's class with a big, red "OK" at the top, a permission slip for a trip to the Iowa Historical Building, and a note to parents about the PTA. And there's also a stapled letter from Mrs. Neal, the music teacher, about the instrument lessons we can sign up for at school, $1.50 a lesson.

In the letter is a list of the instruments we can take—violin, cello, flute, clarinet, trumpet, trombone, and drums. Three different teachers will come to the school on three different days—one for strings, one for woodwinds, and one for brass and percussion. I know the different instruments because Mrs. Neal drilled us on them last year in third grade, holding up big flashcards with instrument pictures. She also taught us songs out of a big yellow book called *Singing and Rhyming* and took us downtown to hear the Des Moines Symphony.

Mrs. Neal is nobody's favorite teacher. She has tight brown curls that look like she just took the curlers out, a squirmy little red mouth, and a voice that sounds all wobbly when she sings "Five Little Pumpkins Sitting on a Gate" to teach us the tune. Plus the fact that every morning after the bell rings she stands up in front of the piano and goes "Good morning, boys and girls" and we have to answer, "Good morning, Mrs. Neal." She's the only teacher at Hanawalt who does that, and I always feel a little sorry for her because I can just hear the other kids thinking how dumb it sounds. But even though Mrs. Neal teaches it, I still like music class.

"Can I take violin?" I ask Mom now as we look at the list. I like the way violins look, all carved, graceful curves, like something out of one of those *Little House* books Mom reads to me, where Laura and her sisters wear long, flowing skirts and ride in horse-drawn buggies, unlike the way it is now, which isn't half so nice.

"Well . . . maybe," she says. "Let's see what your father says." This probably means yes, but first Mom has to do what she always does, which is pick up the phone. She calls Gladys, a friend in her duplicate bridge club, because Gladys's daughter started violin lessons last year. She calls Grandma Harter, whose father used to play "Just a Song at Twilight" on his violin for her when she was little. She calls a couple of music stores to find out how much violins cost. And she calls my Aunt Martha, who tells her that my cousin Judy has an old violin we can borrow.

That night at dinner, Mom tells Dad I want to play the violin.

"That's great, Daughter," he says. "You can be like Evelyn and her magic violin." I don't know who Evelyn is, but I think it must have been somebody on the radio in the olden times before TV. The only violinists I've seen on TV are Jack Benny, who plays really bad just to be funny, and Dick Kesner on Lawrence Welk, whose violin is a Stradivarius, which Mom says is the fanciest kind of violin there is, like a Cadillac in cars.

After dinner, Mom calls Mrs. Neal and asks her all sorts of questions. Does she think I'm big enough to play the violin? Does she think I have a good enough ear? How will I be able to tune the violin when we don't have a piano? As far as I know, my ears have been fine ever since I had my tonsils out last year, so I don't know why Mom asked that. After she hangs up, she tells me I can sign up for violin if I want, as I knew she would.

"But it's not an easy instrument," she says. "You'll have to practice every day. If you're going to play the violin, you can't just *fiddle* around—ha, ha." It's not that funny, but I laugh anyway just to be nice.

The next morning, Aunt Martha shows up in her Oldsmobile 98 with my cousin Judy, who's in tenth grade at Roosevelt High. As they come up the walk, I see that Judy carries a battered brown case under one arm. She sets the case down on the davenport and opens the lid. It's lined with green felt, on which rests a yellowish violin. Judy shows me how to tighten the bow. Then she puts the violin up under her chin and plays the first part of "Twinkle, Twinkle, Little Star." It sounds kind of awful, worse than Jack Benny even, but I don't think Judy took violin very long, which must be why.

When Judy and Aunt Martha are gone, I carry the violin case into my room and set it down on the floor next to my record player and records, almost all of which I got from Judy and her sister Mary, along with most of my clothes and a whole set of Nancy Drew mysteries. Uncle Parker, their dad, is a doctor who delivers babies, and doctors make more money than the executive sports editor at the *Register and Tribune*, which is what my dad is.

Now I have a violin, but lessons won't start until week after next, after everyone has signed up. For the next few days, I open the case now and then just to remember what the violin looks like. At first, I'm afraid to touch it, but after a few days I start taking it out and trying different ways of holding it. By Saturday I've started strumming the violin like a guitar even though I know that's not really how you play it.

I've also figured out that you tune the strings by turning the little black pegs in both sides of the scroll-thing, which looks like a little piece of rolled-up paper. I remember how in music class Mrs. Neal taught us to sing 1-3-5-8-5-3-1, up and down, which she called an "arpeggio." Maybe that's how the violin is supposed to be tuned. I tug at one of the pegs, but it doesn't want to turn, so I twist harder. It refuses to budge. I tighten my grip and wrench it as hard as I can and then a little harder.

There's a sound like a pistol shot, the violin jerks in my hands, and all four strings fly suddenly loose.

I drop the violin onto the bed and race out of the house to where Mom is on her knees planting iris bulbs. Shame sweeps over me as I tell her, between sobs, about the horrible thing I just did. Mom gets up and follows me inside and I show her. She calls up Judy, who comes over and looks at the violin.

The bridge is just broken, Judy says. It was probably cracked already and my turning the peg just finished it off. It will have to go to the music store to be fixed. It wasn't my fault, Judy says, but I know she's wrong, that if I hadn't tried to turn that peg, the violin would still be sitting in its case, as good as new. Remembering that awful pistol shot makes me wish I never got the idea to take violin in the first place, but it's too late to back out. All I can do now is call up my friend Kristine and ask if she wants to come over and play Ginny dolls, so that's what I do.

Chapter 3. Taking Violin

On Tuesday morning, I'm in Mrs. Neal's class waiting to have my first violin lesson. There's just one problem: I don't have anything to play on. Yesterday afternoon, the music store called to say my violin was fixed, but Mom couldn't go get it until today. She promised to bring it to me, but now it's getting late and still no Mom, no violin.

I stare at the door. Mrs. Neal is saying something about key signatures, writing on the board. On the shelf next to the door is a row of black, new-looking violin cases belonging to the other girls who've signed up for violin. They all came from the same music store downtown, which has a plan where you can rent an instrument and the rent will go towards buying it. I wish my parents just got me one of those normal violins, not one in a beat-up old brown case with alligator sides. Finally, at five to eleven, Mom appears in the doorway, sets my violin down next to the others, blows me a kiss, and tiptoes out of the room.

A few minutes later, a man with snow-white hair comes through the door and calls my name. It's Mr. Shaw, the violin teacher. I get up, grab my case off the shelf, and follow him out of the room. The school music room is in the basement, and next to it is a low door frame with no door. It looks like the entrance to an underground goblin's den. Mr. Shaw leads me through the door, stooping a little. We go past some old piled-up desks and into another room where there are two chairs and a music stand. On a workbench is an open violin case with not one but two violins and four bows. One of the violins has a regular scroll like mine, but the other has a funny, bearded Rumpelstiltskin where the scroll should be.

Mr. Shaw has me set my case next to his and open it up. He takes out my violin and looks it over. Then he holds it up to the light and peers into one of the longish curved holes in the top.

"Did you know your violin was made in Germany?" he asks. "Look." I peep into the hole and sure enough, inside is a tiny label with the words "Made in Germany" on it. Germany is not a nice place. My dad helped kill Germans in the war because they tried to put our neighbor Mr. Gruen in a gas oven before he came to America.

Tucking my violin up under his chin, Mr. Shaw braces its scroll on the work bench and draws the bow across the strings. Pitches, first high, then low, siren up and down as the bow see-saws back and forth and Mr. Shaw's fingers fiddle with the pegs. The sounds under the bow settle into plain tones that somehow fit together, though these are not 1-3-5-8. Then, like magic, a song comes pouring out of the instrument as the bow moves this way and that and the fingers twitter up and down the strings. Every now and then a finger stops and Mr. Shaw's whole big hand wiggles like Jello. I've seen this same hand wiggle when Dick Kesner played his Stradivarius on Lawrence Welk.

After a few minutes, Mr. Shaw stops playing and tells me to stand up and hold my left arm up in the air. He sets the neck of the violin between the little line where the pointer finger goes into my hand and the thumb. Then he takes my other hand, curves my fingers over the bow, sets it on one of the strings, and pulls and pushes at my hand so the bow goes back and forth. A faint scratching sound comes out of the violin, nothing like the sweet sounds that Mr. Shaw just made, but he keeps saying, "Good, fine, that's just fine." Finally, he lets go of my hand and I go on making the scratches by myself. Before I leave, Mr. Shaw gives me a slip of paper telling Mom what book to get for me at the music store. I take a dollar bill and a fifty-cent piece out of my case and hand it to Mr. Shaw, and my first lesson is over.

At home, I take my violin out and show Mom and Dad and my big brother Davy how I can tighten the bow and move it across the strings. It doesn't make much noise, but they still clap.

Gambles Book 1 has a blue cover. In the front are pictures of a bald man holding a violin and a bow to show you the right positions. The first few pages of the book have only "open string" notes with no fingers on the strings, and none of them sound like real songs. After I've spent another week on open strings, Mr. Shaw takes slivers of tape and slides them up under the strings of my violin and onto the black fingerboard to show me where to put my fingers down. The slivers wear off after a while, but by then my fingers know where to go and I can play whole tunes.

As my fingers press down on the strings, a deep ridge appears in each of them, and they start to get sore. "You'll get calluses pretty soon and then it won't hurt anymore," Dad tells me. "Baseball players get 'em on their hands from holding the bat, and sometimes other places too if they slide a lot." Dad doesn't know much about music, but he knows a lot about sports.

I practice every day after school, making my way, week by week, through Gambles Books 1 and 2 and eventually moving on to an album called *Let Us Have Music for Violin*. As I progress from "Lightly Row" and "The Bluebells of Scotland" to Schubert's "Serenade" and "The Blue Danube," I keep playing after I've finished my real practicing. I'll start at the beginning of a book and play through one tune after another. I love the titles of songs, the different patterns in the music, and the pictures they make me see. One song brings up a field covered with blue flowers, another a black-haired man strumming a guitar beneath a lady's window, another a church choir marching down the aisle. As each song ends, I turn the page to see what the next one will be.

Mom brags to her friends that she never has to remind me to practice. I never watch the clock, and neither do my parents. Nor do I practice in any special place. I just take my violin out wherever I happen to be and play. My favorite place is in the bathroom, which sounds like I'm in a big concert hall. Dad calls this "acoustics." In the summer, I sometimes practice on the back porch, even though the acoustics there are crummy. At first, I'm afraid the neighbors might complain, but Mr. Gruen says he likes hearing me play because he can imagine he's in a café back in his home town in Germany.

Some kids have musician parents who supervise their practicing, but all mine do is listen. Sometimes when I'm playing in my room, Dad will come in and flop down on my bed and listen until he starts to snore. If I'm practicing in the living room, Mom might pause as she passes through with a pile of laundry and ask me the name of a piece I'm playing. Some nights after dinner I go out in the living room and play a little concert for my parents and Davy. They always clap when I'm finished and tell me I have "talent." I'm not sure what talent is, exactly, but I think it has something to do with *Arthur Godfrey's Talent Scouts* on TV, where they have an applause-meter with a needle that goes up to show how much clapping someone gets, with a prize for whoever gets the most.

After the fourth graders have been taking lessons for a few weeks, we start playing in Mrs. Neal's orchestra, which meets on Friday mornings before school. The only trouble with orchestra is that you have to remember to bring your instrument, your music stand, and your big, cardboard music folder to school with you. I don't know what terrible thing happens to you if you forget, but I know I don't want it to happen to me. The folder is covered with music store ads and has only two books inside—a big blue one and a little green one, both by Lorraine E. Watters, who also wrote our singing books. Mr. Watters is the head of school music in Des Moines, and Mrs. Neal says his books are used all over America.

At the end of every year, the Hanawalt orchestra and chorus present a music program for the PTA. Mixed in with the orchestra part of the program are some solos. The year I'm in fifth grade, Mrs. Neal asks me to play a solo, which makes me feel important. My piece is called "The Young Prince and Princess" from *Scheherazade*. In the music book it tells how the clever queen Scheherazade was married to an evil king who married a different wife every night and had her killed in the morning. Scheherazade survived by telling her husband a different story every night and leaving it up in the air so he'd have to let her live another day to find out what happened next. The stories were so good that in the end the king fell in love with Scheherazade and made her his permanent wife.

The afternoon before the PTA program, I take a bath after school and Mom paints my nails with pink polish. I wear my striped taffeta skirt with the big sash and a white ruffled blouse. At school, the kids gather in the music room and wait to go on stage. First, we march in onto the steps and sing the chorus part of the program in two-part harmony. Then we go back and get our instruments. The orchestra plays a couple of pieces, and now it's my turn.

As I move to the front of the stage, something peculiar happens. My face starts glowing red-hot, like I have a 104-degree fever, my hands are covered with sweat, and I feel stiff and shaky all over. What's wrong with me? Is it the Asian flu again? I had a bad case last winter, along with Dad and Davy and half the school. I'm feeling worse and worse, but somehow, I still get my violin up and play through my piece. Then it's over, people are clapping, the shaking has stopped, and my face feels cool again.

After my parents hug me and some other kids' parents shake my hand and tell me I have talent and we're on our way to Bauder's Drugstore for a hot fudge sundae, I tell them about the Asian flu feeling. They laugh. I wasn't sick, they tell me, I just had something called "stage fright."

"Football players get it all the time before they go out to play," says Dad. "Some of 'em even throw up before a game."

The next morning, the phone rings, and Mom picks it up.

"Oh, hi, Fran," she says in her sugar-sweet telephone voice. Fran is Mrs. George, Janie George's mother, one of the mothers who came up and shook my hand last night. Mrs. George was our Bluebird leader in second grade, and now they talk for a long time while I try to figure out what they're saying.

"Well, wasn't that nice?" Mom says, after she hangs up. "Fran called to say how much she loved hearing you play your violin last night. She said she thinks you have talent and that you're ready for another teacher. She thinks you should take from Janie's cello teacher, who mostly teaches violin. Her name is Mary Sexton. Fran says Mrs. Sexton is a terrific teacher. She says I should call her and see if she can take you as a pupil. What do you say? Should I call her up?"

I'm not sure. I want to take more lessons, but there's only one problem: Mrs. Sexton's name. Once at the dinner table Davy used the word "sex" and I asked them what it meant and they just laughed and wouldn't tell me. Now I know it's a word that makes kids snicker, like the word "breast" in the lullaby we sang in music class. What would they say if I told them my teacher was named Mrs. Sexton?

"This could be a great opportunity, honey," Mom says. "Fran says Mary Sexton is nationally known. What do you say?"

On the other hand, it's summertime now, and I'm going to horseback riding camp with my twin friends Betsy and Barbie, where no one knows anything about violin teachers and anyway, I don't have to tell anybody my teacher's name if I don't want to.

I nod my head yes, and Mom picks up the phone.

Chapter 4. Starting All Over

"Her star pupil got a scholarship to go to some camp for musical kids up in Michigan," Mom tells me in the car on the way to the recital. "Fran said Mrs. Sexton herself teaches a class of teachers there, so she must be really good." Thanks to Mom's phone call to Mrs. Sexton, I now have a lesson scheduled for Friday. We've also been invited to come to her students' end-of-the-year recital at Critchett's Piano and Organ Company on Forest Avenue.

Entering the store, we make our way past the pianos and organs, then sit down in two of the folding chairs toward the back. Up in front is a platform with a baby grand piano surrounded by chairs on which kids of various ages, mostly girls, are seated with stringed instruments. Janie George is there with her cello. Off to the side is a small, gray-haired woman in a navy-blue suit who must be Mrs. Sexton. When everyone's settled, she turns around and welcomes us, announces the first number, and a girl about my age gets up to play.

I cry all through the recital. Each of Mrs. Sexton's violin students plays better than the one before, way better than I ever could, talent or no talent. "I thought I was good," I whimper into Mom's ear. "I'm not good at all. I'm TERRIBLE!"

"Shhhh!" Mom whispers, handing me a Kleenex. "You're already better than half of them and you'll soon be better than the other half." It's not true what she says, but it still helps.

The last soloist is Debbie, Mrs. Sexton's star pupil, a high school girl with brown hair in a French roll, who zips up and down her violin like greased lightning and plays melodies that make you want to fly. After she finishes to lots of clapping, Mrs. Sexton gets up and gives a little present wrapped in red tissue paper to a girl who just graduated from high school. She also gives one to Debbie, for getting a scholarship to go "way up north to the National Music Camp at Interlochen, where it's *cool.*" I watch while Debbie opens her present, a little sewing kit in a plastic case, with tiny rolls of different colored threads. I decide then and there I'm going to get good enough on the violin to get one of those neat sewing kits myself.

I have my first lesson a few days later, and Mom comes along. Mrs. Sexton's house is on Woodland Avenue, down the hill from Callanan Junior High, where I'll be going in the fall as a sixth grader. The house is small and white with a screened front porch, old, but with only one story. As we pull up in front, I hear violin noises coming out through the screens.

After a while the noises stop, and an older boy comes out with a violin case, followed by Mrs. Sexton, who turns to greet us. We're closer now than at the recital, so I can get a better look at my new teacher. She reminds me of a little old lady in a comic book. She's about my height but very thin, with her head and shoulders hunched forward a little. At the back of her neck is a flat bun of gray hair, and she has practically no chin, gold old-lady glasses, and a tiny gold earring through a little hole in each earlobe. I can't keep from staring at the holes, which make my own earlobes throb.

As Mrs. Sexton says hello, I can't tell from her voice if she's glad or mad that we're here. It isn't a warm, cheery voice, but it's not exactly mean either, just sort of grim. It makes me think of Aunty Em in *The Wizard of Oz*, and I wonder if Mrs. Sexton is from Kansas. Maybe that's just the way people from Kansas talk. But she smiles as she leads us into the house, showing some gold teeth along the sides.

In Mrs. Sexton's living room is a baby grand piano, which takes up half the room, and over the fireplace is a huge stuffed moose head, whose antlers take up most of the other half. The floor is covered with oriental rugs, and at the windows are white net curtains. On the wall are two big framed oil paintings, both of swans and lily pads. This isn't at all like our living room on Pleasant Drive, which has pale green carpeting and flowered drapes and a TV set and no moose head or grand piano or swan paintings.

In the dining room is a row of chairs along one wall, and Mrs. Sexton has me lay my violin case across two of them and get my instrument out. She tunes my violin, then asks me to play something. I set the music of "The Young Prince and Princess" on the stand and start to play. I've only gone down about half a page when she stops me.

"Okay, that's enough," she says, in her flat, grim voice. Then she stands there thinking for a moment.

"Well, the intonation is good," she says finally, "but the position of your left-hand needs fixing and we're going to have to start all over on that bow arm. Is that how Mr. Shaw showed you to hold your violin?"

I can't remember how Mr. Shaw told me to hold my violin, since it was almost two years ago, at my first lesson, and he never said anything about it after that.

"All right," says Mrs. Sexton, not waiting for me to answer. "Let me show you. The palm of your left hand shouldn't be up like this"—she raises her palm up flat towards the ceiling—"but down like this"—she pulls her palm down so the fingers and thumb all stick straight up. "Now, hold your hand up straight like that." She twists my hand sideways. "That's right. That's better. I don't know why, but I never had a student come from Roy Shaw who didn't do this," she says, turning to my mom and making her hand all flat again. She turns back to me, sets my violin in the right spot, and adjusts my thumb. "Now, hold your violin up nice and high . . . Good."

After getting my left hand set, Mrs. Sexton turns her attention to my bow hand, which Mr. Shaw never paid much attention to either. Instead of forming a stiff brace on the bow, she tells me, the little finger is supposed to be gently curved, as if I'm holding a ball, and my double-jointed thumb needs to curve too, not cave in, at the frog of the bow—the heavy, squarish part under your hand, where the bow can make a scratchy sound like a frog in your throat. "Relax your shoulder," she says, then shows me how to lead with the wrist as I draw the bow back and forth. Showing me, her hand is like a paint brush in the air, the fingers like bristles making broad strokes, down and up.

All these new instructions come at my brain like Indian arrows attacking a wagon train, but Mrs. Sexton says not to worry, that it will take time to change my habits. "Rome wasn't built in a day," she says. For the rest of the lesson, I play only on open strings while Mrs. Sexton resets my positions over and over. By the end, I'm making bow strokes from one end to the other, leading with my wrist.

Finally, Mrs. Sexton pulls some ancient, crumbling music books out of a file and circles a few baby-simple tunes in them for me to practice. This is all I get to work on until the new habits take hold. Before we leave, Mrs. Sexton writes down the names of a few more music books—a Wolfhardt etude book, a third position book, some simple pieces—for us to get at Miller's music store across from Drake University. We're also to get some new, aluminum-wound "Gold Label" strings, which Mrs. Sexton says will make my violin sound a lot better.

"So, what do you think?" Mom asks me, back in the car. "She really knows her stuff, doesn't she?"

I don't know what to say. I feel like a car that's just had all its parts taken out and put back together a different way. Part of me wishes I could turn back the clock and just play the same as always. But the rest of me is a racehorse tossing its head at the starting gate. I'm going to practice hard and learn all the new habits right away. I'm going to get back to playing more grown-up music. I'm not going to be terrible anymore. I'm going to be as good as Debbie and get a sewing kit. And I'm going to make Mrs. Sexton say I have talent.

I prop my left elbow on the pull-down arm rest, stick my palm and fingers straight up, imagine the violin resting against it, and start making long bow strokes back and forth in the air, leading with my wrist, all the way to the music store.

Chapter 5. Harmony Haunt

After my first lesson, I go to Mrs. Sexton's house by myself every Friday. During the summer, Mom drops me off in the morning, but when school starts at Callanan in September, I keep my violin in my locker on Fridays and carry it down the hill to Mrs. Sexton's house. Its brown case bumps against my leg as I walk, balancing my schoolbooks and zippered music case on my other arm. Mrs. Sexton's door is never locked, and I'm supposed to go right in. I set my case down, take my violin and bow out, and wait for my lesson to begin.

Mrs. Sexton tunes my violin and we get started. First come scales and arpeggios, then etudes, then pieces. Sometimes Mrs. Sexton plays along with me on her own violin, which is made of plain, grayish-brown wood, not fancy like Mr. Shaw's violins. Whatever I'm playing, she constantly corrects my position in her flat little voice, saying the same words again and again, always as though it's the first time. Before long, her words come into my head when I practice: *Get your violin up...Relax your shoulder...Elbow higher on the G-string...Bend your thumb...Keep that little finger curved...Listen to your sound...*

As the weeks go by, new habits take hold, but I never seem to get to the last habit. As soon as I've got one thing down, there's something else. It's like opening a door and behind it finding another door and then another and another. But I sound a little better all the time, and before long I'm back to playing more grown-up pieces.

I love how it feels when Mrs. Sexton circles the title of a new piece to work on or, better yet, when I get a new book from Miller's that's filled with clean pages of black-and-white notes. I love the way when I start something new the blurs of notes slowly come clear like words in a Magic 8-ball. And I love when Mrs. Sexton sticks a little colored star at the top of a page, which means I can let that piece go and move on to another.

After a few weeks of lessons, Mrs. Sexton shows me how to do vibrato. "Put your finger down on the string and hold it there," she says. "Now just move your hand back and forth, back and forth—that's right." At first, I do this slowly, but then she has me speed up the motion until it takes off on its own. For the next few weeks, Mrs. Sexton draws a little wiggly line over the longer notes in my pieces, where I'm supposed to add vibrato. I can do this in my lesson, but I'm not sure I want to do something so weird and wobbly-looking anywhere else. I'd just about as soon go outside in my underwear as do vibrato in public. But when I see Mrs. Sexton's more advanced pupils all doing vibrato, I start doing it too.

Meanwhile, I progress from first position to third and fifth, then to harder positions like second, fourth, sixth, and seventh, playing higher and higher notes, all the way to the end of the fingerboard. By fall, I have a new album of pieces to play, and by spring, I've learned my first concerto, the "Indian Concertino" by George Perlman, which I play first on one of Mrs. Sexton's recitals and then at a "competition" run by the American String Teachers' Association. I don't know why they call it a competition, because you're not competing with the other kids, just trying to get a good rating on the certificate they give you. My certificate comes back with "Superior," which is the highest rating, even though the day of the competition I'm sick with the flu, and when I get home my temperature is 103.

I'm still in bed the next day when the phone rings, after which I hear Mom's voice murmuring off in the kitchen. Finally, she comes into my room. "That was Mrs. Sexton," she says, sitting down and putting her hand on my forehead. "She called to tell me how thrilled she is with your progress. Really, she just *raved* about you. She seems to think you might get to be another Debbie—or better."

This comes as a total shock, because even though Mrs. Sexton always tells me if I'm doing things right or wrong, she never praises me to my face. In fact, she never says much of anything to me about myself, though she loves to talk about other people. "Sandra's too interested in boys right now to practice much," she'll say, or "Jeannie's the baby of the family—I think she's a little spoiled." She even talks about other teachers, especially the public school teachers like Mr. Shaw and the teachers at Drake University, none of whom she seems to think are as good as she is, which must be true, because most of Mrs. Sexton's students sit first chair in their school orchestras, which means they're the best.

During my first summer of lessons, Mrs. Sexton asks if I'd like to play in her "string ensemble," which meets every Monday night, summer and winter, in her living room, and for which she charges nothing. The kids in the ensemble, all Mrs. Sexton's students, range from sixth to twelfth grades. There are usually about twelve of us, and even with all the furniture moved out into the dining room, we barely fit. In my first year, I sit in the back, right under the big moose's head, with a terribly thin girl named Carrie. Both of us have to sit at funny angles to keep our bows from crashing into the antlers on a vigorous up-bow.

Up in front, Mrs. Sexton sits on a high kitchen stool—the kind with steps that pull out—and conducts us just as seriously as if we were the New York Philharmonic, stopping from time to time to give little talks about the music. The music we play is mostly by Italian composers like Vivaldi and Corelli. It has lots of sixteenth notes on which you have to saw up and down very fast, using lots of bow. When I first look at a new piece, the notes are always a big tangly mess, but the more we play the piece, the more the notes get sorted out into phrases.

After I've been in the ensemble for a while, Mrs. Sexton starts teaching me to play the viola, which is played the same way as the violin, but is bigger and has strings tuned five notes lower. This is confusing, as the lines of the music staff have different letter names—not EGBDF but FACEG. By now, I know that Debbie's scholarship to Interlochen was to play viola, not violin, because the camp orchestra is always short on violists. "You might want to try for a scholarship yourself someday," Mrs. Sexton says to me.

Sometimes on ensemble nights, or if I have a lesson on Saturday, Mrs. Sexton's husband is there in the house. His name is Duard, and he looks like a professor, though he isn't one. He works at the John Deere plant, which makes farm machinery, and his hobby is painting pictures. The two big swan paintings on the wall are both pictures Duard painted. Like Mrs. Sexton, Duard wears gold glasses, but while her voice is grim, his is gentle and very precise. Mom thinks the Sextons are a really close couple. She says that's what often happens when couples don't have children. Dad says he can see why they don't have children, but I don't know what he means by that.

Right before Christmas, Mrs. Sexton has her annual party for the ensemble. It's different from other parties in that we bring our instruments and play Christmas carols before we get anything to eat. Then we go into the dining room, where there's a big plate of decorated cookies on the table and paper cups filled with punch. Mrs. Sexton gives us all little presents wrapped in Christmas paper. I get a special, soft yellow flannel cloth for wiping the rosin dust off my violin. The day after Christmas is Mrs. Sexton's "Ensemble Reunion," when her former students come back and play music together and talk about old times. Someday, I'll be coming back for the reunion. During the holidays, my parents and I get a Christmas card in the mail from the Sextons. The address label says

"Harmony Haunt" above the regular address, which is what Mrs. Sexton calls her house, like something out of a Nancy Drew book. She's the only person I know whose house has a name.

As the months go by, I work my way through one book after another, always hoping to play something a little harder. By seventh grade, I've fallen into a regular routine of practicing for an hour every day after school and two hours a day on weekends. I keep a clock on my dresser to time my practicing, but when I'm finished, I often let myself just play. Everything in my old books sounds better and is way easier now than when I worked on it before.

Then, one Saturday afternoon, it happens. I'm playing a new piece called "Cavetine." It's an easy piece, a lovely melody in waltz time. Everything is working just as it should—the bow arm, the fingers, the vibrato—and the notes are going by, when all of a sudden I feel myself lifted off. I'm a bird soaring up and up, feeling a way I haven't felt since I waltzed around the room to "Shall We Dance." I play the "Cavetine" piece over and over, unable to stop.

Someday, after I've gone to Interlochen in the summers and to the University of Iowa and am married with a home of my own, I'm going to be a violin teacher just like Mrs. Sexton. I'm going to have a baby grand piano in my living room and belong to the American String Teachers Association and kids will come to my house every day after school while my husband is at work. I'll have a string ensemble just like Mrs. Sexton's and Christmas parties and ensemble reunions.

And I'm going to give my house a name. Maybe I'll even call it Harmony Haunt.

Chapter 6. The Everyday Me

You might think from everything I've told you so far that the violin is the only thing I ever do, but that's not true. The truth is, I do lots of things that have nothing to do with the violin, day after day, year after year. Because, along with the violin me, there's another me, one that does pretty much the same things regular kids do, which I call the "everyday me." Sometimes the violin me and the everyday me get into tugs of war, but most of the time they just take turns, peacefully coexisting like the Americans and the Russians.

The everyday me takes riding lessons and tennis lessons and swimming lessons and ballroom dancing with Miss Adeline Ogilvie, where she learns to Fox Trot and rock-and-roll with boys in stiff plaid sports jackets. She goes with Betsy and Barbie to the Double A Bar S ranch camp near Ogden, Iowa for two summers and then to Clearwater Camp for Girls in northern Wisconsin, where she learns to sail and goes on three-day canoe trips and builds fires and plays her violin on the camp talent show. She takes Sissy, her white Siberian sled dog, on long walks in the woods with Betsy and gets her shoes all muddy in the creek and discovers a horse on a few empty acres on Cummings Parkway and sneaks into the barn, where she and Betsy take turns sitting on the horse's back and nervously standing guard at the stable door.

She solves math problems and studies grammar rules and does jumping jacks to "Chicken Fat" in gym and learns that the earth's axis is tilted and

George Washington was inaugurated in 1789 and the average life expectancy in India is 42. She teaches herself to type using a *Typing Made Simple* book and types out all Mom's handwritten recipes. She writes reports on Egypt and comets and Andrew Jackson and Archimedes and Buddhism and gives them to Dad to correct and types out whole paragraphs that Dad dictates until she starts to hear Dad's voice in her head and doesn't need the dictating any more. She decorates bulletin boards and goes to assemblies and plays intramural volleyball after school.

She goes to Sunday school at Plymouth Congregational and joins the Youth Club, where they have classes on religion and drama and rhythmic choir and Mr. Major, the Minister of Christian Education, comes into her Christian Living class and tells the girls about things called erections that may make boys not want to dance too close to you. She stays overnight with Betsy, who explains the joke to her about the bald-headed mouse and with Laurel from Youth Club, who shows her the dirty parts in a book called *Lady Chatterley's Lover*. She reads *The Power of Positive Thinking for Young People* and writes Bible verses on little cards and carries them around with her and repeats "I can do all things in Christ who strengthenest me" hoping this will help her to stay on her diet and keep from getting nervous during recitals and after she still goes off her diet and gets stage-fright she throws the cards in the trash.

She babysits for the Krugers across the street and bribes their kids with snacks and scary stories to get them to bed so she can sit on the Krugers' couch munching Oreos and reading a book about Madame Curie for school and falling asleep until the Krugers come home and pay her fifty cents an hour. She reads nurse books and horse books and a book about Eleanor Roosevelt and stays up until 2 AM reading *Exodus* and *Jane Eyre* and *Gone with the Wind*. She resolves to read all the books in her parents' library, starting at the left side of the top shelf and reading her way across through *The Horse's Mouth*, *The Sun Also Rises*, and several other books she doesn't like until she finally gives up in the middle of a hopelessly boring book by Thomas Mann.

She goes to Saturday matinees with her friends at the Ingersoll Theater, where they eat Black Crows and Milk Duds to *Pollyanna* and *The Music Man* and *Gidget* and listen to Moondoggie singing to Gidget after she almost drowns and learn from Gidget's mother that when you fall in love it's like someone hit you over the head with a sledgehammer. She watches *Maverick* and *Donna Reed* and *Ben Casey* and *77 Sunset Strip* and takes turns retelling stories from *The Twilight Zone* with her friends after lights-out at camp.

She rides through the Kansas wheat fields in her parents' new Chevy Impala to visit Dave and his new wife Jeanetta, a big, bossy young woman from West Des Moines, and her new namesake, Cynthia Elizabeth Housh, in San Diego, where Dave is in the Navy. After Dave goes overseas and Jeanetta and "Little Cindy" come back to West Des Moines, she babysits Cindy and starts teaching herself shorthand from a book Jeanetta gives her and quarrels with her and makes peace by letting Jeanetta make her up and do her hair in a bubble and goes with her to see *The Birds* in a drive-in movie theater.

She watches the Democratic convention on TV with Mom and hears Senator Kennedy talk about the New Frontier and watches the debates and sits up half the night waiting to find out who wins the election and watches the inauguration at school and asks herself what she can do for her country. She sits in the auditorium at Merrill, a brand-new junior high to which she transferred from Callanan, and watches the rocket with Alan Shephard somewhere inside it going slowly up on the screen while in the seat next to her Sharon Murphy keeps saying, "This is history in the making!" over and over, and she watches another rocket going up with John Glenn and another rocket and another.

She clips out current events stories from the *Register and Tribune* to do oral reports for social studies on Juan Peron and the Bay of Pigs and James Meredith at a place called "Ole Miss." She listens to guest speakers at Youth Club—a Hiroshima survivor from Japan, some Negro civil rights workers, a man from CROP—and learns a new song called "We Shall Overcome." She hears Dr. Lenhardt tell the congregation at Plymouth that we often make the mistake of thinking we can't do anything just because we can't do everything and that you can always do something to make things better. She hears Miss Hall in English class read the passage from *The Prophet* about how we give but little when we give of our possessions and the quote from Henry James about how you should try to be someone on whom nothing is lost.

She goes with her parents one evening to hear Arnold Toynbee, a famous British historian teaching at Grinnell College for a year, who says that if mankind can rid itself of slavery we ought to be able to get rid of war too and discusses the decline of Western civilization with her parents on the way home. She hears rumors in the school cafeteria that the world is about to end and watches President Kennedy on TV talking about missiles in Cuba and hears her parents talk about making Dad's basement workshop into a fallout shelter and imagines what it will be like living on canned peaches in the basement for two weeks and using a bucket for a toilet. She wonders if the missiles will just target Chicago so all they have to do is survive the fallout or if they will hit Des Moines because of Solar Aircraft, in which case they will all die. She thinks about the flash and being knocked to the ground and then feeling nothing at all—"You wouldn't know what hit you," Dad says—and tries to imagine what nothing at all would feel like, knowing that she can't really do this, nothing being nothing, and prays that it won't happen before she has a chance to fall in love and get married.

She practices kissing her stuffed dog Mimi and her own cold lips in the mirror and her twin friend Betsy, who goes "Ew!" and jerks away. She wraps herself in a towel so it looks like a bathing suit after she gets out of the tub and stands in front of the mirror and discovers that she doesn't look like Gidget, that her thighs are white and puffy and disgusting, and that although her skin is mostly clear and her nose is all right, she has practically no chin. She counts calories and drinks Metrecal and does jumping jacks and wrestles with temptation and buys Hostess cupcakes and big bags of Brach's jelly-nougat candies at Dahls' supermarket and eats four cupcakes and half the candy and hides the rest in her bottom dresser drawer. She brushes her teeth and puts tiny round rubber bands on her braces and teases her hair to make it puff out like Jackie Kennedy's and puts Clearasil on her face to keep from getting blackheads. She wonders if she's ever going to get her period and discreetly refastens her bra when it comes apart in science class and tugs at her new girdle every time it rides up and cuts into her thighs.

The everyday me does all these things and many more, but all the time she's doing them, the violin me is still waiting underneath, dimming whatever the everyday me is doing just a little. Waiting for free time to practice. Waiting for the sounds in my head to come alive in the air. Waiting for the next recital, the next competition, the next concert. Waiting for "Cavatine," "Shall We Dance" moments. Waiting for clapping and talk about talent. And, I'm beginning to think, waiting for the violin to carry me off to another world altogether, a mist-enshrouded Bali Hai in the north woods, where the everyday me and the violin me are one and the same and the music never stops, a place called Interlochen.

Chapter 7. My Swollen Head

It's not my fault if my head is swollen. I didn't start the violin because I wanted lots of compliments, but that seems to be what it gets you sooner or later, and although the compliments can be fun to get, they can also puff your head up like a hot air balloon. I can just see the cartoon of my head getting bigger and bigger until it goes "Bam!" and shrivels down to nothing as I fly crazily all over the room on a Bronx cheer noise. The whole thing makes me a little nervous.

The compliments come in different flavors depending on who the complimenter is. Gushy compliments come mostly from girls. I got lots of gushy girl compliments after I played on the talent show at the Clearwater Camp for Girls: "Oh, Cindy, that was sooooo beautiful! You're sooooo talented! You must be a GENIUS!"

Boys, on the other hand, when they bother to compliment you at all, seem to know only two words to use: good and nice. I got a few of these plain boy-compliments after I played my Seitz concerto on the talent show at Callanan last year, from boys coming towards me in the hall, who mostly spoke in this dumb monotone and called me by my last name, just so I'd know they didn't *mean* anything by the compliment: "Hey, Housh, you played pretty good on that violin" or "Nice job on the fiddle, Housh."

Then there are the compliments the grown-ups dish out, which range from being even more gushy than girls' compliments to very obviously just being polite. Grown-ups' compliments are often a little snootier than kids' compliments, like they're trying to sound really smart, especially if the grown-up happens to be a musician. Like after our quartet played in the Friends of Music concert at Salisbury House—which is this spooky old manor house that some rich family brought over from England to Des Moines brick by brick, complete with suits of armor and creepy portraits—and this man who was about a hundred years old came up to the settee where Shirley and I were sitting and asked which of us had played the first violin part on Haydn's Sunrise Quartet. When I told him it was me, he said, "Bravo! I especially admired your interpretation of the first theme." No kid would ever have said something like that except maybe David Manheimer, who really *is* a genius and took algebra in the seventh grade.

Grown-ups also like to combine compliments with advice about my future, like my Aunt Maurine, who said I should go to Julliard, which Mom says is some special college in New York where concert artists go. Aunt Maurine is a singer and an actress and my favorite aunt.

Whatever the compliment is, I always react exactly the same, which I hate. Of course, I say thank you, but meanwhile, this stupid, silly smile starts spreading across my face while I try like mad to stop it so the complimenter won't think I'm a conceited idiot. It's embarrassing, but I must still like being praised, because every time I see a friend coming towards me after a performance, my heart starts beating like crazy, and I feel like Pavlov's dog, just drooling for another compliment.

Awhile back there was an article in the paper with the headline, "Your Child Needs Praise." The author said kids need to be praised to keep them from getting an inferiority complex, but that if a kid gets too much praise, the boy or girl may turn into a "praise addict." Can you be both a praise addict and a person with an inferiority complex at the same time? If so, I think that's me.

Because even though the violin me gets praised a lot, the everyday me doesn't get much praise at all and sometimes even gets teased. Sure, the everyday me gets good grades, but she's also too tall and wears glasses and has braces on her teeth and a figure like a pear instead of an hour-glass. The everyday me has to wear clothes her mom made or hand-me-downs from Judy and Mary instead of buying new ones at Younkers like Betsy and Barbie, whose father is a rich lawyer and lets them have their own charge-a-plate. The everyday me doesn't belong to the Des Moines Golf and Country Club like they do and has to go as their guest, wearing an awful pink-and-white bathing suit with a *skirt*, which only old ladies wear anymore, while the twins wear brand new two-piece Hawaiian prints.

So even though I get lots of praise about the violin, I still have an inferiority complex. Maybe that's good, though, because it'll make me practice harder. Mom showed me an article about a woman who became a great opera singer who said she got to be such a great musician because she was taller than the other girls and had to do something to make up for it. The funny part is, I know no matter how good I get on the violin and how many people tell me I'm good, it's never going to give me an hour-glass figure or a decent bathing suit or any of the other things that make you popular, but I keep practicing anyhow. It's like I'm trying to get rid of a headache by hitting myself on the head with a hammer, but I can't seem to do anything else, I don't know why. Maybe I just like hitting myself on the head. My swollen head.

Chapter 8. Dreams of Interlochen

Just after Christmas, the year I'm in eighth grade, Mom asks me if I want to go back to Clearwater next summer. For a moment, I almost say yes, remembering singing around campfires and the camp cook's chocolate cake and my favorite horse, but then I stop. At my last lesson, Mrs. Sexton said if I really work hard this year, she might take me with her to the chamber music conference at Interlochen summer-after-next. Her latest star pupil, a high school boy named Jack Simpson, is going to Interlochen this year on a viola scholarship, and after he graduates, it'll be my turn. But if I go back to paddling canoes at Clearwater that will mean seven weeks with no lessons, which might make Interlochen less likely. It's one of those everyday me vs. violin me moments, like in the Robert Frost poem that starts "Two roads diverged in a yellow wood."

Finally, I tell Mom no, I don't want to go back to Clearwater, I want to stay home and take violin lessons.

One evening that summer, Dad comes home and hands me a copy of *Seventeen* magazine someone gave him that has a story in it about Interlochen.

"Suddenly each summer, music fills the air," the story begins, in headlines above a picture of a girl playing a harp next to a lake. Across from the picture are kids playing trumpets and French horns and string basses and pianos and an orchestra in a big outdoor concert shed.

Sprawled on my blue polished-cotton bedspread, I read the *Seventeen* article over and over. It tells how only the most talented young musicians get to go to Interlochen, where they also have dance, drama, speech, painting, and ceramics and about the grand finale concert where they play a piece called *Les Préludes* because Dr. Joseph Maddy, the camp's founder, hopes that for the campers, experiences at Interlochen will be a "prelude to a richer and more fruitful life."

"It's pretty exciting to walk through a grove at three o'clock in the afternoon of a sparkling day and hear the sound of practicing coming out of a cottage—and know there's a fourteen- or fifteen-year-old youngster in there sawing away at his cello for maybe two hours," says some TV guy named Mike Wallace who used to teach radio at Interlochen. "It's especially exciting to know he's doing it because he wants to."

Reading these words, I see a cabin in my mind, somewhere in the woods. It's square, with screens on all four sides and roll-down canvas shades, like some of the cabins at Clearwater, breezy and smelling of pine trees. The cellist looks like Moondoggie from *Gidget*, but he floats off into nowhere and then I'm in the cabin myself with my violin, sawing away for maybe two hours because I want to. Later, somewhere in a blue twilight, the Moondoggie cellist and I are sitting side-by-side and I'm saying, "Nobody at home understands kids like you and me. Nobody understands us the way they do here at Interlochen. I feel as though I was born here, as though I was at Interlochen in another life. I want to stay here forever."

All that summer, I take lessons and practice my violin for at least two hours a day, glancing from time to time at the alarm clock on top of my dresser. Next to the alarm clock is the new wind-up metronome I got for Christmas. When I have a fast passage to learn, I set the marker at a slow speed, then move it up little by little until I can play the passage in tempo. Consequently, I now can play a lot faster than ever before.

I also practice for an hour every day on piano, which I've been taking from Mrs. Grace Walker since September. Getting to do this was a big accomplishment, because we didn't have a piano. It took me a whole year of begging, but I finally convinced Mom to help me get one. As with the violin, good old Aunt Martha came through and offered to lend us the piano they had in their basement rec room, a yellow spinet which is now in our den. After playing the violin for four years, I'm finding the piano easy because I already know how to read music. I went through a couple of John Thompson books in nothing flat, and on Mrs. Walker's year-end recital, I played Beethoven's "Für Elise." What I love about the piano is that you have all the music right there, unlike with the violin, where you need the accompaniment for it to sound complete. I could practice piano all day if I let myself, but piano will never get me to Interlochen, so I have a rule that I can only practice it half as long as violin.

One Sunday evening in July, I'm alone in my room fooling with my little radio, which sits on top of my desk. It's old, but you can get lots of stations on it, even ones far away. Dad painted the radio light blue to match the walls of my room and gave it to me for my birthday last year. I'm twisting the knobs past a lot of static and rock-'n-roll when all at once, I hear it: an orchestra playing music like blue lake water, and a man's voice breaking in, saying, "From the National Music Camp at Interlochen, Michigan, this is 'Best from Interlochen,'" after which he announces a Tchaikovsky symphony.

As the music starts up again, I lie back on my pillows and watch the movie in my mind: the orchestra filling an outdoor stage, the violins and clarinets and trombones, the conductor, Dr. Joseph E. Maddy, waving his arms to make Tchaikovsky fly out of all those different instruments and up to the stars and across the miles of lakes and trees and cornfields and down into my little blue radio in Des Moines, while somewhere in the viola section at Interlochen sits Mrs. Sexton's student Jack Simpson, a real-live person that I know. It's a miracle, and it fills me with awe, as though I've traveled for days and nights following the star with the three Wise Men and suddenly turned a corner and found the Christ child lying in a manger.

At my next lesson, Mrs. Sexton tells me Jack wrote to her that the Interlochen orchestra is going to play a concert at the White House! Stories about the concert appear a few weeks later in the paper, with pictures of the orchestra on the White House lawn, and dancers in white dresses, and President Kennedy shaking hands with one of the kids. In September, at the first ensemble rehearsal, Mrs. Sexton asks Jack, now a senior at East High, to tell us about his trip to Washington.

Jack talks about his adventure as if it was an ordinary trip to anywhere and the president of the United States was just anybody. He tells how the kids boarded the plane in northern Michigan and landed at Dulles airport and went to some army base in Virginia, where they were to stay overnight. And how they went to the White House and got set up on a platform on the south lawn and President Kennedy's helicopter landed just in time for him to get out and shake some kids' hands and make a little speech before their concert. And how he called Interlochen "a most distinguished school" and talked about the importance of the arts in America and said he was sorry he wouldn't be able to stay for their concert because he had to work, but he promised to keep his door open so he could still hear them. "I don't think he got much work done that day," Jack says. And he tells us how they played Tchaikovsky's Fourth Symphony and Strauss's "Emperor Waltz" and a piece by a Japanese composer. And how after the concert, the President came out again and greeted them in the Rose Garden and there was a spaghetti lunch inside the White House, but there was a mix-up and they wound up in a room with no furniture and had to eat their spaghetti sitting on the floor, though it was a very fancy floor and "seemed pretty clean."

Listening to Jack talk, I suddenly realize that in just a couple of years this could be me, going to play for the Kennedys in a repeat performance, maybe with the president himself able to attend this time. It's possible, though it doesn't feel real, probably wouldn't feel real even if it happened to me. It's all too hard to think about, so I don't. Instead, I look at the music on the stand in front of me and start fingering through the notes and wait for Mrs. Sexton to start the rehearsal.

Chapter 9. Interlochen Preview

What's so great about this place? I ask myself as I scramble out of Doris's
Nash Rambler and look around. I thought Interlochen was in the woods, and
instead all I see is a broad expanse of asphalt covered with green-painted park
benches. Nor is the air filled with music as the *Seventeen* article said it would
be. And where's the beautiful square cabin where the cellist saws away for two
hours because he wants to? Nowhere in sight.

What I don't know yet is how big this place is.

It's August,1963, and I'm here with Mrs. Sexton and Doris McFadden,
an older former student of hers who drove us from Des Moines to Milwaukee,
from which we took the ferry across Lake Michigan to Ludington, which is
a couple hours south of Interlochen. The drive up the coast took us winding
through a green cathedral of trees, edging one blue lake after another. Now it's
early afternoon, and here we are.

The three of us make an odd trio: Mrs. Sexton, the little old lady in
her navy blue suit; Doris, who is movie-star thin with a long braid of hon-
ey-colored hair; and me—tall, chinless, glasses-and-braces-wearing Cindy
Housh. Doris is pretty but serious, Marian the Librarian in *The Music Man*,
and Mrs. Sexton is Mrs. Sexton. Neither is a person I can really confide in,
but I have my daydreams for company, imagining all the way up here that
by some miracle we might run into Mark Baxter, a fellow violinist on whom

I have a huge crush and whose grandparents live somewhere in Michigan, I happen to know.

Mark and I played in the same quartet last year, he on first, me on second, and we also both sang at Plymouth in the Matins choir, which his dad conducts, along with playing the organ and conducting about five other choirs. He's like J.S. Bach without the wig, and Mark's mother is one of the best piano teachers in town. With parents like that, of course Mark is really good on the violin, better than me, I have to admit. It's a good thing he's better, since if I was better I'd have absolutely *no* chance with him, not that I have any chance anyway, the reason being that I'm a couple inches taller than he is, which makes me not even a girl in Mark's eyes.

Trouble is, Mark is the only boy I know who can talk about anything but football plays. Mark is smart and funny and talented, which is why half the girls in the choir are in love with him, alas. But actually, unrequited love isn't such a bad thing for a musician to have, as it gives you lots of feelings to pour into the sad pieces.

This trip is just a preview of Interlochen, not the real thing. I'll probably be the only high school kid here, which is not how it would be during the real camp season. But camp ended last week, and every year after camp, a few hundred grown-ups, including Mrs. Sexton and Janice, show up to play chamber music, and I've been invited along for the ride.

Over the next week, I play chamber music every morning with the adults. By 8 am, lists appear on the bulletin board of the players in that day's ensembles, what music they're to play, and the name of their coach. The first morning, my group plays Haydn quartets, which is good for me because of all the Haydn Mark and I played in our quartet back home. But the day after that, I get stuck playing second viola in a Brahms sextet, which is way too hard for me, and the coach picks on me the whole time.

As long as I'm playing music, I feel just like everybody else, but the rest of the time I'm not sure how to act. The grown-ups are friendly to me, but at meals I'm always wondering if they wish they hadn't gotten stuck sitting with a high school kid. Over the next few days, between the various activities—chamber music, a sight-reading orchestra, master classes, concerts, Mrs. Sexton's string teaching class, where I serve as her assistant and guinea pig, and late-night cocoa gatherings—I wander here and there and discover that Interlochen isn't all covered with asphalt.

Hundreds of cabins are scattered amongst the pine trees, though I never see any square, screened ones. The Interlochen cabins for sleeping, mine included, are all shaped like shoe boxes with roofs and seem to have been built from the same blueprints. The cabin where I sleep, along with fifteen grown-up women, has an entryway with a single bed where during regular camp a counselor can sleep, a shelf for instruments, and a coat rack. Beyond that is a big room with eight bunk beds, four on each side, with a shelf at the end of each bed for two people's clothes and personal belongings. In the back is the bathroom, four sinks with mirrors flanked by a toilet on one side and a shower on the other. Not exactly the Ritz, but better than a tent.

Besides the sleeping cabins, there are countless others: rows of little stone-and-brick practice cabins, consisting of one door, one window, one piano, and lots of cobwebs; square wooden cabins that are teachers' studios; scholarship lodges which visitors can rent and where faculty live; and big screened shoeboxes for rehearsals and recitals.

Along with the cabins, I also explore some of the larger buildings, a few of which are open to the elements. The biggest open building is Kresge auditorium, probably paid for by the dime-store people. Kresge's stage has tall glass windows at the back, through which you can see the lake, and above the stage are written the words, "Dedicated to the Promotion of World Friendship through the Universal Language of the Arts." Standing at the back of Kresge reading those words, I imagine a huge orchestra on stage filled with Americans and Germans and Mexicans and Russians and Chinese, all playing a Beethoven symphony. If only everyone could do that, there wouldn't be any wars.

Another open building I wander into is the Bowl, which is just this huge wooden shed with one side missing and zillions of green park benches arranged in the open space in front of it. Somebody here must have gotten a great bargain on park benches, which are everywhere you look. The Bowl is the building I saw in *Seventeen* filled with orchestra musicians playing a concert.

Most of the big, winter-proof buildings at Interlochen are connected so you don't have to go outside much to get from one to another. This makes sense because of the new, year-round school they just started here, the Interlochen Arts Academy. The Academy opened just last year and has only a few hundred students, unlike the camp, which has been around since the 1930s and has over a thousand. The administration building, the three round classroom buildings, and the combination gym and auditorium are all connected by this huge, long "concourse," which is lined with glass display cases and is like a hallway out of one of those nightmares where you run and run and never get to the end.

Separate from the buildings connected by the concourse is another cluster of connected buildings: the Stone Hotel, the cafeteria and kitchen, and the Women's Dormitory. The Stone Hotel is named after a philanthropist named W. Clement Stone, whose picture, which includes his wife, is in the lobby. Mr. Stone has a handlebar mustache and a bow-tie, which makes him look like a magician, and Mrs. Stone has on a satiny, printed dress. The Stone Hotel should be made out of stones like some of the other buildings, given its name, but it isn't. Instead, it's made of plain, gray cinder blocks. The lobby is decorated all in knotty pine, with walls and furniture to match and has a fireplace in one corner. In the basement are the music library and most of the rooms where our chamber music groups meet.

Besides these big, connected buildings there are various middle-sized ones, my favorite of which is the little stone store where they sell music, candy, and something called a "Melody Freeze," which is exactly like a Dairy Queen. I've heard that somewhere there's also a theater for plays and a dance studio, though I've never seen these, and there are whole villages of cabins and other buildings that I haven't seen either, some of them on the other side of the highway, where only boys can go. This camp is HUGE!

My other favorite Interlochen places, though, aren't buildings at all but spaces outdoors. Best is the big, cement sun decker next to Kresge, which overlooks what Interlochen people call Lake Wahbekanetta, though it's Green Lake to everyone else, just like Interlochen's other lake, Lake Wahbekaness, is Duck Lake. The camp lies between the two lakes, which is why this place is called Interlochen. I love to stand at the railing looking out across the shining blue lake water and watch the sea gulls diving for fish and dream about Mark Baxter showing up here just to see what Interlochen looks like on his way home from his grandmother's and seeing me sitting down here by the lake, and being amazed by the coincidence and wondering why he never really saw me before. Other times, I'll just sit on one of the green park benches in the asphalt-covered "Main Camp" area, licking a Melody Freeze and watching people throw coins in the fake wishing well to pay for kids' scholarships.

Part of the Interlochen landscape, inside and out, are the blue camp uniforms that all faculty, staff, and students (when they're here, which they aren't during post-camp) are required to wear (except us chamber-music players, who wear regular clothes). Mrs. Sexton says the uniforms haven't changed since the 1930s. Girls and women at NMC wear short-sleeved light-blue shirts, blue corduroy "knickers" – pants that gather just below the knee, like George Washington wore – and colored knee socks. Boys and men wear the same shirts but with long, blue corduroy pants.

Another piece of the landscape is the famous Dr. Maddy, founder and president of Interlochen, often accompanied by Mrs. Maddy. Dr. Maddy has a reddish, bunched-together face, gray hair, and bushy, gray eyebrows, and Mrs. Maddy has a snow-white bun and looks like Mrs. Santa Claus. Both wear the camp uniform with red sweaters. Mrs. Sexton introduced me to Dr. Maddy in the cafeteria on the first day. He smiled and shook my hand when she told him I was a prospective camper, but I had trouble understanding his words, which ran together kind of fast. I don't know if he remembers me from that brief encounter, but he always smiles and says hello when I see him, so maybe he does.

By the time we leave at the end of the week, I can say I've been to Interlochen, but it doesn't feel that way. I've played a lot of chamber music and made a few grown-up friends and gotten a pretty good look at the place, but that's all. I haven't worn blue corduroy knickers or played in the National Youth Symphony or competed in the mysterious ritual known as "challenges" or made friends with kids from all over like Jack and Debbie got to do. Thus, more than anything in the world, I want to come back next summer, not as Mrs. Sexton's student guinea pig, but, like the Velveteen Rabbit, transformed into somebody real—in this case, a genuine, 100% Interlochen camper.

Chapter 10. Friends and Rivals

This is NOT how things should be. I thought for sure that Mark Baxter would sit first chair in the Roosevelt High School Orchestra and I'd spend my sophomore year as his stand partner and move up to concertmistress after he graduates. But it turns out that Mark isn't even playing violin in orchestra because he got this stupid idea that he wanted to learn string bass. So now, instead of sitting next to me, the love of my life is all the way across the stage, miles from the violins, with his silly, old string bass. This wouldn't be so bad if it meant I got to sit first chair, but it doesn't. Instead, I'm starting out in third chair.

The person who put me there was Mr. Brauninger. The regular orchestra teacher is Mr. Bagley, under whom I sat first chair at Callanan and who's the only teacher I ever saw with a beard. He's a trumpet player who loves his marching band and doesn't know much about strings, as he himself will admit. Meanwhile, the Des Moines Public Schools hired Mr. Brauninger, a new young violinist and string teacher from the Eastman School of Music. I was excited when I heard Mr. Brauninger was coming, but then Mr. Bagley asked Mr. Brauninger to run the string auditions this fall.

The moment I walked into the audition room, I could tell that Mr. Brauninger wasn't going to like me. It was one of those things you just know without knowing why. Most men violinists are short and stocky like Mr. Shaw, but not Mr. Brauninger. He's tall with long arms and hands, a bland face and a reddish crew-cut, the kind of guy who ought to be wearing one of those colored undershirts and playing basketball, not the violin, which is way too little for him. The auditions were in this dead little room, and all the time I was playing, Mr. Brauninger felt too close to me. The room was so dead he could hear even the tiniest little flaw in my sound, which made me nervous, though my Mozart concerto still went all right. Then Mr. Brauninger put some music in front of me and asked me to sight-read, and my brain got tangled up and I stumbled once or twice.

When I'd finished, instead of saying something reassuring, he said, "Your solo was good, Cynthia, but you don't sight-read very well." His voice sounded like he was telling me I had halitosis, and I felt ashamed, even though I know that under normal circumstances I sight-read just as well as anybody else—I just don't sight-read very well with a big, pale, red-haired Frankenstein breathing down my neck in a dead, little room. But, of course, I couldn't tell Mr. Brauninger that.

I knew then that I wasn't going to be concertmistress, and sure enough, on the first day of rehearsal, Mr. Brauninger made an announcement. "We're fortunate to have not one but four outstanding violinists in our orchestra," he said and proceeded to explain that the four of us would rotate chairs, though who knows when that will ever happen. He put Glenda Ferris first, Sandy Ferguson second, me third, and Marian McCallister principal second. This was completely screwball. If anyone besides me ought to start out in first chair, it's Sandy, who played the Mendelssohn violin concerto last year, a really hard piece, but no, he had to put Glenda Ferris first even though she isn't half as good as Sandy and me. I suppose he did that because she's a junior and Sandy and I are only sophomores, but the first chair is supposed to be for whoever's best, not whoever's oldest.

All three of my girl rivals take lessons with teachers at Drake University, as does Mark Baxter. All the Drake kids play in the Des Moines Symphony, and they all hang around together. This made me feel left out until one day I got this great idea to ask Mrs. Sexton to ask Mr. Noyes, the conductor, if I could play viola in the Symphony so I could borrow a Drake viola to use for my audition tape for Interlochen. The real reason, of course, was that I wanted to be part of the Drake kids' clique and spend more time around Mark. Amazingly, this worked, and I'm now a member of the Des Moines Symphony's viola section, sitting on the second-to-last stand with a college girl named Joyce.

When Glenda and Marian find out I'm playing viola in the symphony, they ask me to play in a quartet with them and a cellist named Greta, who also takes lessons at Drake. Of the four of us, only Marian is pretty, with dark curls and a creamy complexion. Glenda is short and bossy, with a blond Dutch bob and glasses; Greta is tall and plump, with freckles; and I'm tall and chinless and pear-shaped. But how we look doesn't matter at all—what matters is how we sound on our instruments. The four of us rehearse on Mondays after lunch, with Mr. Brauninger for a coach, who gives us a Beethoven Opus 18 quartet to work on. We go to an Iowa String Quartet concert together, and Marian, who just got her license, drives us all down to KRNT Theater to play the Des Moines Symphony children's concert, after which we stop in at Noah's Ark for huge concoctions of vanilla ice cream and chocolate fudge sauce and cherries and peanuts and whipped cream. Despite being rivals for both orchestra chairs and Mark Baxter, the girls in my quartet are getting to be my best friends at Roosevelt. As for the others—the normal, non-musician kids—I hardly notice them, and they hardly notice me. I'm not, after all, a cheerleader, a baton twirler, or a synchronized swimmer, the only routes to popularity at Roosevelt, a big school with over a thousand students.

Over the fall semester, life gets more and more complicated. Mr. Brauninger announces that he's starting an all-city orchestra, and I have to play in that, and then he organizes a string ensemble, and I have to play in that, along with Mrs. Sexton's ensemble and Mark's father's ensemble at Plymouth, where I'm also in the choir. And in the school orchestra and the string quartet and the symphony and the sophomore chorus at school. Plus piano lessons and practicing three instruments while the everyday me goes to pep club rallies and Friday night football games and memorizes French vocabulary and reads *Julius Caesar* and studies for world history tests and babysits to make extra pocket money.

You might think with so much going on, I'd have forgotten about Interlochen, but I haven't. I keep seeing those words about world friendship at the front of Kresge stage and imagining myself up there in blue corduroy knickers performing with the National Youth Symphony. As a matter of fact, right now, I'm busy applying to go to Interlochen next summer. I'm learning the first movement of the Hoffmeister viola concerto to play on my audition tape, which Mrs. Sexton will help me make. I also have to fill out some forms and get recommendations from both my private teacher—that's easy—and my school orchestra teacher—that's not so easy. Obviously, I should ask Mr. Brauninger to recommend me, but I keep putting it off. Every time I see him, I tell myself I should just go up and ask, but somehow the words won't come out. The trouble is, I still don't think he likes me, though I'm pretty sure he wouldn't say no or write me a bad letter.

When I start getting tied up in knots this way, I tell myself not to be a paranoid idiot. It would be stupid if I didn't get to go to Interlochen because I was too shy to ask Mr. Brauninger to write me a letter. Enough is enough. I swear, tomorrow I'm going to go up and ask him no matter what. I really, really am.

Well, maybe not tomorrow—maybe the day after that, but no later than that—I swear.

Chapter 11. The Unfinished Symphony

The seats in the Roosevelt auditorium are all empty as I make my way up to the front row, though the lights are on over the yellow wooden stage, and the folding chairs set up for the orchestra. I set my violin case across the arms of two seats and sit down. I'm not sure I should be here. I'm not sure where I should be, because a few minutes ago, just before English class ended, when Mr. Craft was writing our assignment on the board, a boy in our class named Dennis came rushing in and shouted, "The president's been shot!" and everything stopped. Was this a joke? Dennis's eyes had little tear-jewels starting in the corners, which meant it must be true. But how? Where? When? Dennis started saying something about a parade in Dallas, but just then the bell rang, and everyone hurried out into the hall.

I didn't know what to do, so I came here. Orchestra is my fifth period class on Fridays, and tonight we're supposed to play the first movement of Schubert's "Unfinished Symphony" as an overture to the school play, *The Crucible* by Arthur Miller. Next week is Thanksgiving, when the choirs at Plymouth dress up like pilgrims and we sing "Come, ye thankful people come," and I sit at our round dining room table and stuff myself and wait for the relatives to leave so I can practice, and the day after that, the All-State Orchestra starts rehearsing down at the Hotel Fort Des Moines. I've been practicing like mad for the chair tryouts, but who knows now if there'll even be tryouts or All-

State or Thanksgiving or anything. It's like a giant meteor has suddenly hit the earth, smack in the middle of everything.

Soon other kids start showing up in the auditorium. Nobody says much, though you can feel the thoughts flying every which way as we take our places on the stage and start warming up. I look across the orchestra and see Mark Baxter sawing away on his bass as though nothing is wrong and wonder if anyone told him what happened. Finally, Mr. Bagley marches up onto the stage.

"I trust you all heard the news by now," he says quietly as he steps up onto the podium. Instead of starting the rehearsal, he just looks around at all of us, stroking his beard. No one says anything.

"Well, look, people," he says, finally. "I don't know if we're gonna be playing the Schubert gig tonight or not, but I think we oughta go through it just in case—okay? You with me?" Nobody answers, but when Mr. Bagley points to the first oboe, she gives us the A and we start to tune.

After the tuning has quieted down, he raises his arms into a square, the baton comes down, and the cellos and basses rumble out their opening bars, a little out of tune. Our school orchestra is better than most, but that's not saying much. After a few measures, we violins come in on our fast, fluttery sixteenth-notes, two to a pitch, diddle, diddle, diddle, diddle, diddle, diddle, up and down and up and down again until the woodwinds take over with their long tones braiding in and out, also out of tune.

The music goes on, but about half a page down, I look out and see a strange boy coming down the aisle with a slip of paper in his hand, and right away I know what this means. He marches straight up onto the stage and holds the paper out to Mr. Bagley, whose arms drop to his sides. The music peters out, though a French horn in the back gurgles on for a few more beats. Mr. Bagley turns to grab the note and read it, then steps down off the podium and stares at the floor for a long time, as if he's struggling to get control of himself. Finally, he climbs back up and glares at the back wall behind the trumpets.

"Well," he says. "The president just died." His voice sounds angry, as if we're somehow to blame for what happened. We sit very still, watching while he turns away again for a moment and shuts his eyes, then opens them and turns back towards us with a questioning look. It's obvious he doesn't know what to do.

"Well," he finally says, opening his eyes and raising his baton. "Carry on, I guess. Letter C, please." I wonder if he's a Democrat or a Republican.

After a few more bars, Glenda gets up and runs out of the auditorium with her violin, tears streaming down her face, and I remember that her father died just last year. A little later, Sandy runs out after her and then one of the girl cellists. I keep playing, though part of me wants to follow them. It feels like it's important to act just right, if only I knew what that was. Should I run out of the room and cry like the other girls or just carry on with Mr. Bagley? My hands keep cranking out line after line of music, while my mind runs through one scene after another—Jackie Kennedy with her children, Lyndon Johnson taking the oath of office, southern white trash dancing in the streets, Nikita Khrushchev giving the order to launch Russian missiles at the U.S., taking advantage of the crisis, buildings collapsing and the terrible, red fire raining down . . . No, Khrushchev wouldn't do that. Johnson would send missiles back at Russia if he did that—Khrushchev knows that, doesn't he?

President Johnson. I hate the sound of it. Johnson, the ugly, old Texas hick who's probably never been to a classical music concert in his life, moving into the White House with his plump little hen of a wife, and the beautiful, elegant, arts-loving Kennedys gone forever. The White House where now I'll never get to play like Jack Simpson did, whether I make it to Interlochen or not. As if that still matters. As if anybody's selfish, little wishes matter when all the hope has just gone out of the world, when nothing is ever going to be the same again. Because it's not. Even if Johnson turns out to be an okay president and the southern schools all get desegregated and we and the Russians somehow get to be friends and dump all the bombs in the ocean, nothing is ever going to be the same because just like that, something precious has been smashed to bits.

"Clarinets, I need more of you there," says Mr. Bagley, stopping the orchestra. "Letter H please, one more time." He's back in full conductor mode now, but his face is strained, as though held together with scotch tape.

Playing the lovely, liquid first theme with the other violins, I try to make myself cry like Glenda and Sandy. I think about Jackie coming into the White House nursery and taking Carolyn on her lap and telling her that her Daddy died. I think about the president's body in a flag-draped coffin being lowered into the ground and the soldiers saluting as someone plays taps. I remember the poem I memorized in the sixth grade that Walt Whitman wrote after Lincoln got shot: "O, captain, my captain, our fearful trip is done . . . " I think all the saddest thoughts I can muster, but the tears still won't come. It's like feeling a sneeze that won't happen while your nose tickles and burns. I glance over at Mark and see him seeing us, seeing the real girls crying and running out, and seeing me just sitting there sawing away with a face like a piece of wood, as if I were a boy. What's wrong with me?

Finally, I manage a dry sob and run out of the auditorium and into the hall. A girl in a red sweater is weeping into one of the pay phones and two others are huddled on the floor with their arms around each other. I wander the hallways crying crocodile tears until a decent amount of time has passed, then return to the orchestra and finish the piece, which ends just as somberly as it began.

Only then do I realize that we've been playing the "*Unfinished* Symphony," which has only two movements instead of the usual four because Franz Schubert, like John Fitzgerald Kennedy, died before he could finish his life's work. This is a beautiful thought, and for just a moment, the beauty takes the sting out of something terrible, and I know that whenever I play that symphony again, I'll always think of this day.

School lets out after the rehearsal, the play is canceled, and nothing is open on Monday, the day of the funeral. For the next three days, I drift in and out of the living room, leaving only for choir rehearsals and church services. At home, I sit with my parents watching replays of the shooting and interviews with politicians, Republicans as well as Democrats, all saying how shocked and sad they are, and thrown-together biographies of the president, while my violin waits in my room, the clock ticking off minutes until the All-State chair auditions on Friday.

Mom says I should go practice if I need to, and when I can't stand the waiting anymore, I do, but I feel like Nero fiddling while Rome burned and wonder what I'm missing out in the living room. Once, after I go back to the T.V., Dad tells me they just saw a man step out of the crowd and shoot Lee Harvey Oswald, the president's murderer. It's history in the making, and I missed it. I sit down and watch a replay, but it's not the same.

I guess for me the violin is like the security blanket Linus drags around in *Peanuts*. It's a funny thing to hang onto, not soft and cuddly like a blanket, but it's all I've got.

Chapter 12. The Letter

The letter arrives on a Wednesday afternoon in April. I'm just sitting down in my orchestra seat, second chair now with Sandy in first, as Mr. Brauninger finally made good on his promise to rotate us. But I don't even care where I sit at Roosevelt now, because believe it or not, in the auditions for chairs, both Mark Baxter and I got chosen as two of the four rotating concertmasters/mistresses of the Iowa All-State Orchestra, where each of us sat first chair for one of the four pieces on the concert. Glenda got sixth chair and Sandy and Marian were further back in the first violins. Ha!

The best part for me was that I got to sit next to Mark for two glorious days, ending with the concert in the KRNT Theater in front of millions of people. Sitting in first chair in front of a huge orchestra in my blue brocade formal with satin pumps dyed to match and Prince Charming at my side, I was sure that if I lived to be a hundred I'd never be that happy again.

My getting to be an All-State Concertmistress also made it easy for me to ask Mr. Brauninger, who came up and congratulated me, to recommend me for Interlochen. A few days later he told me that he'd written his letter, and that he'd mentioned my All-State victory, bless his heart. So, I guess he must not hate me after all.

Today I'm sitting down in orchestra when a messenger from the office shows up to tell me I have a phone call. Hurrying through the empty hallways,

I wonder if someone died. But when I pick up the phone, it's Mom, and I can tell from her voice that's not it.

"You got a letter," she says. My parents don't usually open my mail, but I gave Mom strict instructions to open anything from Interlochen and let me know about it right away. Now, I feel my heart speed up as she starts to read: "Dear Cindy, We are happy to notify you of your acceptance as a member of the High School Division for the 1964 season of the National Music Camp. We are also happy to advise you that you have been awarded a viola work scholarship to play in the orchestra in the amount of $475." She goes on reading, but the rest is just business and I'm feeling as though I've been filled with rocket-fuel, shooting me off like the kid with go-power in a Cheerios commercial. I race back to orchestra and tell Mr. Bagley and Mr. Brauninger and my violinist friends what happened, knowing that at home Mom is calling everyone she knows with the news. I also know that after she calls Dad, he'll tell his friends at the *Register*, and one of them will want to do a story about me.

Sure enough, the following week, a reporter and photographer show up at school, and they call me out of class for an interview in the office. The next Saturday, there it is, their article, on the special page that features high school kids, next to a story about the girls' track team at Urbandale High School. I had swim class the day of my interview, and my hair looks all limp and stringy. If I ever had a chance to make Mark Baxter like me, that chance is gone if he sees that awful picture.

Reading the article, I feel like they're talking about some other girl who just happens to have my name. It tells about the work scholarship, about what this person named Cynthia Housh had to do to apply to Interlochen and about her studying with Mary Sexton and playing in the Des Moines Symphony and being chosen an All-State concertmistress. Then it quotes this alleged me as saying, "I owe practically everything to my teacher, Mrs. Mary Sexton.

Without her help I doubt I'd have won." I could swear I didn't say the last part of that. Won what? It sounds like I entered a sweepstakes.

What it should have said is that I wouldn't have known Interlochen existed if it weren't for Mrs. Sexton. But of course, it wasn't just Mrs. Sexton who got me that letter, but a whole lot of people, going all the way back to Mrs. Neal in the fourth grade. When I think about all the people who helped me get to Interlochen, it boggles my mind. I can see them standing in rings like on a target. At the center of the target are Mrs. Sexton, my parents, and me. In the next ring are Mrs. Neal, Mr. Shaw, Mr. Brauninger, Mr. Bagley, Mr. Noyes, and my cousin Judy, for giving me my first violin. In the ring after that are Mrs. Walker, Mr. Baxter, and all my other vocal and instrumental music teachers. In that ring too are all my Des Moines music student friends and rivals. And beyond that, in the very outside ring, are all the folks who ever encouraged me, the kids who tossed me compliments in the hallways, the old man at the Salisbury House quartet concert, and everyone who ever clapped after hearing me play.

For me, all these Des Moines people are like Mission Control for an astronaut. I wouldn't be going to Interlochen if it weren't for them, and if I ever get to heaven, I hope they're all there.

Part II
Suddenly This Summer

Chapter 13. Interlochen Corners

Beatles wail out through the speakers about sending all their collective loving to their collective girlfriend "you-oou-ooou" to whom they're going to write letters every day while they're away as our Oldsmobile 88 blasts onto Interstate 80.

The song says just what I'd like to say to Mark Baxter, not that he'd want to hear it. Not after taking little raven-haired, creamy-complexioned, feather-brained Millie Gosling to the senior prom. But that's all water under the bridge, and now here I am in the backseat with Mom, racing away from unrequited love at seventy miles an hour while, unforgivably, next to Dad in the front seat sits not the charming Mark Baxter, but short, stocky, slightly prissy Bruce Simpson.

Bruce is Jack Simpson's younger brother and Mrs. Sexton's pet. He mostly plays piano, but Mrs. Sexton taught him string bass so he could get a scholarship like I got for viola. She never criticizes anything he does, and I even heard her tell him he has perfect pitch.

"Mrs. Housh," Bruce says, turning around and looking from her to me and back again, "please don't feel you have to sit in the back seat the whole way. I'll be *glad* to sit in the back with Cindy. Just say when."

No! I sit very still, waiting for the panic to subside. He's just trying to be polite, I tell myself, but the seeds of fear have already been planted. Can it actually be that he *likes* me?—No! Oh, God, please no. Why, why, why did I open my mouth at that last ensemble rehearsal and invite Bruce to ride with us all the way to Interlochen? What was I thinking?

"Oh, thank you, Bruce," says Mom in her sweetest Donna Reed voice, "but I'm just fine. And we need you to navigate. Maybe later you can help us out and drive for awhile." Bruce nods and turns back to his map while my mother winks at me and I silently forgive her for every unkind thing she ever did.

For the entire rest of the trip, all the way to Milwaukee in the car, over pork shanks at Mater's, seated on top of the Lake Michigan ferry, walking along the breakwater to the Ludington lighthouse at sunset, all the way up through the north woods to the turn-off at the "Interlochen corners" bill-board where US-31 meets MI-137 and into the main entrance, I know exactly where Bruce's body ends and mine starts and make sure I never accidentally brush against him for even a second. This is tricky, because if I carry it too far, Mom is sure to bawl me out for being unkind.

Be that as it may, by the night before we arrive at Interlochen, I have other things on my mind. Not only am I going back to the National Music Camp, I'm going back for real this time. Not as a visitor, not as Mrs. Sexton's guinea-pig, but as a full-fledged camper with a scholarship. A camper to whom glorious things might happen. I might be playing in the orchestra on NBC radio, playing concerts with Van Cliburn, and maybe even going to Washington, D.C. at the end of the summer—not to play at the White House this time, according to a letter we orchestra players received, but on a barge out in the Potomac, at a place called the "Watergate."

Meanwhile, none of these things will happen if I don't make it into the Youth Symphony and instead wind up in the second-string Concert Orches-tra, and the auditions are tomorrow afternoon. The mere thought of the audition makes it impossible for me to lie still in my double bed, especially with my parents a few feet away, listening to every toss and turn. The trouble is, I have absolutely no idea how I'm going to do. I might get first chair or last chair or anything in between. I don't want to wait to find out how my audition goes or what chair I'll get. I want to know NOW, and the not knowing keeps me twisting and flailing in the sheets until my mom finally stumbles out of bed in the dark and brings me a glass of water and one of her big, red Phenobarbital pills.

Both my parents take pills for their nerves. When I was in fifth grade, my dad got depressed and kept imagining he had cancer until he started seeing a psychiatrist named Dr. Cash, who gave him tranquillizers. Mom said I should never tell anyone about this because if his boss found out, Dad might lose his job. Mom never went to Dr. Cash, but her regular doctor gives her sleeping pills, which she sometimes shares with me.

I swallow the pill and slip into a semi-coma, but in the morning, the jitters are back and my head is filled with what-ifs. What if we're arriving on the wrong day and everything's already started? What if the camp people say they made a mistake and sent me the wrong letter and I wasn't really accepted after all? What if my counselor looks at me like I'm from Mars when I introduce myself? What if my audition is so bad that I get last chair in the Concert Orchestra?

As we come up to the entrance of the camp and join the line of cars, it's clear that this is the right day, at least. A girl in a madras headscarf tells us where our two divisions are, High School Boys and High School Girls. We go first across the highway to drop Bruce off, then make our way to HSG Headquarters, a green wooden building just beyond the gate, where I learn that I'm to be in Cabin 16, putting another "what-if" to rest.

Mom follows me into the cabin, where the counselor, instead of looking at me like I'm from Mars, introduces herself as Sue Lamb. Sue is a squat, tan, thirtyish woman with curly, yellow-blond hair. She looks more like a gym teacher than somebody who belongs at Interlochen and gives me a hearty handshake. Sue and Mom chat a little, and I learn that at home, she really *is* a gym teacher and that here at the camp she teaches tennis and swimming.

Now that I know I'm supposed to be here and have met my counselor, I can't wait for my parents to leave so I can start my transformation into a real Interlochen High School Girl, but all at once they start dragging their feet. Mom insists on helping me unpack and make up my bed while Dad waits outside. When the bed is made, Mom and I go back out, but then the two of them stand there and stand there, leaning against the Oldsmobile and thinking of things to say to make me feel guilty for going away.

I'm not sure why I always feel guilty at times like this, but I think it must have something to do with Sally, the girl baby my parents lost to a kidney tumor before they adopted my brother David. Sally was born by cesarean, and back in those days, you could only have one baby that way. But ten years later, my mom's doctor told her she could have a second cesarean after all, and here I am. All of which means that I've never had any doubt that I was loved, the only problem being that sometimes I feel a bit too loved. Like right now.

Sometimes I envy kids with parents who didn't have to go through so much to get them born. First, mine lost Sally, and then when Mom got pregnant with me, she was really, really sick, throwing up for months, as she loves to remind me. She wants to make sure I know how much she suffered to have me, as if it's my fault. And Dad just wants me in the room with him all the time and gets upset if I even close my bedroom door for a little while, which makes me feel all smothery. Now, though, I have a whole summer ahead of me with nobody clinging or making me feel guilty, which is going to be a huge relief, as soon as it starts. If it ever starts.

"It's going to be a long, hot summer without you, Daughter," Dad says. "I wish I could stay up here where it's cool. Maybe we'll just stick around and keep you company." His words set off alarms in my brain, though I know he's just teasing. I promise to write them twice a week and call them every Saturday. I promise to write Grandma and Mrs. Sexton and my friends at home. I promise not to spend all my time practicing and "have a little fun" and to talk to my counselor if I run into any problems. Finally, after kisses and hugs, they get back in the Oldsmobile and drive away.

Then, just like that, I'm alone among strangers.

Chapter 14. Becoming Real

My transformation into a real Interlochen camper starts back inside Cabin 16, which, like the cabin I stayed in during post-camp, contains eight narrow bunk beds spaced four on each side. Between the beds, girls are chatting, unpacking, spreading blankets, and arranging toiletries, while a jumble of violin, saxophone, and French horn noises stream in through the windows, music now truly "in the air," mixed with the excitement of getting acquainted. All around me, I hear girls asking each other the same questions: What's your name? Where are you from? What's your major? Have you been here before?

"Hi, there, bunkmite!" says a voice from below. I look down to see a short, busty girl with shining brown hair and brown button eyes making up the lower bunk.

"Ahm Buffy Jean," she drawls. "What's your naime, bunkmite?" Her voice, though Southern, is low-pitched, more the voice of a cowgirl than a Scarlett O'Hara.

I tell her my name and we ask and answer the usual questions. As we talk, I wonder if Buffy Jean is prejudiced against Negroes. If I'm prejudiced against anybody it's probably Southerners, because of the awful way they treat colored people, beating them up and putting them in jail just because they want to eat at a lunch counter or go to a decent school. I don't know why anyone would want to live in the South. Buffy Jean tells me she's from Longview,

Texas—which is better, I think, than one of those awful states like Alabama or Mississippi, so maybe she's okay—that this is her first summer at Interlochen, and that she's a piano and organ major.

After we've all unpacked, our next task is to go get our uniforms at a gray cinderblock building called "Housekeeping." On the right side of this building is a long line of girls going in one door and coming out another and on the left side a long line of boys doing the same thing. My cabin mates and I join the girls' line, chatting excitedly all the while, getting to know each other better by the minute. Inside the building, we're each given one new-looking pair and one faded pair of dark blue knickers plus four short-sleeved light blue blouses, which is all we get to wear while we're here.

Thus equipped, we hurry back to Cabin 16 and get into our new clothes, including the light blue knee socks we had to bring or buy at the camp store. At Interlochen, I now know, you can tell the different girls and women by their socks: light blue for High School Girls, red for Intermediates, and dark blue for Juniors, University Women, faculty, and staff.

Once I'm wearing my new uniform, all I have to do is pin my round, white National Music Camp name badge over my hip to complete my outfit. The purpose of this badge, according to Sue, is not just to tell people your name, but also to let the ushers know you can attend concerts and other events for free. Thus, the worst thing that can happen to you at Interlochen is to have your badge taken away, which counselors sometimes do to kids they catch breaking the rules.

"Would you believe, I had my badge taken away last year just for sitting on the lawn with my boyfriend's head in my lap," says a black-haired girl on the other side of the room. "They're really paranoid here about boys and girls touching each other, for some reason. I mean, they even have this crazy expression—'NBC,' which stands for 'No Bodily Contact.' Do you believe that?"

This seems weird to me, but since Mark Baxter isn't here, I don't figure it has much to do with me. I'll cross that bridge if and when I ever come to it.

After the big clothes-change, we all go to Sunday dinner in the cafeteria. Meals now are a lot noisier than they were during post-camp, when just a few, quiet adults sat together. Now the whole, big room is filled with the clatter of silverware on metal trays, chairs scraping, chattering teenagers, and shouts from kitchen staff. Dinner is roast pork, mashed potatoes, canned peas, jello salad, and chocolate cake. I gobble it all down, though I know I'll regret this, my stomach being jumpy over my upcoming audition.

By three o'clock, I've picked up my viola—the same one I used in post-camp, thank God—practiced for an hour, and survived performing, in front of the two main viola teachers, a page of Hoffmeister and a half-page of sight reading—which goes just fine, thank you very much, Mr. Brauninger— after which I reward myself with a Melody Freeze before I make my way back to Cabin 16. I have no idea what the viola teachers thought, but at least it wasn't one of those performances that left me wanting to throw myself off a bridge afterwards.

By now, I may look like an Interlochen camper on the outside, but on the inside I'm still not quite full-fledged, not until the all-camp assembly that takes place that night. Kresge Auditorium is packed with campers. On the stage, a row of blue-clad adults are seated in folding chairs. One of them is Dr. Maddy, but I don't recognize any of the others. Finally, a big, solid-looking man with greased-down gray hair gets up and introduces himself as George Wilson, the Vice President of Interlochen, and reminds us that he signed every one of our acceptance letters. After a few words of welcome, Mr. Wilson introduces "a man of vision, whose dream long ago led to all of us being here today, an extraordinarily great man to whom we owe an enormous debt of gratitude, Dr. Joseph E. Maddy!"

Kresge erupts into cheers as Dr. Maddy gets to his feet and walks up to the podium. His speech is fast and jerky, but I can make out most of what he says, which is about the history of the camp. He tells how in the 1920s, when he became a music educator in Richmond, Indiana, there wasn't much instrumental music in the schools, and how he built up his own school orchestra and organized the first National High School Symphony in 1926, with players from 39 states. The kids in the symphony begged Dr. Maddy to start a music camp so they could play together longer than just a few days.

"It was a pretty tall order," he says, "but I couldn't let those kids down, and I told them I'd see what I could do." He tells how he had to find a good location for the camp and how he worked to raise money to pay the bills in the middle of the Great Depression. "A lot of folks back then thought I was crazy," he says, "but I didn't let that stop me." The National High School Orchestra camp opened in June of 1928, and in 1931, after they added a band, a choir, and an opera program, they changed the name to the National Music Camp. The camp kept on growing, broadcasting radio concerts nationwide and adding dance and drama and visual arts programs, and in 1962, the Interlochen Arts Academy, a year-round school for students gifted in the arts, opened its doors, with 124 students attending.

Now, in the summer of 1964, over 1500 campers in four different divisions—Junior, Intermediate, High School, and University—are here to attend programs in all the arts. These campers are from all fifty states plus nine countries outside the U.S. Starting with Alabama, Dr. Maddy has us stand up, state by state, then country by country. Each group of kids cheers as they stand up. I see only a few other Iowans as I get up, and hardly anybody from the South except for Texas, but when he gets to Michigan, half of Kresge stands up.

To end the program, a big, jolly-looking bald man gets up and leads us through the camp song, the words of which are printed on the program:

Oh, sound the call to dear old Interlochen!
Land of the stately pine.
Where stalwart hands and loyal ever greet you,
Faithful for Auld Lang Syne.
Old friends you'll meet,
New ones you'll greet,
A welcome you'll ever find
So sound the call to dear old Interlochen!
Shrine of the muse divine.

I have to guess at the tune, but I follow along, then make my way back to Cabin 16 with my new friends, now a 100%, full-fledged Interlochen High School Girl, inside and out.

Chapter 15. Gifted Youth

"G—I—F . . . T—E—D . . . Y—O—U—TH! Gifted youth! Gifted youth! Forever we will wave our knickers high!"

Campers at the next table chant to the tune of the Mickey Mouse Club song on my first morning of camp, pound on the table with their spoons, and laugh as I gobble down my powdered eggs and soggy toast across from Buffy Jean, who invited me to breakfast with her.

"Hey, gifted youth—that's *us!*" she says, then dashes over to the other table to join the chanters, one of whom she recognizes, leaving her food half-eaten across from me.

She's right, I realize. "Guiding America's Gifted Youth"—stamped on every piece of Interlochen stationery—refers to everyone in this room, including me. Not only am I fifth chair viola in the National Youth Symphony, as I just learned from the lists posted outside the cafeteria, I'm also one of America's Gifted Youth! If that isn't enough to swell your head, I don't know what is.

Half an hour later, viola in hand, I'm climbing onto the tiered stage of the Interlochen Bowl. On each stand is a black folder of music. I wander through the stands until I find "Viola III"—which chairs five and six share—in the second row, just a few feet from the conductor, and sit down in the outside seat. I'm sure I'm in the right place, but I can't shake off the feeling that this is a mistake, that any minute now, somebody is going to come up and tell me to move to the back.

No one does. Instead, a serious-looking boy with big, black glasses, slicked-down hair, and a troubled complexion, sits down next to me and holds out his hand.

"Burt Merrill," he says, in a deep, bass voice. I can't believe he really expects me to shake hands, though I do, of course. Where I come from, handshakes are for politicians and men your parents introduce you to at church, not for greeting other high school kids.

I open our folder and find two half-pages of music—one with "The Stars Spangled Banner" and the other with "Interlochen Theme" handwritten across the top—along with the viola part to Dvorak's "New World Symphony" and a piece called *Tod und Verklärung,* which I recognize as German from the Bach motet we sang in Mr. Baxter's choir at Plymouth. The composer is someone called Richard Strauss. Could he be a relative of Johann Strauss, the waltz king? I open the music and page through it. Yikes! The staffs are black with triplet and sixteenth-note runs peppered with sharps and flats. Now I'm sure I don't belong here.

"It's *Death and Transfiguration,"* says Burt. "Not an easy piece, but don't worry. Everybody fakes runs in Strauss." He tunes his viola and starts playing through the easiest part, which doesn't even look that easy, while I start taking the runs apart, a measure at a time, puzzling out the accidentals.

I've gone through about half a page when a youngish, black-haired man steps up onto the podium, claps his hands, and as the playing peters out, introduces himself, in a clear, tenor voice, as Waldie Anderson, the orchestra manager. His job as manager, he explains, is to take care of orchestra business. He's the person we should talk to if we have to leave a rehearsal or aren't sure where to sit or have problems with the lighting. Then he goes over the rules. We're to be in the Bowl twenty minutes before the rehearsal starts so we can be warmed up and ready to go by eight o'clock. When the concertmistress stands up to tune the orchestra, we're to quiet down immediately, and there's to be no talking while the conductor is speaking. Orchestra will meet every day from eight to eleven, and strings and winds will meet separately in the afternoons from three to four. Sectionals will be held on Thursday mornings from eleven to twelve, and challenges on Fridays at the same time. "If you don't know what challenges are, you soon will," he says, and the old-timers laugh.

After Mr. Anderson has introduced us to the music librarian, who says a few things about practice folders and bowings, he motions for the concert-mistress, a thin wisp of a girl with a mop of light brown curls, to stand up and tune the orchestra by pointing to the first oboist, who gives two A's, one for the strings and one for the winds. "That's Amy Joanou," whispers the brown-haired fourth-chair violist, a girl named Emily whom I met in the breakfast line, "and next to her is Annie Kavafian. They were rivals all last year for concertmistress, and it looks like they still are." Annie is short and neat, with black curls and shining black eyes.

All this time, Dr. Maddy has been standing next to the podium, and now he climbs up and greets the orchestra with a nod, announces that we're to start with the "New World Symphony," opens his score, and raises his arms in the air. As the baton comes down and I start to play, I suddenly realize that I'm not hearing Dvorak. Instead, the strings are playing a raucous fiddler's melody. Dr. Maddy drops his arms and feigns surprise, then stands waiting for the tune to end.

"It's a joke we always play at a conductor's first rehearsal," Emily whispers. "It's the hoedown. Try to play along." Burt and I start sawing back and forth while the melody knits together in my head, and by the time it's over, I've got it, more or less. At the end, everyone laughs, and I hear feet scuffling back and forth on the wooden platforms.

Now the joke is over, and Dr. Maddy raises his arms again, this time for real. His forearms shake, and the baton wobbles uncertainly through the beats as we begin to play. At the beginning, the cellos have the melody, and we violas can fit our notes in around theirs, but a few bars later, the strings have to come in after the fourth beat in the measure on a syncopated rhythm. A strong beat is needed to bring us in together, but all I can see from Dr. Maddy is a fuzzy jerk, and everyone comes in at different times. This keeps happening, but as we go on playing, we begin to listen to each other. By the break I've learned to ignore Dr. Maddy's beats and follow Amy, which is what everybody else is doing.

"Have you heard about the new Maddy doll?" Emily whispers to me. "Wind him up, and watch him follow the orchestra." I snicker, but I can't help feeling sorry for Dr. Maddy, who was probably a good conductor once but now is just too old and shaky.

At ten o'clock, after we've read through the whole Dvorak symphony, Mr. Anderson yells "Take ten!" and the kids around me all start getting up and walking off the stage. I don't need to go to the bathroom, but I take a quick trip up to the camp store window for some Turkish Taffy, which glues my teeth together. By the time I've finished the candy, it's time to go back.

We spend the second half of the rehearsal on the Strauss piece. The syncopated rhythm at the beginning, Dr. Maddy tells us, is supposed to be someone's heartbeat. As we play, I begin to realize that the piece really is about somebody dying. Did Dr. Maddy choose it because he's old and knows he's going to die himself pretty soon? It's a creepy thought, but I'm too busy trying to play the notes to go on with it. The problem isn't just getting the notes, which really aren't as hard as they look, but where to put them. Faking my way through one chromatic run after another, I can see that Burt and Emily are doing the same thing. The runs all sound like mud, and it's hard to believe that we're going to be performing this piece on Sunday night, six days from now.

Between now and then, I'll need to practice like crazy to learn the notes, not just because of the concert, but because on Friday challenges will determine whether I keep my chair or am promoted or demoted. The problem is, when am I supposed to practice? Mornings are taken up with orchestra, and afternoons with theory class, violin lessons, string quartet rehearsals, and more orchestra. That leaves only the evenings, unless I want to go to any concerts, in which case it leaves nothing, and I have to practice the violin as well as the viola. What am I going to do?

During the next couple of days, I figure out at least part of the answer, which is to practice as much as I can during rehearsals. Not that I can play the music out loud, but whenever the conductor is rehearsing the winds, I can finger the viola notes and play them in my mind, which helps. There's also time before orchestra starts and time during the break and an hour before lunch on Tuesdays and Wednesdays and half an hour between string rehearsals and dinner. It all adds up, and since everyone else is as busy as I am, I have a feeling that the secret of doing well in challenges is to make use of these little bits of time.

As to whether anyone else has figured out the same secret, I guess I'll find out on Friday.

Chapter 16. Cabin 16

Meanwhile, over the course of the next week, I get to know my cabin-mates. By the end of the week, I know all their first names and some of the last ones plus some other things about each of them, and I can feel the sixteen of us plus Sue turning into one big family. With all the pressure of rehearsals, lessons, auditions, and challenges, it's good to have Cabin 16 to retreat to, the one place where we don't have to perform and can just flop down on our bunks and read, cry, talk, or just stare into space.

The girls in the cabin are from all parts of the U.S., though mostly from the East and Midwest, especially Michigan, with all the different arts represented among us. There are a whole bunch of black-haired girls from New York and New Jersey, probably Jewish, who say "quoorter" instead of "quarter" and at first seem all the same to me, but as time goes on, they gradually turn into different people. Lindy and Nina are both dancers, quiet and gentle. Merri is an actress and singer who just got the lead in *Little Mary Sunshine* and walks around singing the same phrases over and over. Merri's best friend in the cabin is Jody, a pianist who's always complaining about being flat-chested and puts Kleenex in her bra. Audrey's a sweet, freckle-faced violinist with whom I'm getting to be friends. Ruth is a bassoonist who calls herself "Mama Bernstein" because she likes to give advice. Already, she's fixated on my makeup, informing me that there's a line around my chin where my Cover Girl ends and attacking me with powder puffs.

The rest of the girls are mostly from the Midwest and have different hair colors and accents that sound normal to me, though probably not to the kids from the East. Bess is a quiet blond flutist from Cadillac, Michigan. Melody is a clarinet player from Indiana who bunks with Ruth and always has something nice to say to you. Nan is an artist from St. Joseph, Michigan and practices a neat-sounding religion called Bahai, and another artist is Jackie from Indiana, who's always talking about having to go "throw a pot." Jane, whose bunk is next to mine, is from Detroit, and is a real violist, not just a violinist playing viola like I am, and our section leader. She takes from this terrific private teacher in Detroit named Ara Zerounian.

"He teaches Annie Kavafian and her sister Ida," she says, her voice reverent when she says Annie's name, as though she's talking about a movie star. Annie was a concerto winner for the last three summers, Jane says, and her sister played a Mozart concerto last year with the Intermediate orchestra even though she was only a Junior.

The wild-card in Cabin 16 is Buffy Jean, the only girl from the South, who isn't like anyone else I've met here at Interlochen. Most kids here tend to be introverts like me, but Buffy Jean is the proverbial extrovert. She has a deep, Southern belly laugh and sometimes laughs even at things that aren't that funny, just because she loves to laugh. To me, she seems more like a cheerleader than an Interlochen camper. But although Buffy Jean is about as different from me as a person can be, for some reason, she seems to want to be my friend. She asks me to go to breakfast with her almost every day, though once we get there, she's constantly going off to talk to boys she just met or wants to meet. This makes me feel invisible, though she always comes bopping back sooner or later. In the cabin, she tells me about all the different kids she met, including her various dates, and she seems to know everybody, unlike yours truly, who knows only string players and Cabin 16 girls and goes out on dates only in her dreams.

Over all of us presides the queen of Cabin 16, Sue Lamb, who supervises our sleeping habits (in the morning, the first thing we hear is Sue's voice going, "Crawl out of those sacks, girls!"), reminds us not to put Kotex in the toilet, and organizes activities. Under Sue's leadership, we already have plans to hike to the Cracker Barrel for breakfast some Sunday, order pizza late at night for a cabin party in the big room under the sun decker, and spend a night out on the beach.

Bedtime in High School Girls follows a strict routine. It starts at ten o'clock, when a trumpeter blows a special bugle call known as "tattoo." As soon as we hear the bugle call, the practicing from various quarters stops, the music goes out of the air, and the counselors come out of their cabins and start hustling girls inside. By ten fifteen, we're to be in pajamas on our bunks for Sue's announcements, and lights out is at ten thirty. On weekends, when there are concerts, the times are a bit later, but the same routine still applies.

After the trumpet plays taps and all the naked light bulbs in the cabin ceiling are out, there are a couple of bedtime traditions. First, one of the girls reads something inspirational, which she gets to choose. It could be a poem, a Bible verse, or just a quote. I haven't done a reading yet myself, but I've already chosen my first one. I'm going to read a poem by Henry Wadsworth Longfellow that's in a book I brought with me, the poem that ends,

> *And the night shall be filled with music*
> *And the cares that infest the day*
> *Shall fold their tents like the Arabs*
> *And silently steal away.*

I love those lines, which make me feel all peaceful inside, and I can't wait to read them out with my flashlight in my most inspirational voice.

Then, after the reading, we start to hear "Slumber Music." Sometimes popular and sometimes classical, but always soft and pretty, the music drifts in from here and there beyond the dark windows, played or sung by girls from a different cabin each night. Sue says that Dr. Maddy sometimes brings visitors down to HSG to listen to the slumber music, and we need to think about what we'll do when it's Cabin 16's turn.

As a person who sometimes suffers from insomnia, I soon learn that slumber music—plus exhaustion—works even better for me than pheno-barbital. On Thursday night, with challenges on Friday morning, I'm having trouble lying still, just like in the motel the night before I got here. My mind keeps playing the harder passages of the Strauss over and over, my fingers drumming on the covers, and I can feel my neck and shoulder muscles getting tighter by the minute, but then, all at once, some lovely, silvery voices come rippling in through the screen at the foot of my upper bunk to drown out the notes in my head, singing about reaping and sowing and how good it was to be young and about the green summer leaves calling them home. I turn my pillow over to the cold side and let the voices, crushed stars, stream through me.

Safe in my bunk in Cabin 16 and bathed in music, I feel my muscles slacken and my mind go quiet. Then, as the last verse ends, the voices move off to begin again, echoing from somewhere further down the rows of cabins, then move again and echo one last time, fading into nothing and leaving only the bump of a moth against the screen and a few faint snores in their wake.

Chapter 17. Bloody Friday

"Is there a change?" asks Mr. Bundra, the viola teacher. His voice is dead serious, the voice of a judge asking a foreman if the jury has reached a verdict at the end of a murder trial.

I don't even have to think about which of the two short performances I just heard is better—Jane's or Evelyn's—on the Dvorak passage that Mr. Bundra chose for the tryouts. To my relief, it's not the hardest passage, and I'm sure I can play it myself when my turn comes. Meanwhile, it's obvious Jane is where she belongs, so I keep my hand in my lap with my eyes still shut tight.

"There is no change," says Mr. Bundra.

I open my eyes. The viola teacher is a stocky man with a crew-cut who looks more like a wrestling coach than a classical musician, sitting there on his high stool in the basement of the combination gym and auditorium, the Jessie V. Stone Building, better known as "JVS." Rolled-up gym mats line the walls, along with kettle drums and extra black music stands. In front of Mr. Bundra, twenty violists are seated in two rows of pairs.

Yesterday, he conducted our sectional rehearsal, coaching us through all the hardest passages, but now it's Friday, and these are my very first Interlochen challenges. Before they began, Mr. Bundra explained how they'd work. We'd start at the front of the section and work our way back from first to last chairs, then do the same thing in reverse. The front-to-back part is called "tryouts"—don't ask me why—and the back-to-front part is called "challenges." The first two violists would play, and then we'd all close our eyes and vote about who played the passage better. "If you think there should be a change," he said, "raise your hand." Then, the second and third chairs would play, and so on. "Try to listen closely and be as fair as you can," said Mr. Bundra. "Do unto others as you would have them do unto you."

Now, I sit very still and listen to Evelyn play the same passage again, then Greta. My own turn is coming and my hands are starting to sweat, which makes it hard to concentrate. Neither player sounds much better than the other, and I keep my hand down again. "There is no change," says Mr. Bundra. Then Greta and Emily play. Greta's sound is clear, but Emily's is a little rough, and she stumbles in one spot, sending a flash of hope through me. I know I can do better than that, and I'm next.

When it's my turn, I set my bow on the strings and start to play. My sound is a little shaky, but no more so than Emily's, and the notes all come out clearer. Whether I win or not, I deserve to, I'm sure. I close my eyes. As I raise my hand to vote for myself, I can hear rustling sounds, a good sign. I open my eyes.

"There is a change," says Mr. Bundra and gives me a nod. I try not to smile as Emily and I switch places. She gets to play again before Burt plays, does better this time, and stays in fifth chair. As the tryouts go on down the line, the sounds get rougher, weaker, and less in tune until the last person plays.

Then, suddenly, from the rear of the section, I hear a strong, sure viola sound, with all the notes perfectly in tune. I turn around and look. A tall, pale boy with a big yellowish viola is sitting in last chair. I shouldn't be surprised: I've been hearing rumors about this kid all week. His name is Heinrich, he's from Austria, and he didn't get here until Tuesday and missed the auditions, so they just put him at the back of the section. Everyone knew he might be dangerous, and now he's proving it.

After Heinrich and the next-to-last chair switch places, Mr. Bundra announces the challenge passage, which is from the Strauss, though not the hardest part, on which all of us except Jane would probably sound equally terrible. Heinrich plays the Strauss passage perfectly, then proceeds to outplay one person after another, moving closer and closer to me, a big, viola-playing tank rolling over everything in its path. Before I know it, I too, like everyone else, hear the dreaded words, "There is a change," putting me back in fifth chair after just minutes on second stand, while Heinrich ends up in second chair, leaving only Jane undefeated.

A couple of kids smile and congratulate Heinrich, but he just gives them a stiff nod, as if to say, "But of course I belong on the first stand—where else should I be?" This is not a good way to win friends and influence people. I walk back down the concourse with Emily, my new stand partner. I keep looking at her face to see if she's mad that I beat her, but we're both still in shock about Heinrich, and she seems to have forgotten about my own role in her misfortune.

All the way back to HSG, we pass kids asking each other how they did in challenges. "I went up three," a girl shouts at a boy across the way, "how'd you do?"

The boy points his thumb down and holds up two fingers, shaking his head. "Not my day," he says. I feel sorry for the boy. It must feel awful to have to sit in a lower chair than you started out in, but of course next week he'll have a chance to move back up.

It's still too early for lunch when I get back to Cabin 16. After exchanging challenge reports with my cabin mates, I go over to the sun decker, settle onto a bench, and think through the morning's events. Challenges, I've been told, were Dr. Maddy's invention. The story goes that before he became a music educator, he was a violist in the Minneapolis Symphony and resented the fact that in professional orchestras, promotions are based on seniority, not on how well you play. So, when Dr. Maddy started directing school orchestras, he wanted competition to be fair, and challenges were the result. Along the way, he figured out that getting kids to constantly compete also made them practice harder. It's like factories in the U.S. making better quality cars than they make in Russia because in the U.S. everybody has to compete and under communism people get paid the same whether they work hard or not, which makes them lazy.

Personally, I'm not sure if I'm going to like challenges or not. To be sure, it's fairer than Mr. Brauninger deciding where we belonged after one measly audition in the fall and keeping us there all year long. And it's good to know that I still have seven more chances to work my way up to first chair. That's bound to make me practice harder, but whether it will make me happier is something else. The whole thing could be pretty hard on your nerves. I'm afraid I'll start having nightmares about going down and down. And what about the kid who keeps trying week after week to get out of last chair and never succeeds—isn't so much losing going to make him want to quit? There must be a reason they call this "Bloody Friday."

Then, too, it seems like this constant competing is bound to affect the way campers feel towards each other. If I beat people are they going to hate me the way you could just feel everyone hating Heinrich? How are we supposed to play and live together with everybody always trying to outdo everybody else? And what about the music? Won't that get lost in the shuffle?

Mrs. Sexton told me that when Debbie was here, a girl in her cabin was so upset after she beat her in challenges that Debbie quit trying to move up. "She just didn't think orchestra chairs were worth hurting people's feelings over," Mrs. Sexton said. "To Debbie, all that really matters is the music, not where she sits."

I have to admit, I'm not Debbie. I want to win this game, and I'm going to try as hard as I can to get first chair viola by the end of the summer. But if I'm ever in Debbie's situation, I like to think I might at least consider doing what she did, that I might put being a good person before having to win. I like to think that anyway.

Chapter 18. Interlochen Sunday

On Sunday morning, we get to sleep a little later and there are sweet rolls in the cafeteria for breakfast. Instead of wearing the usual shabby blue shirts, we wear our own white ones with our best knickers, and after breakfast, Buffy Jean and Bess and I go to Kresge for the non-denominational service.

We can hear a brass choir playing as we pass between the cinderblock walls at the back of the auditorium and sit down on a couple of green park benches. After the brass choir finishes, a girl on the stage gets up and strikes some chimes three times, which is apparently the signal for the choir, seated in rows behind some adults in folding chairs, to sing:

> *The Lord . . . is in his holy temple,*
> *The Lord . . . is in his holy temple.*
> *Let all the earth keep silence,*
> *Keep silence befo – ore him.*

For an instant, I feel something shimmer in the air, as if God is trying to materialize, right here in Kresge.

Then the organist starts to play "My Country, Tis of Thee," and we all stand up to sing. The service includes "The Lord's Prayer," so I guess it's meant mostly for Christians even though it seems like half this place is Jewish. Can Jewish kids at Interlochen go to Friday night services in Traverse City? I wonder. Or do they have something here for them? Do all the Christian music and prayers here make them mad? I've never heard any of the Jewish girls in my cabin complain, but at home, Ricky Zerin's mother walked out of the Hanawalt auditorium when we sang Christmas carols, she was so mad. But Ricky's father was a rabbi, so she was probably extra aware. Rabbi Zerin used to come to school and teach us about Jewish holidays, and one time the Plymouth Youth Club went to visit his temple, which had the Ten Commandments and some scroll things up front instead of a cross. Other than that, it didn't seem that different from a church. . .

Daydreaming about the Zerin family, I miss half of Dr. Maddy's "message," which is called "Foundation for Learning" and was probably something about positive thinking and the power of prayer, like in that Norman Vincent Peale book I read in junior high. Finally, after we've sung "Holy, Holy, Holy," a man named Clarence Stephenson gets up and reads a closing prayer in a deep, radio announcer's voice. The prayer is called "A Camper's Prayer," and I breathe in every word, clichés and all, feeling the prayer's inspiration flow all the way out to my fingertips.

"God of the hills, grant us strength to go back into the cities without faltering, strength to do our daily tasks without tiring and with enthusiasm, strength to help our neighbors who have no hills to remember.

"God of the lake, grant us thy peace and thy restfulness, peace to bring into a world of hurry and confusion, restfulness to carry to the tired whom we shall meet every day. Content to do small things with a freedom from littleness, self-control for the unexpected emergency, and patience for the wearisome task, with deep depths within our soul to bear us through the crowded places.

"Grant us the hush of the night time when the pine trees are dark against the sky line, the humbleness of the hills who in their mightiness know it not, and the laughter of the sunny waves to brighten the cheerless spots of a long winter.

"God of the stars, may we take back the gifts of friendship and of love for all. Fill us with great tenderness for the needy person at every turning. Grant that in all our perplexities and every-day decisions we may keep an open mind.

"God of the wilderness, with thy pure winds from the northland blow away our pettiness; with the harsher winds of winter drive away our selfishness and hypocrisy; fill us with the breadth and the depth and the height of thy wilderness. May we live out the truths which thou has taught us, in every thought and word and deed.

Amen."

That afternoon, we play our first broadcast concert. Big signs are placed outside all the entrances to Kresge that say, "Quiet, please, broadcast in progress." On the stage, technicians fiddle with microphones, moving them here and there among us, then asking the orchestra to play short passages to test out their sound equipment. When everything is in place, Dr. Maddy stands waiting for the signal to start, while behind some big, glass windows above one side of the stage, an announcer is saying things we can't hear. Finally, a man in headphones points at Dr. Maddy with a big, sweeping gesture, and Dr. Maddy raises his arms to conduct the first movement of the Dvorak. The seats in front of us are almost all empty, yet we're playing for a huge, invisible audience. It's like playing for God, and I'm not sure if I like it or not. God doesn't clap, and I miss that part.

What I don't know yet is how much clapping we're going to get tonight. The Sunday evening concert is in the Bowl, which is packed with campers from all divisions, and their only job is to applaud. Playing in the Bowl is really different from playing in Kresge. The acoustics aren't nearly as echoey, as it's just a big wooden shed surrounded by trees. But this feels more like we're all together in nature, so I can see why they still have our concerts here.

The program starts with "The Star-Spangled Banner," which we have to stand up to play. Then comes the Dvorak, and after that the Strauss. It feels good to be able to play at least some passages rather than faking. The piece starts off on somebody's death-bed, but after some crazy, swirly death-struggle parts, it ends with a beautiful, slow melody up in the stratosphere, obviously the "transfiguration," though you can't tell from the music what the person is being transfigured into. It could be an angel or maybe a butterfly or a new baby if you believe in reincarnation.

Playing the lovely, triumphant melody, I don't care anymore about Heinrich beating everybody in challenges or whether Emily will beat me back next week or whether I can beat Evelyn and Greta. I don't care about anything but the music and everyone playing together and the colored lights in my head, and when I'm old and on my death bed, I think I'll ask them to play me a record of *Death and Transfiguration* so I can compare it with what it's really like when the time comes and see if Strauss guessed right.

At the end, the kids in the audience all stand up and clap and yell bravo, which more than makes up for the silence at the broadcast recording. Dr. Maddy bows and shakes hands with Annie, who beat Amy in challenges and is now concertmistress, and has us all stand up. Then he goes out and the people clap some more and he comes back and we stand up again and he goes out and comes back and we stand and sit and stand and sit until finally the clapping dies down and Annie hands her violin off to Amy and climbs up onto the podium to conduct the Interlochen theme.

Retrieving the baton gingerly from the conductor's stand, Annie raises her right arm and awkwardly beats out the four-beat pattern, keeping her other arm at her side rather than using it to gesture like a real conductor would. The theme is a lovely, liquid passage from Howard Hanson's "Romantic Symphony," which he wrote one summer when he was here at Interlochen. It's played to introduce all the broadcasts, and I heard it myself back in Des Moines on my little blue radio. Playing the music for the first time here at Interlochen, I know that we'll play it at the end of every concert, and when we play it for the last time in August, it will make me cry. And I know, too, that for the rest of my life, whenever I happen to hear this music, whether I'm sitting in a concert, or in the car, or listening to the radio before going to sleep, I'll find myself back on the stage of the Bowl, the shining lake water at my back, with Annie Kavafian making her awkward four beats in the air, as the lights twinkle on between the trees.

Chapter 19. Happiness

As the summer rolls on, I realize that despite the pressure of having to learn millions of new notes every week and cold sweats and diarrhea on Friday mornings, I'm now happier than I've ever been in my life. And unlike the various happinesses I've experienced at home, which have usually been about just one thing—getting what I wanted for Christmas or winning first chair in All-State, for example—the happiness I feel at Interlochen is about a whole lot of things.

Not that I'm happy every minute. Not with mosquitoes and rain dripping through the roof of the Bowl and onto my viola if I'm not careful and the bat in Cabin 16 that Sue brained with a tennis racket and Heinrich beating me in challenges and the backaches after long rehearsals. But none of these things is important enough to cancel out a much bigger, general happiness stretching over everything like the roof of a huge circus tent.

Ever hear the story of the ugly duckling? Well, that's me. I was an ugly duckling back in Des Moines, but here at Interlochen I'm a swan among swans. At home, looks, money, and sports were all that mattered to high school kids, but here the popularity criteria are different. Not that those things don't matter at all, but at least they're not number one. Instead, what really matters is how good you are on your instrument or whatever you do in the arts. Fat kids,

kids with pimples, even kids who are just, plain ugly can be popular here if they're great pianists or violinists or actors or whatever, which means everybody has a chance to be somebody. At home to really count, I'd have to have an operation to make me four inches shorter and a lot skinnier, with a pair of B-cup boobs and a new jaw-line tacked on, and meanwhile win a sweepstakes to buy all the right clothes, plus a wig made of decent hair instead of these nothing-colored wisps, but at Interlochen, all I have to do is practice.

In other words, for everybody here, there's hope. Lots and lots of hope, swirling around in the air along with the music. Hope to get a higher chair, hope to win the concerto competition, hope to go to Julliard, hope to get a seat in the New York Philharmonic or even make it as a concert artist. It's everywhere, and there's nothing like going up in challenges to give you a nice, big dose of it. I should know, after making it past Evelyn and Greta last week to third chair, where I get to sit for the Van Cliburn concert. My next hope is that I can beat Heinrich and make it onto the first stand, which I think I might if I practice hard enough. As for beating Jane out of first chair, well, even hope has its limits.

And I'm not really a violist anyway, I'm a violinist, so what do I care? What I really want is to win the concerto competition on violin and get to play a solo with one of the orchestras. Not that I have any more chance than the proverbial snowball in hell. Sure, I managed to convince Mr. Hardesty, my violin teacher here, to let me audition on the Mozart D Major, but that only raises my prospects from zero to one in a thousand. I know I shouldn't have such a negative attitude, but it's hard to be positive when Mr. Hardesty only said the audition would be "a good experience" for me, which translates into "don't get your hopes up because you're not going to win." But a girl can dream, can't she?

Speaking of dreams, I have a new crush! His name is Jeffrey Higgenbottom, and he plays the trombone in the Youth Symphony. I met him when we passed out programs together for the Concert and Guide Service, which is what I do for my work scholarship, though he mostly ignored me and talked to the other boy working with us. Jeff has hair like President Kennedy's and wears glasses and sounds smart when he talks. But what really caught my attention was that he seemed kind of shy, like me.

That afternoon during the broadcast concert, I glanced back at the trombones and there was Jeff in a red sweater, with a big, brass trombone bell next to his head and his mouth all smushed from blowing on the mouthpiece. I couldn't believe it—fate had thrown us together twice in the same day! The sight of him made everything go all wavery, like an out-of-focus TV screen, and I had to shake myself out of it to come in at the violas' next entrance. After the broadcast, I floated back to Cabin 16 and spent the next half hour imagining scenes in which Jeff and I tell each other how shy we are. Of course, I don't even really know the guy—he may already have a girlfriend, for all I know—but at least my new crush seems to have erased Mark Baxter from my mind, a lost cause if there ever was one. Now I can start fresh, and who knows—maybe Jeff even has an inferiority complex like I do.

Another reason I'm so happy is Lake Wahbekanetta, alias Green Lake. Whenever I want to wallow in romantic thoughts or get inspired, I go down to the sun decker next to Kresge and sit on one of the green park benches. Gazing out across the blue-gray water and feeling the lake breeze on my face always brings up calm, quiet music in my head, the Largo from the New World Symphony, for example. Watching the tiny wavelets turn over one by one to the English horn solo, I can see the ghosts of Indians cutting towards me across the water in their birchbark canoes, and everything shimmers. It's called being one with Nature. I'd give anything if Jeff would come up behind me and see me being one with Nature and maybe even sit down next to me, but of course that never happens. Instead, a couple of bratty Intermediates are sure to show up blabbing into my thoughts and spoiling my mood.

Love and acceptance and Nature are all great happiness-makers, but of course, the biggest reason that I'm so happy at Interlochen is the music. Lots and lots of new music, a whole new set of amazing pieces every week. Dvorak, Strauss, Tchaikovsky, Wagner, Sibelius, and Copeland so far, plus some composers I never heard of, and this is only the third week. Not that I'm happy every minute in orchestra. There are those impossible passages you practice and practice and still can't play and the times you come crashing in during a rest and the conductor glares and the times when you sit and sit while some other section goes over a difficult passage and even in performances there can be whole pages of music you play through without feeling a thing. But in every performance there are also certain spots that you wait for, knowing that when you get to them it will be as though the whole orchestra has been filled with helium and all the chairs have levitated a few feet above the stage like some magician's assistant.

Moments like these make any other form of happiness seem cheap by comparison, but it's probably a good thing they're just moments. If they weren't, my brain might blow a fuse or something. I guess composers must know that, which is why they always put a lot of boring stuff between the mountain peaks. Some days, though, when I'm in just the right mood, the in-between stuff isn't that boring but just feels good in a quieter way. I guess that must be what they call contentment. It's the kind of happiness my parents seem to have, the kind philosophers recommend, more than the mountain peak kind.

I'm not sure which kind of happiness is better, but I love thinking about it. Once when I was going on about the meaning of happiness in Cabin 16,

Ruth laughed and said to me, "Cindy, would you *please* stop being so philosophical?" I laughed too, but maybe she was right. Maybe the best way to be happy is never to ask yourself if you're happy and just go ahead and do things. But then, what's the point of being happy if you don't know you're happy? And if you never ask yourself if you're happy, how are you going to know?

Chapter 20. Van and Lucy

I suppose I should be nervous, but I'm not. Here I am, third chair viola, up near the front with a world-famous concert artist standing just a few feet from me, but it doesn't feel like any big deal. He's just a human being, after all, who eats and sleeps and uses the bathroom just like everybody else. So now I'm tuning my viola and playing through the hard parts like I always do before rehearsals, showing off just a little in case the world-famous concert artist should happen to glance my way.

I recognized Van Cliburn right away even though I never saw him in person before. Van Cliburn. It always seems to me like he doesn't have a first name, that he has one of those last names that starts with "van," like Ludwig van Beethoven. But no, Van is short for his middle name, Lavan, his first name being Harvey, or so I read somewhere. Harvey Cliburn sounds like a real hick—you can see why he didn't want that—but why not Lavan? Whose idea was Van, anyway? His mother's probably—they say his mother goes with him everywhere and runs his life.

I never saw Van Cliburn in person before, but, of course, I saw his picture on the cover of *Time* magazine after he came back from Russia. Above his picture it said, "The Texan that conquered Russia." It was the year after that Sputnik business, when the teachers started giving us more homework, but then Van went to Moscow and won the Tchaikovsky competition. He played the Tchaikovsky Concerto and the Rachmaninoff Third, and the Russians gave him an eight-minute standing ovation. The judges had to ask Khrushchev if they could give him first prize, even though he won it fair and square. They were probably afraid they'd be shot or something, but Khrushchev just asked them if Van was the best and when they said he was, he said, "Then, give him the prize!"

The other time I saw Van Cliburn was on *What's My Line*. After he signed in, Dorothy Kilgallen asked him if he was in show business, and he answered in a funny voice that made him sound like an old German professor so the panelists wouldn't recognize his real voice. "You might say that," he said. This threw them off and the audience laughed when Miss Kilgallen asked if he ever played in nightclubs. They asked him if he'd been on the stage and he said no, except for a "limited performance," and after they'd given up and taken off their blindfolds and laughed, he said that when he was fifteen years old he'd played Lazarus in a biblical play and "never quite got over it."

This cracked me up because Van really does look like somebody who just came back from the dead. He's tall and very thin and pale, probably because he's spent his whole life in a practice room and never been out in the sun. His hair is ash blond and kinky like Negroes' hair, which I can't help wondering about, though if Van Cliburn, the big hero, has any Negro blood it would be the deepest darkest secret in the world, of course, especially since he grew up in Texas like Buffy Jean.

Van won the Tchaikovsky competition in Russia, but he's not playing Tchaikovsky on our concert. Instead he's playing a concerto by an American composer named Edward MacDowell, the same guy who wrote "To a Wild Rose." Then he's going to conduct the "Romantic Symphony" by Howard Hanson, another American composer, and *Peter and the Wolf* by Prokofiev, a Russian, which Lucy Baines Johnson, the new president's daughter, is going to narrate. One Russian piece and two American pieces to illustrate friendship between the two countries, I suppose. Too bad there won't be any Russians here to appreciate it.

Russians or no Russians, we're going to play two concerts on Thursday—one in the afternoon for the whole camp and one in the evening, which outsiders pay to come to. Van comes every year to play and conduct a benefit concert. I don't know how this happened, exactly, but I heard someone say Dr. Maddy got introduced to Van's mother, and that was that. One great thing about Dr. Maddy is that he seems to be able to talk anybody into doing anything for the camp.

Right now, he's up on the podium with his arm over Van's shoulder, which doesn't reach, since Van is way taller than Dr. Maddy, and after he introduces Van, we all clap. Then Van turns to the orchestra and says he's delighted to have a chance to work with us again, that it's always a thrill for him to come to Interlochen and meet so many talented young people, and he says all sorts of other gallant things in his precise, gentle voice with just a slight drawl from his Texas days.

We spend the next hour rehearsing the symphony, which Howard Hanson wrote while he was here at Interlochen and which contains the theme that we play at the end of every concert. Van doesn't just have us play through things, he stops quite a lot and makes us go over certain passages until we get them right. He doesn't yell at anyone, though, and is always a perfect gentleman and talks to us as respectfully as if we were the New York Philharmonic and not just a bunch of kids.

During the break, I go out to the bathroom and on my way back, I hear two boys from the orchestra talking about Van. "So whaddya think of him?" one asks.

"I think he's a great pianist, but he's *obviously* no conductor," the other says. He may be right, but I can't help feeling annoyed. I want to ask him how he knows so much about conducting and if he's a conductor himself, which I'm sure he isn't. Why do boys always have to pretend they know everything?

When we get back after the break, a short, pretty girl with shining brown hair is sitting on a stool in front of the first violins with her feet tucked under the seat. Lucy Baines Johnson is wearing a regulation blue shirt and knickers, the best ones the uniform ladies could scrounge up. Buffy Jean—who, being Buffy Jean and from Texas, has already managed to have her picture taken with both Van and Lucy—told me that Lucy's staying at the Stone Hotel and that a couple of guys in suits follow her everywhere she goes. Since everyone else here has on blue and blue, they might just as well have "Secret Service" stamped on their backs. Poor Lucy must feel like she's in a zoo.

Climbing back onto the podium, Van extends his hand out towards Lucy and says how delighted he is to work with her, a fellow Texan, and we all clap some more, and then it's time to rehearse *Peter and the Wolf*.

"Earrrly one mornin'," Lucy reads, in her soft, southern voice, "Peter opened the gate and went out into the big meadow."

"Da, da, dada da Da . . ." The violins send Peter skipping away, as we violas glide along beneath them.

"On the branch of a big tree sat a lil' burrrd," says Lucy while we're still playing Peter's theme.

"No," says Van, holding up his hand like a traffic cop. "Not yet." Lucy starts again, but this time she waits too long and comes in after the flute is already chirping away on the bird theme. After four or five tries, she gets it right, but then she misses the next entrance. Before long, the problem is obvious: Lucy can't read music!

Van stops the orchestra and spends a few minutes conferring with Waldie, our manager, while we sit fidgeting. What will happen? Are they going to tell Lucy she can't do the narration and send her back to the White House disgraced? What will President Johnson say if they do that? Will he do like Harry Truman did when he got so mad at that newspaper critic who didn't like his daughter's concert and wrote him a nasty letter? Will Johnson get mad at Dr. Maddy and try to close down the camp?

But Waldie just walks over and stands next to Lucy and gives her the cues. This enables us to get through the piece, but it's going to look pretty weird in the concert.

Fortunately, that's not how things turn out. Waldie sits in the front row with a score and cues Lucy from there, which doesn't look too bad, and no one shows up from the White House to shut down the camp. Everything goes smoothly, Lucy does a fine job, and of course the MacDowell piano concerto is fabulous. Van gets a huge standing ovation from the campers, and that night we do the whole thing over to a packed auditorium filled with outsiders whose ticket money helps pay for our scholarships, and Van gets another huge standing ovation, and we all clap and cheer and shuffle our feet on the floor, and he plays a couple of encores before Annie finally gets up to conduct the theme.

Then, the next morning, we have a plain, ordinary rehearsal with Dr. Wilson conducting, and it's as if Van and Lucy were never here at all and I dreamed the whole thing.

Chapter 21. The Call of Destiny

Well, they say you should hitch your wagon to a star, and I have. Stars are awfully high up, though, and I hope I don't come crashing down.

It all started one night after dinner when Buffy Jean and I were standing at the sinks in our cabin getting ready for the evening. I was brushing my teeth, and Buffy Jean was smearing some white stuff on her face before re-doing her make-up for the fortieth time. She'd been bragging about how Mr. Elsasser, her organ teacher, had arranged for her to go to the new Interlochen Arts Academy for high school next year, when suddenly, out of the blue, I heard myself say, "Hey, maybe I'll see if I can go too."

As soon as the words were out of my mouth, I wondered why I'd said them. Was it because of all the stories Grandma Harter used to tell about her years at St. Mary's in Minnesota? And Mom used to say that when she herself was growing up, she dreamed of going to boarding school, though her family was too poor to send her. Already, several girls in Cabin 16 who got scholarships went to Housekeeping to be measured for their Academy "dress uniforms." For a moment, I pictured myself in a blue blazer and gray skirt, carrying a stack of books across the campus amidst trees turning red and gold.

"Oh, do!" said Buffy Jean, jumping up and down. "We can be room-mites!"

I wasn't sure how I felt about the roommate idea, given the fact that Buffy Jean and I have absolutely nothing in common, but I figured I was about as likely to wind up going to the Academy as being selected for an astronaut program, so it wasn't going to be an issue. To go to the Academy, I'd not only have to get accepted, I'd have to get a huge scholarship AND somehow manage to talk my parents into letting me go, probably the biggest stumbling block of all. So, I said sure, I'd be glad to be Buffy Jean's roommate and she gave me a hug before we went off to the Melody Freeze, where she immediately ran after some boys she knew, leaving me to go to the concert by myself.

All through the concert and in bed that night and the next morning in orchestra rehearsal I kept thinking about what I'd said to Buffy Jean and wondering why I'd said it. Then, as soon as the rehearsal ended, I found myself heading over to the admissions office in the Maddy administration building thinking, I must be crazy to be doing this, but still doing it for the simple reason that I couldn't stop. It was as if somebody had pulled a switch and moved me onto another track. I guess this must be what they mean by the "Call of Destiny."

The receptionist set me up to meet with an admissions counselor that same afternoon. Randy Saks was a handsome college guy in a black-watch plaid blazer who reminded me a little of the blond detective in *77 Sunset Strip*.

"So why do you want to go to the Academy?" he asked as we sat down at a table covered with colored brochures.

"Well, I really love the camp, and I'd have opportunities at the Academy I wouldn't have at home," I heard myself say. "I mean, why wouldn't I want to?"

Randy told me that he himself had graduated from the Academy, in the very first graduating class. He picked up one of the brochures and leafed through it, showing me pictures of science classes and skiing, orchestra rehearsals and dormitory rooms. The Academy classes were small, he said, which meant you really got to know your teachers. And they'd hired a fantastic new conductor for the orchestra. His name was Thor Johnson, and he was the former conductor of the Cincinnati Symphony.

"It can feel pretty isolated up here in the winter," Randy said, "but you get a whole month off at Christmas and three weeks in the spring." I figured I wouldn't mind the isolated part if guys like him were there, plus I'd heard that my big crush, Jeff Higgenbottom, would be an Academy senior. I hadn't actually talked to him yet, but in a whole year, who knew what might happen . . .

I asked Randy about the application process. It wouldn't be difficult, he said. Since I was already at the camp, I wouldn't have to audition. I just had to have my parents fill out the blue forms he gave me and send them in right away. And generous scholarships were available, based on parents' ability to pay.

Leaving the admissions office, I went straight to the pay phone outside HSG Headquarters, scrounged through my purse until I found a dime, and dropped it into the round slot at the top of the phone. I had no idea what I was going to say, but I dialed zero and told the operator I wanted to place a collect call to Des Moines, Iowa. The phone rang only a couple of times before I heard Mom's voice.

"I have a collect call for anyone from Interlochen, Michigan, will you accept the charges?" the operator asked her.

Mom's voice sounded scared as she answered. She probably thought something terrible had happened, getting a call in the middle of the week like that. Outside the nearest cabin, a French horn was blaring.

"Hey, Mom, it's me," I shouted into the phone.

"What's going on?" she shouted back. The French hornist stopped playing and started fiddling with her valves, then set the horn down and disappeared inside her cabin.

"Nothing, really," I said. "I just have a question to ask you." What was she going to say? Would she get mad? Would she say I had a lot of nerve even to suggest such a thing? Or would she burst into tears? She might, but I still had to ask and get it over with. If she said no, I'd be disappointed, but then it would be over and I could get back to sanity instead of pipe dreams. For a moment, I almost hoped she would.

"Oh?" she said, "What's that?" It was a good thing, I thought, that Dad wasn't home. Dad would probably talk me down before I even had a chance to finish, but Mom, with her boarding school dreams, might actually listen. And if I persuaded her to let me apply, she'd be the one to talk Dad into it.

"Well, you see . . ." I began. I was stalling, putting off saying the words, though I could feel them pressing to get out. "They have this boarding school here during the year, the Interlochen Arts Academy it's called . . ." The words kept coming, gathering speed. "I've been talking to some kids who are going in the fall and it sounds really fantastic. The classes are really, really small, and they have great teachers and orchestra concerts every week just like they have in the summer, which means you learn a huge amount of repertoire. Some of my friends in my cabin have gotten accepted already. I know you'll think we can't afford it—the brochure says the general fee for the year is $2950—but the kids who need them have been getting huge scholarships. Our first chair viola got a full scholarship—room, board, tuition, everything. I don't know if I can get a scholarship that big or not, and you don't have to decide now whether you'll let me go. All I'm asking is, can I put in an application and see what happens? That's all I want right now, is just to apply, that's all . . ." I was talking faster and faster, out on a limb that might snap at any moment.

"Oh, honey," Mom broke in. "I don't know. Even if you could get a scholarship, I just don't know if your dad and I could stand to have you leave home.

We'd miss you too much. We're just not ready for that, not yet. You're so young, honey. I don't know."

"Yes, well before you make up your mind," I said, "I should tell you one thing the admissions guy told me, which is that Christmas vacation is a whole month long and you get another three weeks in the spring. And if you let me go, I promise I'll spend every minute of vacation with you and Dad, but if I come home and go to Roosevelt I'll always be at rehearsals and you'll hardly ever see me, so in terms of actual minutes you'd really see me about as much if not more . . . "

"And what about Mrs. Sexton?" Mom broke in. "Don't you think she'd be sad to lose her best pupil? Have you thought of that?"

I hadn't thought of that, and a wave of guilt swept over me at wanting to desert Mrs. Sexton after all she'd done for me. I told myself that I wasn't Mrs. Sexton's only good pupil. I told myself that if I left, Cheryl, her second-best pupil, would get to be Mrs. Sexton's star. I told myself that if the Academy helped me succeed, this would be a feather in Mrs. Sexton's cap. None of these things made the guilt go away any more than anything could make the guilt go away about wanting to leave my parents, but guilt or no guilt, I knew I couldn't keep from applying to the Academy if they let me, and I knew that in the end they would let me. It was just something that had to happen no matter how much pain and guilt it cost any of us, a Call of Destiny, and by the time we ended the call, Mom had agreed to talk to Dad.

After I hung up, I went off to my theory class, followed by afternoon orchestra rehearsal in the Bowl. We were starting to practice for the final concert of the season. I'd been excited about playing my first Brahms symphony plus the big, end-of-camp extravaganza of Liszt's *Les Préludes*, but this afternoon I barely knew what we were playing. Although my body was sitting in third chair in the Bowl with my viola, my mind was floating around out in space as I imagined what my parents might be saying to each other, the crying, the anger, the "how could she do this to us?" If it ended there and they didn't somehow go through it all and come out the other side, I'd be doomed to another year of Mrs. Sexton, Mr. Bagley, Mr. Brauninger, and plain old Roosevelt High, the thought of which was becoming more and more unbearable by the minute. "Don't get your hopes up," Mom had said before she said good-bye, but I knew I already had.

An hour later, I was back at HSG Headquarters, where there was a note in my mailbox to call home. This time both Dad and Mom were on the phone, presenting a united front, as they always did, though Mom did most of the talking.

"Well," she said. "We talked it over, and we'd just about decided to tell you no, but then I called Mrs. Sexton. I really thought she'd agree that you'd be better off at home, but she said, "Well, if Cynthia wants to play in a professional orchestra someday, there's really no better start she could get than that." Mom's voice sounded grim, echoing Mrs. Sexton's.

"Is that what you really want, Daughter?" Dad said. "You want to leave us and spend the whole winter up there in that frozen wasteland?"

I told him I'd never wanted anything more in my life and that I would love him forever if he'd just let me apply.

"Well, I guess there's really no reason you shouldn't *apply*," said Mom, who was now on my side, though just barely. "After all, what do we have to lose? Just because you apply doesn't necessarily mean you're going to end up there. I just hope you're not disappointed if it doesn't work out, that's all." She was saying just what I'd been telling her in our earlier phone call, but I knew that if I were accepted with a big enough scholarship, they'd let me go, and I knew they knew that too.

"I'm not making any promises," said Dad. "It depends on what kind of scholarship you can get. If the tuition is what you told your mom, you'll need to get at least a couple thousand or we can't afford it and that's final."

I told him I understood that and that I had forms they needed to fill out that I'd send them right away by special delivery.

"You're the best parents in the world!" I burst out before we hung up, after which I heard only a growl from my dad.

"We want you to be happy," said Mom. "We love you so much and this is so hard. I just hope you appreciate that."

"I do," I said, meaning it with my whole heart. "I really, really do."

Chapter 22. Les Préludes

Whose idea was it to make Franz Liszt's tone poem, *Les Préludes*, the big grand finale for zillions of kids to play at the end of camp? You'd think they'd have chosen something easier. This piece is dastardly difficult, but they've been ending with it every summer since 1928, and here we are in the Bowl getting ready to play the 1964 version.

Of course, everybody doesn't play the whole thing. The Youth Symphony (which, as of tonight, has been renamed the "International Youth Symphony") plays the whole thing, but the High School Concert Orchestra and the Intermediates and various bands and choirs all start up somewhere in the middle to make the last pages loud, louder, loudest for a big, super-extravaganza effect to end the camp season—for everybody except those of us who get to stay for post-camp and fly to Washington, that is.

Regular camp has actually been ending for the last couple of weeks. It started ending last week with the concerto winners' concerts, one night of them with the University orchestra and one night with us. Listening to the winners, I knew just what Scarlett O'Hara meant by "pea-green with envy," they were all so good, but when Annie played Saint Saens' *Introduction* and *Rondo Capriccioso*, I was so inspired I almost forgot to be jealous. She didn't have the greatest violin, but every note was perfectly in tune and so musical it made you want to cry.

Watching Annie toss off run after run like it was nothing, her little torso bobbing and swaying and her black eyes flashing, I suddenly knew what I wanted more than anything in the world. I wanted to win concertos and play like that on Kresge stage, mesmerizing millions of people. I don't know if I can ever get that good, but if I work hard, maybe I can come close, especially if I can go to the Academy and win concertos there as a first step, but I'm not going to let myself start thinking about that right now or I'll go crazy for sure.

The concerto concerts were the beginning of the end of camp, but the final, final end is tonight's concert, better known as "Les Préludes," though the Liszt piece isn't the only thing on the program, which started with our orchestra playing Dvorak's *Carnival Overture* and Brahms' Fourth Symphony. Now all the extra players are filing onto the stage with their instruments. I'm sandwiched between Evelyn and the cellists, with my elbows squeezed down to my sides and absolutely no room for bowing, as more and more kids take their places. I hope the floor under us is good and strong.

Everybody on the stage except the Youth Symphony kids will be gone by tomorrow, after which we have an amazing week ahead of us. Van Cliburn is coming back to conduct a couple more concerts plus some recordings we'll be making for RCA. Meanwhile, the Philadelphia Orchestra will be here for a music festival and Eugene Ormandy is going to conduct us in a rehearsal and we get to go to their concerts every night until we finish the week off by flying to Washington for the concert on the Watergate barge.

Now, finally, everyone is on the stage. Behind me are long rows of clarinets, trumpets, flutes, and trombones. I scan the trombone row for Jeff but only manage to locate a small patch of his forehead. After we tune, I hear the applause starting as Dr. Maddy makes his way in through the violins, climbs up on the podium, and bows. The audience, crammed with parents here to pick up their kids, is already clapping like mad, and we haven't played a note yet. Dr. Maddy turns to the orchestra and raises his baton, and a moment later, every instrument in the huge ensemble is poised in position—string players with thumbs pressed against our fingerboards for the two pizzicato notes that start the piece, wind players inhaling, percussionists standing at attention, harpists with fingers splayed across their strings for their first chords—all waiting.

Then the baton comes down, and hundreds of index fingers reach out at the same moment to pluck a string once and pluck it again to make two fat raindrops, miraculously together: "Plink! Plink!" The viola notes are open C-strings, mine blurring slightly in my line of vision as it vibrates.

A moment later, my bow moves over the same string as we join the violins in a slow, smooth arpeggio, stair-stepping upwards to where the woodwinds glide in on a series of chords.

A few beats of silence, then two more pizzicato notes, another arpeggio, and more woodwind chords, then one arpeggio after another rolling up and down in big, slow sparkling waves of sound. My bow sweeps back and forth in a sea of others, all going the same direction. Harps come wheeling into the swelling ruckus with more sharps and flats now, crescendoing up to one long, unison arpeggio, then a measure of staccato eighth notes chopping back and forth at the frog of the bow, chop chop chop chop chop chop chop chop, until we're finally there, at a brand new section labeled "Andante maestoso."

It means "slow and majestic"—for everyone else, that is, but not for us, the upper strings. For us, it means line after line of flailing up and down in more and faster arpeggios, struggling to keep our fingers in sync with our bows, while behind us, flanks of trumpets blare out one fanfare after another. Finally, at a place marked "L'istesso tempo," the flailing ends as our bows glide into a new section of long notes harmonizing with the second violins on the first real melody of the piece. For us and the seconds, this is a blessed relief, but the poor firsts are still noodling up and down and around the melody on fast, slurred notes, murky pea soup, probably too hard for anybody but Annie and Amy to really play.

It won't be long now before we come to the first Place, a passage in this piece that I always wait for, just as I always wait for Places in any piece that isn't nonstop boredom. In some pieces, like Tchaikovsky symphonies, there are lots of Places, and in others there are only a few, but there's almost always at least one, and in this piece there are a couple. At the first Place I'm waiting for, we violas get the melody, which starts out like "The Bear Went Over the Mountain." The trouble is, once I've discovered a Place in a piece, everything else is just a path to it with a lot of brambles to get through. And in this case the Place isn't much, not like a Tchaikovsky melody or some of the Places in Rachmaninoff that make you think you could die happy if an H-bomb went off right then. This one isn't Rachmaninoff, but it's enough, a few sips of cool water during a long, hot walk. And after that there's still the other Place to look forward to—the grand finale, of course—not a Place where you're a bird soaring up over a lake but just the boom-boom way you feel when you got an A plus on a test and race home to tell your mom about it.

Next to me, Evelyn leans forward to turn the page, missing a few bars, and now at last we're there, at Place No. 1, which is marked "con sordino," meaning I have to snatch my black wooden mute up from the edge of our stand and slide it down over my bridge before the melody begins. Now at last, here we are, our melody swelling and easing, up and down, and I feel the warm buzz of my muted viola under my ear for eight long bars before we go noodling off into triplets and the woodwinds snatch the melody away from us and the first Place is over.

My hands feel sticky under the hot lights, and sweat is starting to pour down my face as we come then to a whole page of tremolos, tiny back-and-forth shivers of the bow on each note, rising and falling, shiver, shiver, shiver. This is where my back always starts to ache. The trouble with violas is they're so God-awful heavy. Is this part supposed to be a storm? Were those jaggedy chords we just played bolts of lightning?

When the concert's over, I'm going straight to the Melody Freeze, though I suppose everyone else will too and there'll be a huge line. If this were a rehearsal, we'd be giving each other backrubs. Alas, no time for that now, with the fast chromatic scales coming down and the crashing chords, chop, chop, and more tremolos until finally we come to a place marked "un poco piu moderato" and a measure with a big "6" in the middle, which means we're to count six bars out, with only the woodwinds and horns playing.

"One two three four, two two three four," I mouth silently. "Three two three four, four . . ." Wait. Did I already say four? I glance over at Evelyn, who looks back at me and raises four fingers—no, it's all right. Now, in front of us, Jane is raising her viola, bringing the section in for some long, soft notes leading into the "Allegretto pastorale," where a solo horn player calls across a green meadow to a solo oboe, who answers back, two birds' love calls, followed by a clarinet and a couple of twittering flutes, back and forth, the birds calling and calling over our long, soft, arm-killing notes and rests.

Then, as we come back to "The Bear Went over the Mountain" theme, in the violins this time, I glance up and there they are, girls in red and blue dresses, the dancers moving across in front of the orchestra, shifting and floating beyond Maddy's red-clad bulk, floating up the aisles, dancing between the rows, everywhere, even on the roof, I've been told, as we saw through passage after passage, the notes getting blacker as the music builds and builds, violins slithering up and down insanely fast scales, trumpets calling back and forth, tympanists hammering, more and more instruments and singers joining in, flutes trilling furiously, bows sawing back and forth in one long unison passage of eighth notes in the strings, and one long explosion of fireworks sounds, pinwheels and roman candles and great tarantulas of sparkles all going off at once, my heart going like mad as we saw crazily up and down the arpeggios and the dancers bob and whirl to the final chords, a huge amen blaring out from the winds to end the piece.

The crowd is on its feet clapping and cheering as Dr. Maddy comes out again and again, bowing and shaking hands with all the first chairs and having us stand, sit, stand, sit, and having the solo winds stand up one at a time and pointing back to the percussion and the harps and then at all of us again, bowing and bowing until he finally hands the baton off to Annie and steps off to the side. Annie climbs onto the podium to conduct the theme one last time and the Bowl falls silent. As we start to play I see that all around me girls' cheeks are wet and I feel my own throat knot up under my viola. I want this melody to last forever, want to keep things exactly as they are now, this orchestra, this viola section, Cabin 16, Interlochen, life, but all of it is going forward and there's nothing I can do to stop it. All I can do is keep playing note after note until the very last one, drawing my bow all the way out to the tip to hold it and hold it until Annie finally cuts us off with a tiny circle in the air.

Then the lights twinkle on between the trees, and the 1964 National Music Camp season is over.

Chapter 23. The High A

This is stupid. I'm sitting here on Kresge stage rehearsing with Van Cliburn, who's going to both play and conduct Prokofiev's Third Piano Concerto with us in the first ever Interlochen Summer Festival, which is amazing, but all I can think about is what might be going on over at the Academy admissions office. Every time I go back to HSG, I check the Cabin 16 mailbox and, finding nothing, feel my insides tighten a little more, like an E-string gradually being tuned up to a high A. If this goes on much longer, I swear I'm going to snap.

Van's piano has a glass top so we can see him conducting as he plays. He called playing and conducting Prokofiev's Third "just a stunt, really," but I think he was being modest. It seems to work pretty well, actually, maybe because the piano and orchestra mostly play at different times. Van will play for a little while and then one of his long, spidery arms comes up and waves some beats in the air, but a moment later he's back down on the bench hammering away at another jangly passage, which isn't helping my nerves one bit.

To quote Peanuts, I CAN'T STAND IT!!! As soon as this rehearsal's over, I'm going to march over to the admissions office and ask them what the committee decided. It's going to feel a little like opening your presents before Christmas, and I just know that if I go ask instead of waiting, things will turn out badly, but I can't help it. Enough is enough.

When I get to the Maddy Building, I'm sure the secretary will tell me nothing has been decided, but to my surprise, she smiles and hands me a letter. I open it with trembling hands and read:

> *Dear Cindy:*
> *It is my pleasant privilege to announce that you have been ac-cepted as a member of the Interlochen Arts Academy student body for the 1964-65 season.*
>
> *The Scholarship Committee has awarded you $1450 to be ap-plied on the general fee for the entire academic year.*

That's as far as I get. Instead of going on, I read the second sentence over and over, hoping I somehow read the number wrong. The secretary must wonder why I'm not jumping up and down with joy. She can't know that for me, getting admitted isn't enough; the scholarship has to be $2000, Dad said, and $1450 isn't $2000. Forcing a smile, I thank her and stumble out of the Maddy Building and down to the lake, my thoughts flailing around like a drowning non-swimmer.

I knew it, I think. I should have waited. If I'd waited for the letter to come in my mailbox, it would have said $2000, not $1450, but because I got impatient, I'm being punished.

$1450. How did they do that? How did they manage to arrive at the ex-act amount to keep me stranded as long as possible between heaven and hell? If it was $1850 or even $1750, it would almost certainly be enough, whatever Dad said. If it was any less, there would be no hope at all, but at least it would be over. As it is, I've been left hanging onto a tiny thread of hope like a spider over a void, waiting, waiting, waiting. I CAN'T STAND IT!!!!!!

Back in HSG, I place another collect call to Mom, who answers on the first ring. In a dead voice, I read her the opening lines of the letter.

"It's not enough, is it?" I ask through tears, to keep her from saying it herself. "Dad said it would have to be $2000."

"Well, I . . . I'm afraid it might not be, honey," Mom says. "I just don't know how we could manage so much . . . We'll have to see what your father says, but I just don't know . . . "

Neither do I. In fact, I haven't the slightest idea how much money Dad and Mom really have. I know things like how much my allowance is and how much they paid for my camp tuition, but I don't know any more about what's in their savings than I know what mechanisms make a bottle of Tab come out of the pop machine after I put a dime in. I'm hopelessly at the mercy of my parents' willingness to risk losing their house and winding up on the street, but I have no idea how likely that is to happen.

Of course, if I were a better person, I'd tell Mom to forget it right now. I'd tell her that even if they can manage the extra $550, I couldn't possibly allow them to make such a huge sacrifice. That's probably what she would have said in my place, she who dropped out of Grinnell College during the Depression to help her own parents. Isn't it enough that I've already broken my parents' hearts by telling them I want to go away without condemning them to a life of poverty too? Would my going to the Academy mean Mom would have to wear stockings with runs in them and Dad would have to quit playing golf? But alas, I'm not my sweet, self-sacrificing mother, who has no idea what it's like to walk around with this selfish, red lobster-thing inside of you that makes you always have to go after what you want. If I told Mom to forget it, she might protest like grown-ups always do when someone offers to pay the check in a restaurant, but she might not, and I can't take that chance. The red lobster won't let me.

It was useless to talk to Mom without Dad there, I realize, as I hang up the phone. And the worst part is, I can't just go sit on a bench and think things over. Instead, I have to be back on the stage of Kresge in ten minutes without having had any lunch, not that I want any.

Wiping my tears away, I grab up my viola case and make my way down the steps towards Kresge stage. Don't let yourself hope, something inside me says. If you do that, you'll just feel even worse when Dad says no. Forget the Academy. You're going back to Roosevelt and that's that. Don't hope, don't hope, don't hope.

Settling into my chair next to Evelyn and playing through one passage after another, I think about getting off the plane from Washington and falling into my mother's arms. I think about Mrs. Sexton and wonder if she'll be glad I had to come home after all. I think about the next orchestra audition with Mr. Brauninger and wonder if my sight-reading will go any better. I think about orchestra at Roosevelt with no Mark Baxter, who graduated in June, and not caring whether he's there or not when all I want is to get back to Interlochen. More and more thoughts roll through my mind, not a single one of which makes me feel the least bit better as Annie finishes tuning the orchestra and the choir files in and Van Cliburn gets up to conduct a final run-through of Vaughn Williams' *Serenade to Music*.

After the baton comes down and begins weaving the instruments into a lush carpet of mingled sounds, the choir comes in on Shakespeare's velvety words:

How sweet the moonlight sleeps upon these banks!
Here will we sit and let the sounds of music
Creep in our ears: soft stillness and the night
Become the torches of sweet harmony.

Music. They're singing about music, the soloists now singing speeches from Shakespeare's *The Merchant of Venice* about waking Diana with a hymn and the affections of a man with no music in him being "dark as Erebus" and the choir celebrating the joys of music, a perfect piece for Interlochen, where so much music sleeps upon these banks, though lakes don't have banks, I think, only beaches, not that it matters. Not that anything matters. As the music goes on, two big tears slip down my two cheeks, streaking my Covergirl makeup and making my nose run. I won't be able to wipe it until we get to a rest, but so what? People will just think I'm crying because the music is so beautiful, people who know nothing about the Academy and the fact that a week from now I'll be eating a bologna sandwich at Mom's kitchen table, with Interlochen nothing more than a lovely dream, knowing I won't be back here for a whole, long year.

"When you come back, Cynthia," Mr. Brauninger said before I left, "bring a little of Interlochen with you." The corniness of his words made me cringe at the time, but now they come back to me. How can I take "a little of Interlochen" back to Des Moines? I wonder. What did he mean by that?

Then, miraculously on the last page of the piece, I know. On that page, Nancy Jaynes's silvery soprano solo glides up and up across the intervals, holding and holding a single long, sweet, crystal-clear, high A like a white bird flying above the clouds, a note that somehow holds within it all the special Places I've waited for in every piece, and the shining lake water, and the stars over the beach the night Cabin 16 slept out and we took turns reading poetry aloud with a flashlight, and the slumber music, and the lights twinkling on after the theme—a note so lovely I swear I'll remember it forever if I live to be a hundred and three. And as long as that one beautiful note hangs in the air, nothing else matters—not the Academy, not Mr. Brauninger, not Mrs. Sexton or Jeff Higgenbottom or Mark Baxter or Kennedy or Khrushchev or my parents or LBJ—nothing in the world matters any longer until, finally, the voice flutters down again to fold its grey-white wings.

Then, as the choir echoes back the words "sweet harmony" on a lush major chord to finish the piece, I know that everything is going to be all right. Everything I came to Interlochen for I've been given, and I can take it all home with me. If I have to spend next year at Roosevelt instead of the Academy, I'll be disappointed, but I'll survive and make the best of it. Maybe Mrs. Sexton will let me learn the Mendelssohn Concerto, and I can take piano lessons from Mark's mother, Mrs. Baxter, who's supposed to be a great teacher . . .

When I get back to HSG headquarters, there's a note in my mailbox to call my parents. This time, both of them answer.

"Hey, what's new?" I ask in a cheery voice, as if this is just an ordinary call and I'm not waiting to hear which way my whole life will go.

"How badly do you want this, Daughter?" Dad asks. Then, as the Hallelujah chorus spontaneously fills my head, I know that it's really going to happen, that I won't be going back to Roosevelt after all, that I'll be coming back to the Interlochen Arts Academy, even as I also know that if I didn't just spend the last two hours talking myself into feeling all right about going back to Roosevelt, this wouldn't have happened, life being the way it is.

"More than anything in the world," I say, Roosevelt or no Roosevelt.

"Well, we've been doing some more figuring," says Mom, "and your dad thinks we can manage it—barely."

"We'll have to use some of the money we saved for your college," Dad says, "which means you'll have to get a scholarship in a couple of years or maybe not go to the college you want, maybe even have to live at home and go to Drake . . . "

"That doesn't matter," I say. "I can get scholarships lots of places if I graduate from the Academy. And I'm going to get all A's and practice really hard and get first chair so I can go anywhere . . . "

"If we're going to let you go, Daughter," Dad breaks in, "it's only on two conditions. You are to write us two letters every week and you are to call home every weekend no matter what."

"Oh, I promise," I say. "Cross my heart and hope to die. I'll write you every day if you want." Once again, I tell them they're the best parents in the world, and once again, I mean every word.

"We'll need to get you some clothes," Mom says, already starting to plan. "You'll need a warmer coat up there, and some flannel nightgowns . . . "

I'm sure that as soon as we hang up, she'll be calling all her friends to discuss my wardrobe for school, just as I know I'm going to give myself a huge hug and go dancing through the woods, squealing out my news to everybody I meet.

The late 1950s in Des Moines, Iowa: Posing in our backyard are my parents Betty and Leighton Housh, my brother David, and yours truly, front and center.

During my first camp summer, I played the viola in the National Youth Symphony.

Cabin 16 girls in our Sunday uniforms. I'm the tallest girl in the back row. Our counselor, Sue Lamb, is standing on the far left, "Buffy Jean" is below her at the left end of the second row, and "Jane," our principal violist, is next to her.

Practice cabins are scattered throughout the Interlochen woods, each "consisting of one door, one window, one piano, and lots of cobwebs."

The "sundecker," where I sat dreaming and being "one with nature."

Dr. Maddy conducting during his last years.

Van Cliburn at the piano, rehearsing for our benefit concert.

Waldie Anderson helping Lucy, President Johnson's daughter.

Les Préludes, the final camp extravaganza, complete with dancers.

Thor Johnson "motivating" me during orchestra rehearsal.

Here I'm playing principal second with stand-partner "Nancy" and principal violist "Jane," wearing our red blazers while on tour.

Waldie Anderson teaching a wind class in the Interlochen Honors Musicianship Project in the basement of the Jessie V. Stone building.

Dr. Maddy and me, with my "awful hairdo."

Byron Hanson, hero of my senior recital and Interlochen archivist who helped me with this book.

Dr. Maddy's public funeral service in the Jessie V. Stone building, with lots of greenery.

"Buffy Jean" and me, hanging out at the Interlochen Arts Academy's 50th reunion.

Part III
At School in the Woods

Chapter 24. Intermezzo

A few days later, I'm sitting next to Audrey, my violinist friend from Cabin 16, on my very first airplane ride, from Traverse City to Washington. Audrey has flown before and shows me the little paper barf bags in the seat pockets. When the plane takes off, I'm afraid I might have to use one, but after it gets all the way up it doesn't feel like we're moving at all. I'd imagined flying would feel like racing downhill on your bike, but this is more like being in the dentist chair, just as noisy, though without the drilling. Meanwhile, the big squares of countryside edge along down below, growing bigger as the plane descends until, with a bump, we're on the runway.

Dr. Maddy is on the plane with us, wearing this rust-colored tweed suit that looks about twenty years old, which it probably is, since he mostly wears blue corduroys. After the plane lands at Washington National Airport, he stands in the aisle and says good-bye to the orchestra. He won't see us until tonight, he says, because he has to go meet with some "folks over in the government." I wonder what that's about. Is the orchestra going to play at the White House again?

I've been to California and New York City and Boston on family vacations, but this is the first time I've been to Washington, DC, and I can't wait to see all those big white buildings I've seen pictures of. After we check in at the hotel, we take a bus tour of all the monuments and other famous places, ending up at Arlington Cemetery, where we get out and join this huge line snaking all the way up the hill to pass by the eternal flame in front of President Kennedy's grave. There's a little breeze and the flame flickers, but it doesn't go out and isn't supposed to ever, even if it rains. What would the cemetery people do if the flame accidentally went out? I wonder. Maybe it already has and they managed to keep it a secret.

After we get back on the bus, I hear kids talking about where they were and what they were doing when they got the terrible news. Audrey tells me she was at the orthodontist's and I tell her about Mr. Bagley and the "Unfinished Symphony." It's hard to believe that only two years ago the Interlochen Youth Symphony played for the Kennedys on the White House lawn, the summer Jack Simpson was here.

This year's concert at the Watergate isn't anywhere near the White House but on a barge in the Potomac with the audience sitting along the shore. We play *Death and Transfiguration* and some patriotic stuff and accompany a couple of concerto winners from other countries to show how international Interlochen is. There isn't a lot of room on the barge, and the floor under my chair rocks as we play, which makes bowing interesting, but we get through it all right, and the people clap a lot.

The next morning, I fly back to Des Moines from Dulles airport. Coming down the steps onto the runway with my violin case, I feel like there should be a crowd here singing "Hello, Dolly" to me, given all that's happened, but it's just my two parents, looking a little smaller and older than when I left them. As soon as we're in the car, Mom starts in about what clothes and things I'll be taking back with me to the Academy. Dad says he's going to give me one of his portable typewriters to write my two letters a week on and that I can also take his little transistor radio so I'll have a connection with the outside world.

When we get home, several fat envelopes from Interlochen are lying on the hall table, along with a pink envelope containing a note written in Buffy

Jean's curly-cue handwriting saying she got my postcard and how glad she is we can be roommates. One of the Academy envelopes has a copy of the student handbook in it. The introduction was written by the Dean of Students, Mr. Robert Murphy, who quotes Dr. Maddy's motto in all caps: "DO THE RIGHT THING AT THE RIGHT TIME." The point of the book is obviously to tell you the right things to do in all sorts of situations—like what to do with your dirty towels and where to get your mail and where to go if there's a tornado warning.

The next week, despite the Academy costing more than my parents can afford, Mom and I go on a huge shopping spree at Younkers department store. I get some light blue, long-sleeved Oxford-cloth shirts to wear with my knickers and some white ones to wear with my Academy dress uniform, three packages of white Lollypop underpants, three plain white bras—size 34 AA, alas—a new slip and girdle with extra garters, four flat boxes of nylons, brown penny loafers and black flats, a pink mohair sweater, a powder blue pleated skirt and matching sweater, two flannel nightgowns, and a beautiful black formal, the first I've ever owned that didn't come from my cousins. It's the most clothes I ever got at one time in my whole life.

To add to all these treasures, Grandma Harter starts knitting me a red, white, and blue argyle sweater which she's going to send me for my birthday in November, perfect to go with my dark blue knickers. She also makes me an appointment for a permanent at the beauty parlor she goes to so I can arrive at school looking stylish.

The Shinn and Lorenz Beauty Salon is in the Equitable Building, the tallest building in downtown Des Moines. Its waiting room is decorated in dusty rose, with potted palms and Parisian scenes on the wallpaper. On the coffee table are magazines with pictures of women's hair-styles. There are sleek page-boys, bouffant Jackie Kennedy hairdos, Donna Reed flips, charming pixies, and elegant French twists, all full-bodied and shining. Thumbing through the magazines, I can hardly wait to see my own hair looking like one of these.

The Misses Shinn and Lorenz, two old maids in identical pink smocks, make a big fuss over me all afternoon, cutting and snipping and curling. Finally, Miss Shinn hands me a mirror and they both stand back to watch my reaction. I hold the mirror up and freeze. Mounds of frizzy kinks press against my skull in the style of a seventy-year-old trying to look like Shirley Temple in *The Good Ship Lollipop.* And the worst part is, I have to pretend to be delighted so as not to hurt the ladies' feelings.

My mother, after getting over the initial shock, does her best to console me. "Permanents are always a little frizzy at first," she says. "It'll calm down after a few weeks." Meanwhile, to keep from barfing every time I look in the mirror, I dig through my dresser drawers and find a triangular madras scarf that covers most of the frizz.

A week later, I'm on my way back to Interlochen to start my junior year, hideous hairdo and all.

When my parents and I arrive, we go straight to the girls' dorm, where Mom and I meet Mrs. Jewell, the housemother, and a couple of grandmotherly dorm counselors. Mrs. Jewell, a pleasant-looking, middle-aged woman, consults a list and directs us to Room 256, a second-floor room with a powder-blue door, the doors on the hallway all being painted different pastel colors. I knock lightly on the blue door, which flies open, after which I'm immediately enveloped in a Texas-sized hug.

"Hey, it's my roommite! Hey roommite! Do y'all believe we're actually *here?!* Buffy Jean is still in her red-and-blue quilted bathrobe with her hair set in rollers. As she stands back to look at me, her mouth drops into a surprised "O."

"Your hair," she says, after a pause. "Cindy, what on *earth* did you do to your *hair*? It's so curly—I mean it's not that bad, really, it's just so . . . different. Did you get a permanent or something?"

When I tell her I made the mistake of going to my grandmother's beauty parlor, she collapses in laughter, clutching her arm to her stomach and snorting, her huge bosom jiggling in front of her. Like I said before, Buffy Jean's laugh is a deep-pitched belly laugh, straight from the diaphragm, and before long it's infected me and even my mom with hysterics.

"Well," says Buffy Jean, wiping her eyes. "I bet I'm the only girl at Interlochen who can say she has a French poodle for a *roommite!*"

Chapter 25. Another Interlochen

After my parents help me unload and bid me good-bye, Buffy Jean and I spend the rest of the morning getting settled in our new room, which has bunk beds, a Danish modern chair, a long plank that forms two desks with shelves up above and drawers between the desks, and a closet with built-in drawers and shelves. Next to the room is a bathroom with a door at the other end that opens into another bedroom, making up a two-room suite.

Buffy Jean takes the lower bunk and I take the upper one, and we show each other our clothes as we unpack. She raves over my new black formal, but she has more fancy sweaters than I do and not one but two dress coats from a store in Dallas called Neiman Marcus, one coat which she says is a copy of a coat that Lucy Baines Johnson wears. Buffy Jean's father is a big executive at Texas Eastman, and she says executives' kids at his company have to dress and look just right and belong to the country club and go to all the right parties, which makes me kind of glad my dad is just a newspaperman, not a big executive. We may not have a membership at a country club, but at least I can dress and act like myself and not have to worry so much about what people think.

After we've put everything away while singing "Chances Are" along with the Johnny Mathis album Buffy Jean plays on her stereo, we get into our new dress uniforms—navy blue blazers and gray skirts with white blouses—and go down to the cafeteria for Sunday dinner. The place is much quieter than in the summer, with lots of empty tables and only one line instead of two. Joining us at our table are our suitemates, Lynn from New Jersey, who plays the viola, and Sarah, a voice major from New York. Both girls are seniors and seem nice, though it's hard to know what someone's really like until you've lived with them for a while, Mom always says.

After lunch, Buffy Jean and I go for a stroll across the campus, which is not at all the same place it was in the summer, when it was crawling with kids carrying instruments and eating Melody Freezes. Now we see just a few students here and there, all in dress uniforms or dress clothes, most of the music is gone from the air, and all the summer practice cabins are locked up tight. It's like someone waved a magic wand and presto: Another Interlochen!

All through lunch and our walk, I keep glancing around hoping for a glimpse of Jeffrey Higgenbottom, but so far he hasn't turned up. Is he really going to be here? Of course, it doesn't much matter now, since there's absolutely no chance he'll fall in love with me with my hair looking like this. Tonight, I'm going to wash it about six times and see if that helps.

Before I can do that, though, I have to get through our first orchestra performance as part of the opening "convocation." This includes some welcoming speeches and Buffy Jean's teacher, Richard Elsasser, playing an organ prelude and postlude, in addition to both the wind ensemble and the orchestra playing overtures after just one short rehearsal. Ours is Wagner's Overture to *Die Meistersinger*, which Dr. Maddy conducts. When I look at the seating chart before the rehearsal, I discover, to my dismay, that they have me down to sit third chair viola. I don't even have a viola, and I applied as a violin major, so either this is a mistake or somebody was trying to trick me. If so, it doesn't work, because I march right up to the podium and tell Dr. Maddy that there's been a mistake and I'm supposed to play violin at the Academy, not viola. He says I can play violin if I want, but I'll have to sit at the back of the second violins.

So now I'm stuck on a stand all by myself, and it's hard to see Dr. Maddy from back there, but I'm sure I'm better than the kids around me, so it's only a matter of time before I can move up in challenges. And even if that doesn't happen, I'd still rather play violin than viola. If they gave me a choice between first chair viola and last chair second violin for the rest of the year, I'd still want to play violin. Viola's okay for the summer to get a scholarship, and a good violist like Jane Cleveland can make a lovely velvety sound, but you can't really soar on a viola like you can on the violin, and anyway, why would I want to spend the rest of my life playing Hoffmeister when I could be playing Mendelssohn and Tchaikovsky?

After I'm settled at the back of the seconds, I glance back at the brass section and see Jeffrey sitting there with his trombone next to two other boys. Just knowing Jeffrey's there gives me a good feeling, like I've come home. Nothing can happen right now, but there are nine long months until Jeff's graduation, so who knows?

On Monday morning, we have our first real orchestra rehearsal with Dr. Thor Johnson, our new conductor. Dr. Johnson is a giant of a man, both vertically and horizontally. At the rehearsal, he wears the usual camp uniform, with his pants hitched high up around his non-existent waist, and the back of his mostly bald head is covered with slicked-down strawberry blond hair. This is his first real day conducting us, and he's all jollity and enthusiasm, listing off all the wonderful pieces we're going to be playing this year. I can't help feeling, though, that there's something ominous about Dr. Johnson's first name, Thor being the Norse god of thunder and lightning. Time will tell.

"All right, people," he says, picking up his baton and opening the score in front of him. "Let's get to work!" We spend the first rehearsal reading through the music we'll be performing on Sunday—Beethoven's Eighth Symphony, Debussy's *Afternoon of a Faun*, and Tchaikovsky's *March Slav*. Even though we're just sight-reading, I can already tell that Dr. Johnson is way better than any of the conductors we had last summer. Not only is his beat much easier to follow, you can also tell from his face and his gestures exactly what feelings are there in the music, and somehow you have no choice but to express them his way. Maybe that's the Thor part of the equation.

That afternoon, we have meetings with Mr. Frost, the guidance counselor. I'm taking English, American history, French, biology, and advanced algebra. Plus orchestra and private violin lessons. I go straight from the counseling office to the bookstore, where I'm given a big pile of books. My favorite is the American lit book, which has a black cover and is about three inches thick, with everything in it from Puritan journals to Hemingway. There's also a little spiral book for English called *Word Clues* that's supposed to help us expand our vocabularies for the SAT. Buffy Jean got her books too, consisting of *Word Clues*, a skinny little Latin book, and a book for history of the arts, but she doesn't seem very interested in them.

On Tuesday morning, I have to get up at 5 a.m. to do my first work scholarship assignment, which is to help in the cafeteria at breakfast. When I get there, breakfast is being served to the cafeteria staff and student helpers. After we've finished, Mrs. Davis, the head cook, shows us where to get clean white aprons and hairnets, which make us girls look not much different from the old ladies who work here full-time. At least now, nobody can see my seventy-year-old hairdo. My assignment on the first day is to help this plump, red-haired matron named Pat with the toast-making. Pat, who has a voice like an army drill sergeant, teaches me to make toast very fast on a contraption consisting of vertically arranged wire grills that rotate up, down, and around, with three pieces of toast falling off onto a little tray at the bottom every few seconds: plop, plop, plop. I'm supposed to load the slices of bread in, take them out, dip them in melted butter, and toss them in a metal serving pan while the toaster continues to rotate: plop, plop, plop. This requires more coordination than I'm naturally blessed with, and a few pieces end up on the floor before I begin to get the hang of it.

After my breakfast shift, I report to my first class: American history with Mr. Thurston, who looks like he slept in his clothes after staying up late reading about the Civil War, with wire glasses and a cowlick. Then comes algebra with Mr. Chase, a young man with a black crew cut and funny, long sideburns. Then French class with Mr. O'Brien, a small, neat-looking man who talks to us only in French and addresses us as "Mademoiselle" or "Monsieur" So-and-so, until noon. After lunch comes biology with Mr. Hood, curly-haired and fatherly, who assigns us to lab groups and draws pictures of amoebas on the board. My last class is English with Mrs. Chase, Mr. Chase's thin, pretty, intellectual-sounding wife. On the board is a definition of Puritanism by a writer called H.L. Mencken which I copy down: "Puritanism is the haunting fear that someone, somewhere, may be happy." Our first assignment is to start reading a novel about Puritans called *The Scarlet Letter*, which looks kind of hard and kind of gloomy.

Classes are over at two o'clock, and I load my books into my new blue canvas bookbag, throw the bag over my shoulder, and head back to the dorm to get my violin. Everything is brand new, and I can't wait to start working on the assignments the teachers gave us. I always love the first few weeks of school, before the tests and term-paper deadlines start spoiling the joy of pure learning. And here the classes are all small—only ten or twelve kids in a class—which makes me feel special, like one of those kids who star in movies and go to classes between scene shootings.

Orchestra rehearsal is from 2:30 to 4:30, while kids not in the orchestra go off to dance or art studios, the drama theater, or downstairs to practice. After that comes "physical activity"—a hike—then dinner and "study table" in the cafeteria from 7:30 to 9:20, where the girls and boys are kept separate. A big screen is pulled across the part where the boys are, and I can't help wondering if Jeffrey's back there. I managed to do my algebra problems and French homework after dinner and spend study table time reading the biology and history chapters, which means I'll have to sign up for late study in the basement tonight until eleven to start *The Scarlet Letter* for English. And I didn't get to practice at all today—yikes!

Somehow, tomorrow, I'm going to have to find a way to work on the orchestra music, because challenges are on Friday, and I have to try to get out of last chair. The only good part is, there's no place for me to go but up!

Chapter 26. My Big Mouth

$%*$@! I'm so mad at myself I could barf!

I just said something very, very, very stupid, and as a result, I'm now in big trouble. In the words of Ralph Kramden, "I've got a BIG MOUTH!"

It happened tonight when I ran into Dr. Thor Johnson, alias TJ, which is what we students call him behind his back, in the cafeteria after challenges. It's Friday, and normally we have dress dinner on Fridays, where we wear dress-up clothes and sit family style with a teacher at the head of the table, but there was an early concert this week, so the powers-that-be decided to make it cafeteria style.

Before dinner, I came waltzing into the cafeteria. I'd been sitting second chair, second violin all week, since the previous Friday's challenges, in which I went roaring up through the section just like Heinrich did in the violas that time, and I beat everyone but Nancy Morrison, who stayed in first chair. After that, in rehearsals, I could feel TJ's eyes on me, sizing me up. I practiced every minute that I could, and this Friday I beat Nancy too and moved up to principal second. I tried not to act too happy, and Nancy was a good sport and congratulated me, and so did some of the other kids in the section, and for a few hours, life was beautiful.

Then, tonight in the cafeteria, as I got up to the front of the line with my head still swollen to twice its usual size and was about to hold out my tray for spaghetti, whom did I see standing next to me but Dr. Johnson, who motioned for me to go ahead of him with a gentlemanly flourish.

"How did you come out in challenges today, Cynthia?" TJ asked. It was the first time he'd called me by name. Struggling to keep my tone casual, as if this happened every day of the week, I told him I'd gotten first chair.

"Well congratulations!" he said, his face going all smiley and twinkly. "I thought you would. I've been watching you!" TJ turned back towards the food and reached for a roll while I struggled to keep the silly compliment smile off my face.

I said my thanks and went on through the dinner line and was about to sit down when suddenly some evil demon came out of nowhere and made me turn back towards TJ, who was filling a glass with milk from a spigot on the big, silver machine.

"Sir, by the way, excuse me, I just wanted to ask you ..." He looked up at me, letting the milk spill over. "I just mean ... I'd like to know ... now that I'm first chair second, I mean ... when can I challenge the firsts?" The words sounded all wrong, out of place. That "by the way" had been downright weird. What would he think?

Dr. Johnson set down his tray and stood looking at me, his eyes narrowing. "Oh, don't you worry about that, Cynthia," he said. "You can just stay right where you are. There's lots you can learn from leading the second violins. I'm sure you'll do a fine job."

"Oh, well I ..." I said, desperate to fix things, "I just thought ... I might be, well, you know, more ... motivated." As soon as the word was out, I knew it was a horrible mistake. The maestro was no longer smiling.

"Well, Cynthia, if *that's* what you want," he said, in the tone my dad used when he told me to stop crying or he'd give me something to cry about, "I'll be glad to motivate you."

"I'm sorry, I ..." I began again, but it was too late. Dr. Johnson had already turned away and was talking to one of the trumpeters.

I fled to an empty table over by the windows, as far away from them as I could get. The longer I sat there toying with my spaghetti, the worse I felt. Thor Johnson had started out as a jolly giant in rehearsals, but already we were seeing another side of him. He had a habit of picking out one kid and launching a tirade at him in front of the whole orchestra, going on and on about how the kid had "no conception of this music, no conception at all." So far that student hadn't been me, but now that I'd opened my big mouth, I was sure it soon would be, now that I'd asked to be "motivated" and made a total fool of myself. Now I was in for it, and there was nothing I could do.

And to make matters worse, TJ had apparently doomed me to playing second violin for the rest of my life. From what he said, I might never be allowed to challenge the firsts, which wasn't fair. Dr. Maddy had started challenges at Interlochen because he wanted competition to be fair. Everybody else in the orchestra except the first chairs could go up in challenges if they worked hard, but not me, oh no, not Cynthia, no matter how hard she worked. *Cynthia* could only go down, never up. It wasn't fair!

I'd been so happy when I came into the cafeteria, I thought, and then, just because I'd said one little wrong thing, in the blink of an eye, my happiness turned to dust. Now, the only way to stay safe was to never, ever let myself feel that happy again and never let my head get so swollen up with pride, inviting the proverbial fall.

And along with that, I also had to learn to keep my mouth shut. My BIG MOUTH!

Chapter 27. After Lights Out

"Cindy?" Buffy Jean's voice comes out of the dark from the lower bunk, breaking into my dreams for the third time tonight.

"Cindy, do you think Kenny Jacobs is cute?"

"I don't know," I say. "He's all right. I never thought about it." Kenny sits behind me as third chair second violin, but his major is composition. He's the only kid I know who's writing a symphony, which means he must be a genius, but to me he's like a brother.

Kenny should probably look for another genius to go with him, not a society girl like Buffy Jean, but when it comes to choosing girlfriends, even genius boys don't seem to care much about brains. Take the way Kenny acted at dress dinner last Saturday night when he was sitting across from Buffy Jean. She had on her fire-engine red sweater with laces across the bosom and her black, fishnet hose, which was all it took to make genius Kenny act like an idiot, showing off for Buffy Jean by mimicking his high school English teacher, a little old lady named Mrs. Duderstadt, reciting in a silly old lady voice, "I think that I shall never seeee . . . a poem lovely as a treeee . . ." until her giggles drowned him out.

Then, all day Sunday, Buffy Jean kept going, "I think that I shall never seeee" over and over in the same silly voice. One thing I've learned about Buffy Jean is that once she gets something funny in her head, she never stops repeating it, trying to get laughs even after the joke is completely stale. I bet when we're both real old ladies in our eighties, she'll still be going, "I think that I shall never seeee . . . a poem lovely as a treeee . . . " hoping the other people in the nursing home will laugh.

"We went for a walk by the lake this afternoon, and Kenny told me about his symphony," Buffy Jean says now. "I think I'm getting a crush on him, he's so funny, we just laughed and laughed. And we signed up together to be on the same bus for the Mackinac Island trip. Ya'll should sign up for that bus too. We'll have a riot."

"I already signed up for a bus," I tell her. "I don't know if I'm on your bus or not, but actually . . . " Be careful, something warns me, but I can't keep from going on ". . . I mean there's someone else I sort of . . . want to be with."

"Someone else?!" Buffy Jean sys. "A boy? Who? Cindy, what're ya'll telling me?"

"Well, yes, a boy, of course. Someone I sort of . . . like."

"And you didn't tell your own roommite? Why ever not? Who is it? What's his name? Do I know him? Is he cute? Where did you meet him?" Her questions come at me in a fast blizzard.

"His name is Jeffrey," I say, "and I didn't exactly meet him yet. Not really. I mean, we were on concert service together a couple of times last summer, but we didn't really talk. It's just a silly crush, that's all, nothing serious. Forget it, it's not important."

"Jeffrey who? Jeff Bosworth, that bass-clarinet player? He's sort of cute."

"No, not him, this Jeff plays the trombone. He's in orchestra. He's . . . "

After a soft knock, the bedroom door swings open, making a patch of light on the floor. It's Miss Winfield, our dorm counselor, tiptoeing in and sweeping her flashlight around the room.

She whispers good-night, but we both stay still and silent. My big brush rollers are digging into my scalp. I pry two rollers away from each other, creating a small, rollerless patch that I can just barely manage to lie on. My hair will have a flat place there tomorrow, but I'm too tired to care.

"So, your Jeff plays the trombone—what's his last name?"

"He's not my Jeff, not anyone's Jeff as far as I know. And I don't want to tell you his last name because I'm sure you'll laugh."

"Oh, I won't—I promise I won't." She will, but I've already said too much, so I might as well finish.

"Well, all right," I say. "It's . . . would you believe . . . Higgenbottom." It's the first time I've used the expression "would you believe," which started with some art student seniors with long, straight hair and then spread through the dorm.

"Higgenbottom? Ha, ha! Higgenbottom, Higgenbottom. It sounds like some ol' dwarf in a fairy tale. Ha, ha!"

"Buffy Jean, you promised you wouldn't laugh."

"I'm sorry, I can't help it, ma roommite has a crush on a boy named Higgenbottom. Ha, ha, ha"! Her deep belly laugh shakes the whole bed.

"It's not that funny. It's not as though his name was Piggy or something," I say, but I'm starting to giggle myself. I can't help it.

"I think I know who you mean now," says Buffy Jean, after our giggling has died down. "He's pretty cute, and he's tall enough, and serious like you are, which is good. But don't you think he might be just a little . . . well, a little stuck-up? I mean, he always sounds like he's trying to be so intellectual, and he hangs around with superior beings like Suzy Smock and Lily Robbins, either them or the brass-players' clique, who all think they're so cool . . . "

"Oh, I think he's just shy," I say. "People who are shy are often misunderstood as being stuck-up. A lot of people think I'm stuck-up too when really, I've just got a big inferiority complex. I bet Jeff has one too."

"So okay—what's your plan?" Buffy Jean asks.

"Plan? What plan?" The idea of having a plan to catch a boyfriend is completely foreign to me, having been brought up to think that the boy should have a plan to catch me, not the other way around.

"I mean, how're you goin' to get to know him if you don't have a plan? You've at least got to get to know him. D'you want to spend the rest of your life wondering whether or not Jeff Higgenbottom liked you back? Do you want me to talk to him for you?"

"No!" I say, slamming both fists down on the mattress at my sides. "Oh, God, no, Buffy Jean, please, please, please don't ever do that! Don't ever tell anyone, please!" I bend over the side of the bed and give her a pleading look through the dark.

"Calm down," she says. "I was just kidding. Of course, I'd never do that. I'd never tell anyone in a million years. Your secret is safe with me."

Listening to Buffy Jean's protests, I'm one hundred percent sure that sooner or later she'll tell Jeffrey how I feel, but then I think maybe that wouldn't be such a bad thing. At least I wouldn't have to spend the rest of my life wondering, like she said.

Later, after Buffy Jean finally stops talking and her breathing slows down, I lie in my upper bunk on my rollers with my eyes wide open and my brain cranking out one thought after another. What Buffy Jean doesn't understand is that for me boys are a whole different ballgame than they are for her, for the simple reason that she's short and wears a D-cup and I'm tall and wear a double A-cup. Plus the fact that she's rich and can buy all sorts of fancy sweaters to wear with her knickers and has a sexy Southern accent while I have boring, Iowa sweaters and a boring, Iowa accent. In other words, Buffy Jean has sex appeal, and I don't.

Given all that, you'd think I'd be jealous of Buffy Jean, but strangely enough, I'm not. If she just wore a B-cup instead of a D-cup, I probably would be, but a D-cup is almost as bad as a double-A. A D-cup can blind boys to everything else but that. Boys are so stupid that if a girl wears a D-cup, they automatically assume she's some kind of scarlet woman, not the kind of girl they'd ever get serious about, and that's not the way I'd want them to think about me.

But Buffy Jean's D cup does mean she can do things I can't. If I were Buffy Jean, I'd just go up to Jeffrey and start talking to him. Watch for a time when he's sitting alone in the cafeteria and put my tray down in front of his, say hello, ask him how he is, maybe pay him a compliment. Boys love compliments, they say, and they love to talk about themselves.

But I could never ever do that, and it's not just because I'm not sexy like Buffy Jean and am afraid Jeffrey might go "Yuk!" and run away. It's also because if I did that it would spoil something. If I went up to Jeffrey and started a conversation, even if by some miracle this led to him asking me out, it wouldn't mean what I wanted it to. The only way it would mean anything was if Jeffrey came up to me, not if I went up to him, and all I can do to try to make that happen is talk to him with my eyes, not with words, and meanwhile keep putting myself in places where I know he'll be, like in the library before his English class with Mr. Dilly or in the dinner line, which he always joins at about 5:25, in hopes that he might someday decide to speak to me first.

That's all I can do, and in the meantime, I guess I'd rather just content myself with dreams, standing on the sun-decker looking out at the lake or lying in my bunk listening to a certain song over and over and imagining that glorious, pink-and-gold moment when Jeffrey finally tells me that he's loved me all along. My favorite dreaming song is "If I Loved You" from *Carousel*, sung by this whispery quartet of boys called "The Lettermen" on one of Buffy

Jean's 45s. The song isn't exactly right for me—it's about being afraid to tell somebody you love them rather than not being able to talk to them at all—but it's close enough to carry me off into a blue haze, lying back on the pillows and imagining the perfect moment of revelation again and again, not knowing if it will ever come to pass.

Chapter 28. The Hammer of Thor

"First violins and violas, letter L, one instrument, people, one long line, only mezzo-forte until the crescendo up to the szforzando in the firsts: da da da da da da da DA!"

Dr. Johnson raises his baton and glances from firsts to violas and back again while I sit with my own violin on my knee, straight across from Suzy Smock, the concertmistress, right out there where the audience—and TJ—can see me instead of buried next to the firsts the way the principal second usually is. TJ has his own way of arranging the orchestra, putting us over there so the cellos can face the audience to create a richer sound.

I glance back at the trombones, but Jeff is looking down at the floor. I look up at the clock. Three forty-four. Only forty-six more minutes and I will have survived another Thor Johnson rehearsal—or not.

The piece is Tchaikovsky's *Romeo and Juliet* overture, which we'll be performing on Sunday's concert, along with a Haydn Symphony and a modern piece by someone I never heard of named Cecil Effinger. TJ has us play a lot of pieces by people I never heard of, mostly Americans, though one of our concerts this fall was all Japanese music. Miss Kleinschmidt, who teaches senior English, read a lot of tiny little poems by someone named Basho while the orchestra played and there was an exhibit of Japanese prints in the Fine Arts Building that Mr. Cruithards, the cello teacher who lives with TJ, brought over from Japan. The notes in the Japanese music weren't hard, but the rhythms were, and since I have an awful sense of rhythm, it goes without saying that I got yelled at in those rehearsals. At least the rhythms aren't so hard in the Tchaikovsky, though there are some fast runs I'm still faking.

Bringing the section in after rests is about my only job as principal second— unfortunately, since rhythm is what I'm worst at. If this were a professional orchestra, I'd also have to mark the bowings for everyone to copy, but TJ has his own set of parts for most pieces, in which the bowings are already marked just the way he likes them. TJ is very particular about bowings, unlike every other conductor I ever played under.

Now, in the air above me, the baton jabs out a forceful up-beat before coming down like a hammer hitting a nail, bringing in the first violins and violas on a couple measures of sixteenths, after which the firsts go on by themselves, not too bad, after which the violas come in and dissolve into a scrambly, scratchy mess. TJ instantly drops his baton-arm to his side and stands glaring down at the section, turning the violists to stone with his eyes.

For a moment he just stands there, and you can see him struggling to get control of himself. Finally, he heaves a massive sigh.

"All right, people," he says, "again, slower. Da da da Da da da da Come on—better, better, better, people." His tenor voice crescendos upwards on the three "betters" and punches the word "people."

He raises his arms again. Sweat stains are spreading across the armpits of his light blue shirt, and beads of sweat are dripping down his face. I inch my chair back a little for fear one of the drips will fly down on me. Then the white baton comes down again, jabbing and poking—down, across, back, up, down, across, back, up in a four-four pattern until the violas' scrambling starts again and it stops with a jerk.

Again, TJ stands stock still, but this time his eyes are shifting from one stand of violists to another as though looking through papers in a file. Someone is about to get it—who will it be? Finally, his glare fixes on the fifth chair violist, a pimply, miserable runt of a boy.

This has been one of TJ's worst days ever. The rehearsal is only half over and already he's bawled out one of the horn players just for asking a simple question and blasted the first chair harpist. Now, here he stands, high on his wooden box, a blond god hurling thunderbolts down on poor Lenny Wilcox, telling him he has no conception, no conception at all of what it means to play this music.

Finally, the storm ends, and TJ tells us to go back to the beginning of the piece. "Better, better, better, people!" he intones for the fourth time that day. I glance over at the trombones again and for a moment Jeff's eyes lift and seem to almost catch mine, but then they drop away again as he gets ready for an entrance.

"Second bassoon, quiet, too loud!" shouts Dr. Johnson. "It's *piano!*"

. . . *three two three four, four two three four, five two three four* . . . I sit at attention, counting the measures until the seconds are to come in on our four little pizzicato notes. Are we supposed to come in along with the firsts or by ourselves? I look across the stage at Suzy but get no clue. I go on looking at her, trying not to hate her.

Suzy Smock is good. Suzy Smock is really, really good. Suzy Smock is a senior and won concertos last year and plays all her solos perfectly and never, ever misses an entrance or gets yelled at like the rest of us do. Suzy Smock is thin, with milk-white skin and shining black hair. Suzy Smock is president of the student council and gets all A's in her classes and has a tall, cute boyfriend, the first chair French horn. In other words, Suzy Smock is perfect, which is why, as I sit staring at her shining hair while my mouth counts out the measures, I wish more than anything that Suzy would make some huge, embarrassing flub, preferably during a concert, a flub so horrible that TJ would not only yell at her but send her over here to rot in the second violins so she can see what it's like and, of course, move me over to take her place as concertmistress.

Stop it, I tell myself. If you were a good person, you wouldn't be thinking these thoughts. You don't even know Suzy Smock, and besides, what has she ever done to you? If I were a good person, I'd be glad for Suzy Smock's successes, but I'm not. I'm a person with a grasping red lobster inside me, a person who wants for Suzy Smock to mess up, or at least to have a chance to challenge my way up through the first violins so I can sit next to Suzy Smock and turn her pages and get to be part of her circle of perfect friends, including Jeffrey Higgenbottom, as if that could ever happen.

Which, of course, it couldn't, thanks to TJ and that stupid, horrible thing I opened my big mouth and said about being "motivated," the thing that showed TJ my true colors, selfish and competitive and just wanting to get ahead instead of caring only about the music the way Suzy Smock probably does. So here I am, a month later, doomed to eternal "motivation" at the head of the second violin section, getting yelled at every time I don't come in and having to defend my chair every single week in challenges. It's not fair, but there's nothing I can do about it, not if I don't want to get squished like a little bug by that huge, sweating, Norse god on the podium. My only choice is to try to do the best job I can for the sake of the music, which is all that matters, I tell myself for the umpteenth time, knowing that if I can get myself to believe that and forget about challenges and Suzy Smock maybe, just maybe, TJ, seeing my transformation, might change his mind and let me challenge the firsts, all of whom, of course, care only about the music, unlike yours truly, the selfish opportunist.

Meanwhile, with all these thoughts rushing through my head, my mouth has gone on silently counting measures. Ten two three four, eleven two three four, twelve two . . .

Was that eleven or twelve? Did I skip a number? I catch the eye of Nancy, my stand partner, and look at her lips, but they aren't mouthing measure numbers. I mouth "thirteen" and give her a questioning look, but she just shrugs. I put my violin up under my chin, wait for the right place—that wasn't it, was it?—and then suddenly the music stops and TJ's blue eyes are fixed on me as he stands there puffing and panting, and I know that once again, I'm going to get it in front of the whole orchestra. *If that's what you want, Cynthia, I'll be glad to motivate you,* he said. Me and my big mouth. Why, why, why?

"Well, Cynthia?" TJ starts out. "Fancy meeting you here. Please, please, do come in, by all means. What do you want—an engraved invitation? If you don't come in, how can you possibly expect your section to come in?"

I stare into the music, fixing my eyes on a big, black whole rest hanging down from a line under the number "2." My cheeks burn and I feel suddenly chinless and fat, the flab on my thighs pressing into the chair.

"If you had any conception at all of this music, Cynthia," says TJ. "You couldn't possibly have missed that entrance. You couldn't have missed that entrance if you'd wanted to. But obviously, you have no conception, no conception at all. So, all right, people, let's go back to letter L and see if Cynthia can stop wasting rehearsal time and bring her section in at the correct place this time."

We go back, and I try to count measures, but this time all I can think about is how stupid and incompetent TJ made me look to everyone in the orchestra, and I come in a measure early, and again TJ stops the orchestra and glares at me.

"All right, Cynthia," he says. "Are we going to waste the rest of this rehearsal repeating this section just for you? If you don't have any conception of the music, could you at least try to understand what it means to be a section leader? Obviously, you have no conception of leadership, no conception at all."

We start again, and this time, I start whispering the numbers louder and louder, punching each one with a nod of my head so TJ can see how hard I'm trying: "One Two Three Four Two Two Three Four . . . "With each measure, I whisper louder, thinking *It's his fault if I didn't come in right, his fault for saying mean things, his fault that I can't concentrate* and getting madder and madder: "ONE TWO THREE FOUR TWO TWO THREE FOUR . . . " I spit out one number after another and next to me Nancy is also counting, and when it's time to come in, we both come in on our four pizzicato notes which are, after all, supposed to be with those of the firsts, and the whole section follows, and the music flows on.

Then something crazy happens. When I hear the whole orchestra playing Tchaikovsky, it's as if a big wheel inside me jars loose and all my anger changes to pure energy and all of a sudden I'm playing for everything I'm worth. When it's over, I'll be angry or scared or something else, but right now, I'm just playing and playing, at one with the rest of the orchestra, catching the rhythm from Suzy, as good a violinist as Suzy, as good as anyone in the world, holding my violin high in the air, leading MY section, and sawing out all the hardest sixteenth-note passages and the soaring Tchaikovsky melodies as TJ's hand sculpts them in the air, a rapturous look on his face, carrying us higher and higher, the whole orchestra at one with the hands and the face and the sweating body, the violins and the clarinets and the cellos and the trombones, all of it coming together so nothing matters but the music, ploughing up hill and down, billowing and soaring and folding back in on itself.

At the end, TJ stands looking down at us with his arms hanging at his sides for a moment. Sweat is running down his face and his arms and his back but it doesn't matter anymore how he looks, nothing matters but the thing that just happened.

"That's better, people," he says to the whole orchestra, laying his baton down on the stand and folding his arms. "That's the way an orchestra ought to sound."

Then, as I glance up, one blue eye in TJ's sweaty face fixes on me and winks.

Chapter 29. Autumn Collage

Time, time, time. There's never enough time!

I have an English paper due tomorrow and a French quiz and a bunch of algebra problems I still haven't done and challenges and my lesson coming up for which I've hardly practiced and a required assembly tonight and I'm behind with my two letters to my parents. If I could just have 48-hour instead of 24-hour days, life would be perfect. But as it is, everything keeps zipping along way too fast, with me running along behind trying to catch up.

* * * * * * * * *

In the woods, we return to reason and faith. There I feel that nothing can befall me in life—no disgrace, no calamity (leaving me my eyes), which nature cannot repair. Standing on the bare ground—my head bathed by the blithe air and uplifted into infinite space—all mean egotism vanishes. I become a transparent eyeball; I am nothing; I see all; the currents of the Universal Being circulate through me; I am part or parcel of God.

I read the words from Emerson's "Nature" over, sitting in the upstairs lounge of the girls' dorm and feeling the currents of Universal Being circulate through me at five o'clock in the morning. The only part I don't get is the transparent eyeball, which seems kind of gross. I keep seeing this disgusting glass eyeball in a jar of water, like something out of an Edgar Alan Poe story, even though I know that's not what it's supposed to mean.

*   *   *   *   *   *   *   *   *   *

"Ecology," Mr. Hood writes on the board. "Does anyone know what this word means?" No one says anything. He defines it for us, but I'm daydreaming about Jeffrey and miss a couple of phrases, though I hear enough to get that it has something to do with the balance of nature and birds eating worms that eat bugs that eat microbes. Then Mr. Hood leads us out into the red-gold woods and takes a shovel and turns over some dirt and points out all the different forms of life—the tree roots, the dead plants, the insects—that are in just that one section of dirt, and talks about how they all affect each other, which is kind of fascinating, when you think about it. Walking down the concourse to English class, I say the new word a couple more times: "Ecology, ecology."

*   *   *   *   *   *   *   *   *   *

"Bzzzzzzzzzzzz!" goes Buffy Jean loudly in the breezeway, signaling that she sees Jeff up ahead, getting into the dinner line. (The signal for Kenny, whom she's now dating, is "Bzzz bzzz bzzz bzzz!") Jeff turns around and glances back at us for a moment, then turns away again as Buffy Jean stands giggling in the doorway and I gesture like mad for her to be quiet.

*   *   *   *   *   *   *   *   *   *

Da da da   Da da da   Da da da   Da da da ... I turn the metronome up a notch and practice the triplets in the Mendelssohn concerto a little faster. My lesson with Mr. Chausow is tonight, and I can almost play this passage in tempo. The fast parts in this piece are a lot of work, but the melodies are the next best thing to flying and make me glad I stuck with the violin instead of switching to viola. I'm going to practice every minute I can on this piece and get good enough to win concertos this spring and again in the summer so I can play in Kresge with the orchestra like Annie Kavafian did, which is what I want more than anything in the world. I can do it! I can do anything! ... da da Da da da Da da da Da da da ...

*   *   *   *   *   *   *   *   *   *

"The big news today is that Nikita Khrushchev has been deposed," Mr. Thurston says, which I guess means Khrushchev lost his job. I hope it doesn't mean his being stolen away and never seen again, because even though he said he'd bury us and banged on the table with his shoe at the UN after that U-2 thing and tried to put missiles in Cuba, I still feel like he's sort of a friend because of how he came to Des Moines that time when I was in the sixth grade. That was a few years after my dad's golf partner Lauren Soth wrote the editorial in the *Register* saying he thought Russians and Americans should share ideas about farming. Somebody in Russia read Mr. Soth's article, and the next thing we knew, Mr. Soth was off to Russia himself, along with my friend Mary Plambeck's dad, who reads the farm reports on WHO, and when they came back they showed us colored slides of their trip, and a couple years later Khrushchev himself showed up on Des Moines TV news parading through downtown and going to visit some farm and talking about sausages with Harry Bookey, a classmate of mine, at his dad's meat-packing plant, all of which made him seem like a nice, jolly grandfather even though I know he wasn't really. Now, Khrushchev's out of the picture, and for a moment, I think about telling Mr. Thurston and the class about him and Mr. Soth and Mr. Plambeck, but the teacher's moved on to talking about the Constitutional Convention and anyway, I'm afraid they might think I'm crazy and made it all up, so I don't.

*   *   *   *   *   *   *   *   *   *

"I said spiccato, Cynthia, not staccato," says TJ. "Better, better, better, people." I move my bow to the middle and start making it bounce on the sixteenth notes and the Tchaikovsky *Serenade for Strings* comes to life.

*   *   *   *   *   *   *   *   *   *

If I sit here on this bench and gaze out at the lake will Jeff come by and see me on his way to his waiter job in the cafeteria? The sky is plain light gray, with a long-armed V of Canada geese honking across it, and the water is an unappetizing brown, but I'm Emerson crossing the bare common in snow puddles with the currents of the Universal Being flowing through me, glad to be alive, though I'd be even gladder if Jeffrey Higgenbottom would just walk by and speak to me, even if it's just to say hello. Two months already, and still not a word. I overheard him telling someone he's applying to Oberlin. Maybe I'll apply there too, which would give me three more years of chances if he starts there next year and I go the year after that.

* * * * * * * * * *

"I feel happy, I feel healthy, I feel terrific!" the whole school chants at the assembly before sitting down and listening to W. Clement Stone, one of the head trustees, lecture us for half an hour on PMA, which stands for "Positive Mental Attitude." Not that everyone here really feels happy, healthy, and terrific, I don't suppose. You could have gone down in challenges or broken up with the love of your life or just found out that your dog died, but according to Mr. Stone, you're still supposed to say this stuff over and over because if you repeat it enough, it gets to be true. Personally, I don't have much faith in it, given my past failures with Norman Vincent Peale, plus the fact that I have a ton of homework that isn't getting done right now, PMA or no PMA. So why, you may ask, am I and everybody else sitting here listening to a lecture on PMA? For the simple reason that Mr. Stone, this super-rich Chicago insurance executive who wears a handlebar mustache, smokes cigars, writes positive thinking books with a guy named Napoleon Hill, and is what Dad would call a "character," gave most of the money for Dr. Maddy to start the Academy, and considering what he did for us, I guess listening to him spout his pet theories for half an hour is the least we can do. He's like one of those screwball uncles that everybody has to humor because he's family. Someone told me you can get a free copy of Mr. Stone's book, *Success through a Positive Mental Attitude*, in the hotel lobby, though of course I wouldn't be caught dead reading it.

* * * * * * * * * *

In the Fine Arts Building, the two visitors, a man and a woman, are both pale and saggy looking, as if they've never had any sunshine or exercise in their lives.

They're the first real Russians I ever saw, faculty from the Moscow and Leningrad conservatories on a tour of American music schools. Dr. Johnson introduces them and they tell us, in broken English, about their schools in Russia, and I'm thinking how probably they wouldn't even be here if it weren't for my dad's friend Mr. Soth, and everyone is being super-polite, doing our parts to end the Cold War, when all of a sudden this skinny, freckled little eighth grader with black braids named Bobbi Lebowski raises her hand and asks, "So, what's it like to have to live in a country where you don't have any freedom? Do you ever wish you could live in a democracy like we do?" and the whole audience collectively gasps, while the visitors look as if they didn't understand the question, though they're probably just pretending.

"Oh, I'm so sorry, I'm afraid we're out of time," says TJ, getting to his feet and acting as if Bobbi hadn't spoken at all. He thanks the visitors and they thank us for inviting them and everyone goes away relieved except Bobbi, who keeps saying, "Why didn't they answer my question? I don't understand. I think that was really rude of Dr. Johnson not to let them answer!" while the two girls on either side of her keep poking her in the ribs to try to get her to shut up.

* * * * * * * * * *

On election night, the boys come over for a party in the basement of the girls' dorm, with popcorn and hot chocolate, and we watch the returns coming in on the big TV as Lyndon Johnson gets state after state, which is a big relief, since Goldwater would almost certainly have started a nuclear war, and that would have been the end of that. Mr. Thurston is there and has some kind of a game set up that a bunch of boys are playing, with maps and colored chips to represent armies trying to take over the world. Jeff is playing, and I consider joining in, but none of the other girls is playing and world conquest has never appealed to me much, so I don't.

* * * * * * * * * *

"Look at me," sings Buffy Jean along with the record on Sunday morning. Outside the windows, the first snow is sifting down through the bare branches, as she and the record sing on about a kitten up a tree and not knowing their hat from their glove. By the time we leave for dress dinner, the tune is playing itself in my mind with some of the words and goes on even after our concert that afternoon, during which I think Jeff might actually have caught my eye across the orchestra and not looked away. Now I see him walking up ahead of me on the path next to the lake and I'm floating along behind his dark red ski jacket amidst the falling flakes, wanting nothing more than what just might have happened, the song playing away in my head, perfect for the misty way I'm feeling, "and too much in love."

Chapter 30. A Whole Month Off

"I told Grandma we'd come over to see her this afternoon, and they want you to bring your violin and play for them, of course," Mom tells me as she lowers two strips of bacon onto my plate and pops a slice of Wonderbread into the toaster.

I'm still a little tired from the long trip home yesterday, flying first from Traverse City to Chicago in a little propeller plane on North Central Airlines, which took forever because it kept landing in all these little towns in Michigan, then finding my way through O'Hare Airport to the United flight to Des Moines, on which a couple of bleached-blond, blue-suited mannequins served us doll-sized portions of food on plastic trays. Finally, the lights of the gold Iowa capitol dome loomed up into the plane window and a little while later we were on the ground.

Now, here I am, spreading toast thickly with peanut butter while Mom lists off all the various social engagements she's got planned for me. These involve not only family, but also Mrs. Sexton, Mr. Baxter, my Roosevelt friends, and three of her own friends who've invited us to a bridal shower, a neighborhood coffee, and a potluck dinner. And, of course, we've got all the Christmas shopping and wrapping and baking and decorating to do.

All of which makes me wonder when I'm ever going to practice, not to mention do all the homework the teachers gave us before we left. My Mendelssohn has to be note-perfect by the time I go back, plus I'm supposed to read an abridged version of *Moby Dick*, review all my French vocabulary, do the rest of the semester's reading for history and biology, and work a bunch of algebra problems on some sheets Mr. Chase handed out. Some vacation! On the morning when I visit Mrs. Sexton, I play my Mendelssohn for her while she struggles through the piano part. She doesn't say whether she thinks I've improved or not, which hurts my feelings a little, but she invites me to come to her annual Christmas party and tell everyone about my Interlochen adventures. She also asks me to come over and play quartets one evening with her and some friends. Playing second violin, with Mrs. Sexton on first, I suddenly make a strange discovery: Mrs. Sexton may be an excellent violin teacher, but she really doesn't play that great herself! Not that she plays out of tune, and she's pretty good at sight-reading all the notes, but her sound is a little weak, not the kind of smooth, rich sound the best violinists at Interlochen make. I wonder why I never noticed this before, and it makes me a little sad.

Christmas comes and goes, my old Roosevelt quartet takes me out for pizza, and I play a Handel Sonata at Plymouth with Mr. Baxter and sing with the Matins Choir on Christmas Eve, though it doesn't sound so good to me after hearing the choirs at Interlochen, and when I see Mark Baxter marching in with the adult choir, I don't feel a thing, thanks to Jeff Higgenbottom.

By New Years I've almost memorized my Mendelssohn and am over halfway through Moby Dick, which leaves me with only one problem: my parents. It seems like all Mom cares about is my not embarrassing her by wearing the wrong shade of nylons and she's always hinting that she wants me to help her in the kitchen and acts like a martyr if I don't but never comes out and asks, which drives me crazy! And Dad resents every minute that I don't spend talking to him and accuses me of being an "intellectual snob" every time I don't want to watch some silly TV program. What does he mean "intellectual snob" anyway? He himself read Will Durant's *The Story of Philosophy* and is always bragging about the history books he reads, so who is he to talk? What really bugs me, though, is the way they always stick up for each other, making it two against one every single time. Mom gets mad at me for not being more affectionate towards Dad, and Dad gets mad at me for not taking Mom's hints to help her. I don't know why I can't do what they want, but I just can't, which makes me hate myself, which makes me hate them for making me hate myself, at least temporarily.

Usually when they get mad at me, I keep my mouth shut, for fear of making them so mad they won't let me go back to Interlochen, but sometimes I can't help myself. Like the other night at the dinner table, for example. It started when the phone rang and I got up and answered it. It was my Roosevelt friend Glenda asking if I wanted to go to a concert with her and Marian. Of course, when I got back, Dad just *had* to ask who it was.

"Oh, just somebody," I said, which he said was rude, and then he used this as a starting point for listing all my many crimes since I got home. Then Mom chimed in and told me that I'd embarrassed her by being snotty to one of her friends at the wedding shower she dragged me to. The friend, a Mrs. Twist, who had fake blond curls despite being about a hundred years old, had asked me, in her fakey little-girl voice, if I wasn't just thrilled to be home from school and having the time of my life, and I just answered, "Yeah, sure" and didn't say anything after that, so the conversation ended kind of abruptly. Of course, I wasn't about to tell her the truth, which was that I was sick to death of being back in Des Moines and couldn't wait to get back to Interlochen. Actually, I don't think Mrs. Twist really cared what I said, but Mom still had to bawl me out for my "rude behavior" afterwards plus having to use this trivial incident to put her two cents in with Dad just to show us both whose side she was on, which you can be sure wasn't mine.

Then Dad, who was already mad at me about my alleged "attitude" said that he just knew that if they sent me to "that place" that it would turn me into an intellectual snob who thought she was too good for "all us poor, uncultured Iowans" and Mom said that I had to learn that there are more important things in life than getting good grades and being able to play the violin, that I still had to learn how to get along with people and if I didn't learn how to get along with people, it wasn't going to matter if I was at the top of my class and the greatest violinist in the world, I was going to have a miserable life.

At which point, I opened my mouth and told them all I really wanted was to go back to Interlochen, where I had no trouble at all getting along with anyone and didn't always have people mad at me who didn't understand me and would never, ever understand me no matter how hard I tried to please them. I got up from the table and went running off crying to my room and slammed the door and sobbed as loudly as I could to make them feel good and guilty and maybe even stop being mad. Then, a little while later, Mom knocked on my door and came in and put her arms around me and told me she loved me and Dad said he was sorry too and took us to Bauder's drugstore, where he and I had hot fudge sundaes and Mom had a diet coke.

After that the three of us got along better for a few more days, and I got the rest of my Mendelssohn memorized, but now I can feel their mad thoughts starting to build up again, which would probably lead to more scenes if it weren't for the fact that tomorrow Buffy Jean is flying in from the Dallas airport via Kansas City to spend a couple of days with us before we both fly back to school.

Alas, when I wake up the next morning and look out the window, the air is thick with white, infuriating fog. All day Mom keeps calling the airport as one flight after another gets delayed and I'm just sure that Buffy Jean will have to fly back home to Texas, leaving me to suffer through three more days of fights with my parents before I can finally get away. But in the afternoon, we get the word that Buffy Jean's plane is going to "try to land" and a little while later, there she is, coming down the steps to the runway in her red Niemen Marcus coat, and we all go rushing out to meet her. She gives me a great big hug, we're both talking a mile a minute, and my parents take us out for dinner at the Prime Rib for some good Iowa beef and we stay up until after midnight talking and giggling.

The next morning, Mom drops us off downtown, and we have lunch at Babe's, then make our way over to Younker's department store, where we buy fishnet hose and charms for our charm bracelets and diaries for 1965, then on down the street to a candy store that has different kinds of sweets in bins. Coming out clutching white sacks filled with candy, we notice a big sign in front of a drug store that says, "Sale: 25 bars of soap for $1." This seems like a great deal to us, so we go in and buy the twenty-five, strongly perfumed, pink-and-white bars, which we think is hilarious. The only problem is, when we go to pack the following evening, we remember that we can't have over forty pounds of luggage each, and both of our suitcases, when we weigh them on the bathroom scales, are a little too heavy.

Consequently, when we leave for the airport in the morning, our pockets, purses, and flight bags are all crammed with bars of perfumed soap, and every time we see someone near us sniffing the air, we look at each other and giggle.

Chapter 31. Long Winter Nights

"W . . . L . . . S—in Chicago!"

Unbearably cheery voices buzz out of my little transistor radio to attack my frazzled brain in three-part harmony. This is final exam week, and except for a brief spell when I pretended to be asleep before last night's bed check, I've been studying for twelve hours straight: from seven to ten last night in our room, from ten-thirty to twelve in the girls' dorm basement, from twelve-thirty to five illegally on the bathroom floor with towels stuffed under the doors, and from five to seven legally out in the upstairs lounge.

My head aches and my heart's beating a little fast, but thanks to the No-Doz from the Traverse City drugstore, courtesy of one of Buffy Jean's admirers, my mind is still pretty clear. I know how to solve all the different kinds of algebra equations, and I can draw a diagram of a cell, complete with nucleus, and list all the phyla of plants and animals and say what DNA and RNA stand for and how they relate. Math and biology are today, tomorrow is English and American history, and Thursday is French, after which I'll be gloriously, ecstatically free!

The exams are all given in the cafeteria, scheduled by subject area, with the math classes on Tuesday from 9 to 11 and the science classes from 1:30 to 3:30, the English classes on Wednesday morning, and so forth. On the first day, I get through the math and biology finals all right, but the English test the next morning is much harder. I don't know why I'm having so much trouble when English is normally my best subject. Could it possibly be because, after two nights straight on No-doz, my eyes are half-swollen shut, the only way I can read the test is to put my head about two inches from the paper, and everything seems weird and unreal? Leaving the cafeteria, I have absolutely no idea how I did, but at least I stayed conscious and got through it. By afternoon, I feel a little better, and the history test is mostly multiple guess, but French the next morning is something else, with my brain feeling like a mule lying down and refusing to go a step further.

I thought when I was done with my last test I'd be ecstatic, but instead all I can think about is my bed. My beautiful upper bunk, with its regulation beige bedspread, electric blanket, cool white sheets, and foam rubber pillow, waiting up in our room to transport me back to sanity. Alas, the bed will have to wait, because we still have orchestra rehearsal before dinner.

When I do get back to the dorm, I go straight to bed, only to discover that I can't sleep. All I can do is lie there worrying about how I did on that awful English test and about challenges on Friday, for which I haven't practiced at all, and about whether the No-doz has wrecked my brain. Finally, Buffy Jean, who hardly studied at all for her exams despite having taken No-doz too on the second night—why, I'm not sure, as she spent most of the night doing her nails—comes in from ice skating and climbs into bed just before lights out.

She falls asleep unusually fast, considering this is Buffy Jean we're talking about, but I lie there with my eyes still open, listening to her regular breathing and the heating vent switching on and off, knowing that beyond the black windows the snow is piling up, and imagining what it must be like for the squirrels and rabbits out there in the ecology of the cold, dark woods.

I'm just starting to drift off when suddenly, from the bunk beneath me, I hear the words, "I'm not psycho, I'm just HUNGRY!" in Buffy Jean's silliest little-girl voice. It's one of her favorite quotes from some *Peanuts* cartoon, which she repeats any time anyone says either the word "hungry" or the word "psycho" and on countless other random occasions as well, way past being funny. Now, though, she's saying it in her sleep, or at least pretending to, and I wait to hear what comes next so I can tell her tomorrow what she said for a good laugh. I've done this before and find it fascinating, whether it's real or not. Maybe, if I can't make it with the violin, I'll be one of those psychologists who interpret people's dreams.

"My roommate's a wizard," Buffy Jean announces, switching subjects in a singsong, sleep-talking voice. "Just like . . . the Wizard of Oz. Hello, there, Wizzie." It makes sense that Buffy Jean would dream about Oz, given the fact that earlier tonight our suitemate Lynn was singing "We're off to See the Wizard" while telling us about a production she was in, but I'm still suspicious.

"Both teams are on the field now," Buffy Jean goes on. "Wizzie has the ball. Go! Go! Wizzie . . . She's the only player on the field with a pink rose on her helmet . . . " Her voice fades off, then comes up again, giving a play-by-play account of a football game in which I'm apparently the star quarterback. In the morning, I tell Buffy Jean what she said in her sleep and she laughs and swears she doesn't remember anything, but I still think she was play-acting. That thing about the pink rose was just a little too good to be real.

After I've finally gotten enough sleep and survived challenges, I have a long, deliciously free weekend, during which Buffy Jean starts calling me Wizzie all the time, we go skating on the frozen lake, and I spend an afternoon in one of the knotty-pine chairs in the Stone hotel lobby reading *King Lear* in front of an open fire and glancing out at the falling snow every now and then. On Thursday evening there are sign-up sheets on the bulletin board for the next afternoon's ski trip to Sugar Loaf Mountain. It sounds like fun, but if I went skiing, I'd be sure to break an arm and wreck my violin career, so I don't sign up.

Late Friday night, Buffy Jean sits up in the lower bunk, jerking me awake. "What was that?" she asks. "There's something going on out there--I swear I just heard something." She stumbles out of bed and puts her ear to the door and I climb down and stand behind her. Is this just another one of her jokes?

"I hear voices," she says, "and they're not all female!" I can hear them too now, getting closer and louder, though still hushed.

We open our door a crack and peek out. Two boys are coming slowly down the hall carrying Melanie Carstairs towards her room, and it looks like she's asleep. What are they doing here? Boys aren't ever allowed upstairs in the girls' dorm, not ever. And why are they carrying Melanie? What's wrong with her? Is she drunk?

"She'll be all right," says Mrs. Jewell, coming down the hallway behind the boys and their burden. "Just put her in her bunk and we'll take care of her. The doctor's on his way. No, not there—it's that room over there. And that's Joyce's room there, off to the right." She turns and points as two other boys pass by with another sleeping girl.

"Hey," Buffy Jean calls out. "What's going on? What happened?" She starts to go out into the hallway to ask, but Mrs. Jewell waves her back.

"It's all right, girls," she says. "We had a scare, but everything's under control. Go back to sleep." You'd think she could at least tell us what happened, but no, she says to go back to sleep, as if anyone can after that. Buffy Jean and I spend the next hour theorizing, but we don't find out what really happened until the next morning at breakfast.

"When the driver told the kids to get off, nobody moved," Kenny tells us. It was the ski trip bus, he explains. Some carbon monoxide seeped into the bus from the rear and put everybody but the driver to sleep. The driver got out and started yelling, and the boys and counselors came out of their dorm and carried all the kids off the bus and laid them out in the snow. Everyone woke up all right, but they all had headaches and some of them threw up.

The following Tuesday, I get my exams back and, amazingly, learn that I got an A on the English test! I got A's on most of the others too, except for a B-plus in French. When Buffy Jean sees that I'm on the honor roll, she says, "See, I knew I was right to call you Wizzie!" and gives me a hug. She herself got a D in Latin and is still on study table, which would make me want to commit hara-kiri, but when Buffy Jean tells me about her grades she just laughs and goes off to build a snowman with some ninth grade boys she hangs around with.

The second semester starts that day. I have a different biology teacher this semester, Miss Appelhof, and a different English teacher, Mrs. Danneker, who teaches composition. My advanced algebra class was scrunched into one semester, and this semester I have statistics with Mr. Chase, which actually seems kind of interesting. He reads to us from a book called *How to Lie with Statistics* that tells about all the phony ways politicians use numbers to prove whatever they want to prove, and he says we're going to take a field trip to Traverse City to see a real computer at the university there.

All that week, our orchestra rehearsals are extra-long, because on Sunday we're leaving for our first tour. It's just to some places in Michigan, starting out in Ann Arbor, where the University of Michigan is—but Mr. Thurston says Ann Arbor is a great place to buy either records or books. There's not much point in my buying records when I can listen to all of Buffy Jean's any time I want to, but I can't wait to see what's in those book stores!

Chapter 32. Spring Storms

"Wizzie, you're going to kill me!" Buffy Jean announces from the doorway of our dorm room, where I've been pacing back and forth, memorizing notes for a test on the Civil War. She slips out of her dripping, olive green, canvas raincoat and holds it gingerly away from her. Outside the rain is coming down in sheets, washing away snow piles and turning them dirty gray.

"So what terrible thing did you do?" I ask.

"Well," she says, "You're not going to like this, but . . . " She drapes the hood of her green canvas raincoat over the bedpost and drops her book bag onto the bed.

"But what?" Buffy Jean's eyes are dancing in a way that worries me. What did she do?

"Well, I just saw Jeff Higgenbottom in the breezeway and . . . "

I knew it, I think, I absolutely knew this would happen, Buffy Jean being Buffy Jean. Oh, why, why, why did I ever open my big mouth and tell her?

" . . . all I did, I swear," she's saying, "was I just went up to him and said, 'Do you know Cindy Housh?' and he said, 'Well, sort of, but not really,' and I just said, 'Well SHE KNOWS YOU!' and then I ran away! That was all, really. You should have seen his face!" Her laughter is that of a mad arsonist watching a house burn down—my house, my hopes.

And things had been going so well lately too, ever since that perfect moment during *Tristan and Isolde* in the Ann Arbor concert in Hill Auditorium, when I caught Jeffrey's eye across the lush chromatic swirls of the music and for once managed to hold his gaze long enough to be sure he really was looking back. And although he didn't sit next to me on the tour bus but instead sat with his brass-playing buddies, after we got back—was I imagining things?—it seemed like I saw him looking at me more and more, and once he even sat down at my table in the library, though neither of us said anything.

Finally, just a couple of nights ago, I was serving this vomity-looking casserole in the dinner line and he stopped in front of me and looked at the food and said, "Tell me, does it grow?" and I said, "No, but look out, it might bite you," and we both laughed before he moved on. It wasn't much, but it was a start. And now, stupid Buffy Jean just made it so I can never, ever look at Jeff again, much less speak to him.

"I'm sorry," she says. "I just couldn't stand it anymore. I couldn't stand watching you pining away after this stuck-up ol' trombone player without doing anything about it. I just had to do something." Buffy Jean kicks off her loafers and flops down on her bunk.

"But just saying I know him?" I say. "Why would you do that? If you felt you had to talk to him, why couldn't you at least act like an adult, not somebody's bratty kid sister?"

"I don't know," she says. "It just sort of came out that way. Anyway, now the cat's out of the bag, and who knows. Maybe now he'll finally start trying to get to know you."

"Yeah, sure," I say. She could be right, I tell myself, but deep down I know that's not going to happen, that it probably never would have happened, really, Buffy Jean or no Buffy Jean, not to a tall girl with glasses and no chin who wears a double A-cup.

For the next few days, I try to concentrate on my work and forget about the whole thing. And, alas, not only am I right about nothing good happening between me and Jeff, on top of that, a few nights later, something horrible happens instead.

The boys are serving in the dinner line, and Jeff is up at the end manning the tea and coffee machine. I'm looking forward to asking him for some tea when some boy I don't even know—some trumpeter, I think, though not in the orchestra—slops some orange Jello with shredded carrots onto my tray and says, in a teasing voice, "Jeff Higgenbottom's up ahead."

"So?" I say, giving my best I-don't-know-what-you're-talking-about look.

"Just thought you might be interested," he says. When I get up to where Jeff is standing, I march right past him without stopping to ask for tea after all.

That's just great, I think, as I set my tray down with my back to the serving line. Now, just because Buffy Jean opened her big mouth, I'm the laughingstock of the entire brass section. Thanks a lot, Buffy Jean.

Meanwhile, in these months of dreary snow puddles, it seems like a lot of people at Interlochen have been having problems. I've heard the words "I'm depressed" spoken more than once. Even Buffy Jean seems down because of her troubles with Kenny, who's long since broken up with her, or at least tried to. Now, every night after lights out, I have to listen to her talk about how mean Kenny was to break up with her, about how all he ever wanted to do was work on his silly symphony, and on and on about all Kenny's crimes. I ask Buffy Jean why she wants to be with him if he's so terrible, but she ignores this and keeps chasing after him. She even tries to make me act as go-between, and when I refuse, we have a big fight about it and for a couple of days Buffy Jean and I barely speak to each other. Then, after Mrs. Jewel posts sign-up sheets for girls who want to room together next year and I've all but decided not to room with Buffy Jean again and am having fantasies of having a nice, normal roommate who doesn't drag me into all her personal melodramas, Buffy Jean comes in and informs me that she just signed us up to room together again and hugs me as if the fight never happened and, of course, I hug her back and that's the end of that.

But the thing with Jeff is still all messed up, and when we go on the spring tour to Indiana and the University of Illinois and Orchestra Hall in Chicago (not all that exciting, as I've already been to Chicago tons of times—I wish we could have gone to New York or, better yet, Europe!), I deliberately sign up to be on a different bus than his, just to show him and his friends that I don't care. But after we get back, Buffy Jean comes in one evening and reports that a trumpet player named Ricky Small, the same guy who made that comment in the dinner line, told her that the boys in their brass player clique just don't think that "your roommate" meets their standards to be Jeff's girlfriend. According to Buffy Jean, to meet these standards, a girl has to be friendly and outgoing, not just get good grades or be a first chair. She doesn't have to be beautiful, but she has to "make the most of what she has," Buffy Jean says, though I'm not sure this last part isn't just her way of trying to get me to let her make me look like a Texas cheerleader.

After delivering this report, Buffy Jean goes cheerfully off to study table singing "Mrs. Brown, you've a got a lovely daughter," as if she hasn't just dropped a bomb on the person who's supposed to be her best friend at Interlochen. I already have a bad cold, and I spend the next two hours in bed crying and blowing my nose instead of practicing or studying. The worst part is, I know that what Buffy Jeans said is true. I'm not really good enough for a boy like Jeff. I'm tall and fat and ugly and have no chin and no one will ever, ever love me and I might as well just go on lying here wasting away to nothing until some guys in white coats come to drag me away. Rage rises up in me at the injustice of it all.

"God, how I hate myself!" I say aloud through clenched teeth. "I hate myself! I hate myself!" My words ring out, but no one can hear them, and now the silence is broken by the sound of a trombone doing long tones in the trombone teacher's basement studio two floors beneath our room and I wonder if it could be Jeff, not that it matters now.

Then, suddenly, I know what I have to do. It won't help, but I still have to, I don't know why. The next morning, I sniffle my way through French class, in which Ricky Small sits in the row behind me. Chanting conjugations with the rest of the class, I'm getting almost as nervous as I do before challenges. The minute class ends, I rush to the door and stand waiting.

"Can I speak to you for a moment," I say, blocking Ricky's path as he comes out.

"Yeah, sure," he says, looking down at the floor. "What's up?"

"Ricky," I say, in my most miserable, hoarse cold-voice so as to make him feel as guilty as possible about beating up on someone who's already deathly ill, "do you have something against me?"

"I don't know what you're talking about," he says, with a sideways glance. "Why would I have something against you?"

"Well," I say, "It's just that . . . I wanted to ask you about . . . about those things you said to Buffy Jean about me. You know what I'm talking about? She told me what you said about me. Why did you say those things? What did I ever do to you? I mean, you don't even know me." The more questions I ask, the stronger I start to feel, and I like this feeling.

Ricky gives me another "Who—me?" look, but it's fake, and I can see that he knows I know it's fake, and I can't help feeling a little sorry for him. Suddenly I realize that he's about a foot shorter than I am and has a face covered with pimples and isn't even a good enough trumpeter to play in the orchestra and I can't imagine any girl ever wanting to go out with *him*, much less the kind of paragon he described to Buffy Jean.

Feeling better and better, I stand there looking Ricky straight in the eye until he finally looks back.

"Oh, that," he says. "I didn't say anything much really, nothing that terrible. But I'm sure that Buffy Jean, being Buffy Jean, probably exaggerated. You know how she can be." His voice has a pleading sound to it, but I'm not going to let him off that easily. He probably has a huge inferiority complex, or he should have given the fact that he's ugly and stupid and untalented and evil and doesn't even get good grades in French, but still . . .

"Yes, well I thought you'd like to know that she always passes on what people say about me," I say and turn to walk away. "And you can tell your stupid friends that too," I call after him.

Putting Ricky in his place helps my pride a little--pretty good for somebody with an inferiority complex, I tell myself-- but it doesn't get rid of my cold. Feeling sicker by the moment, I head towards the Stone Building and drag myself up to the infirmary, where Mrs. Pauley, the big, motherly nurse, gives me an excuse to spend the rest of the day in bed.

Finally, when my cough is almost gone and I can breathe again, a few nights later Buffy Jean comes prancing in with more news. She was walking down the concourse, she tells me, when Jeff came up and asked to talk to her.

"He said he had a question he wanted to ask me and I said, 'What's that?' and he goes, 'What's really going on with your roommate? Why is she always looking at me?' and I said, 'Well, you know what I said before, I mean she's got kind of a crush on you, that's all' and he goes, 'Well, but she doesn't even know me,' and I said, 'That's true, but she'd like to get to know you,' and then he said, 'Buffy Jean, have you seen me with any girls this year?' and I said, 'No,

I haven't,' and he said, 'Well, there was a time when I did think about trying to get to know her, but I'd decided this year I wouldn't date any girls because my grades aren't that great and it was all I could do to try to get into a decent college, so I haven't tried to get to know her, and that's why.'"

Buffy Jean's words have a ring of truth to them, and I'm pretty sure she isn't making this up. The only question is whether Jeff really did think about trying to get to know me or was just saying that to be nice. I guess I'll never know.

After that, everything feels flat and dull, and of course I can't look at Jeff anymore. All I can do is practice my Mendelssohn concerto every minute I can spare. The competition is next week, and I'm going to show them all. I may not be beautiful on the outside, but there's beauty on the inside that can come out when I play. And who knows—maybe Jeff will be there and some of it will even get out to him and make him sorry he didn't try to get to know me, at least a little sorry, anyway.

Chapter 33. The Concerto Competition

Sunday, May 2, is a day of cloudless blue sky, a good omen. The day of my Big Triumph, I tell myself as I climb out of bed.

Tonight, I'll be playing the first movement of my Mendelssohn concerto in the competition to get to play a solo with the orchestra. It's sounding pretty decent, and I think I may actually have a chance to win. Mr. Chausow seems to think so, too. And if I do win, I'll then have a good chance to fulfill my dream of winning concertos in the summer like Annie Kavafian and playing my piece with the International Youth Symphony. And if that happens, I'm sure to get into Julliard next year and maybe even wind up as a real concert artist and wear beautiful dresses and take tours all over the world and appear on late-night talk shows. I could let my imagination go on and on along that track, but I mostly don't as I know that's dangerous. Right now, I just need to think about tonight's performance.

Of course, there are also scary thoughts I could get into about tonight if I let myself, but I'm not going to. I can't let myself think about who else is trying out or who might be there and what they might think or about winning or not winning or, most of all, about whether I'm going to be nervous or not, because once I start thinking about that, pretty soon I'll be getting nervous about getting nervous, and then it's all over. As FDR said, "The only thing we have to fear is fear itself."

So, instead of driving myself crazy, I've been practicing Mr. Stone's "PMA" ("Positive Mental Attitude") all week. I've been imagining myself in building C7A, the big warehouse-type dwelling where the auditions are being held, striding out to the piano as if I own the place. After taking my time to tune when Mr. Pedersen, my accompanist, gives me the A, I set my violin up under my chin and place my bow at the tip, poised for the first up-bow. Then, as the piano begins to ripple, I glide in as smoothly as a blue heron taking off over the lake. From that point on, the music almost plays itself, with fast passages tripping along under my fingers, the tricky octaves on the first page perfectly in tune, melodies soaring, the wheeling arpeggios in the cadenza spectacular, fireworks in the night sky, and all the beauty inside me pouring out through the music, the best I've ever played in my life, until I reach the last, perfect notes, ending with a flourish as the audience begins to clap and yell "Bravo!" And, of course, Jeffrey is in the audience, and my performance will make him see me with new eyes and fall madly in love with me. When I start thinking that, though, I know I've crossed the line from PMA into hopeless daydreaming.

Today, after breakfast, I go down to the lake and sit gazing out at the sparkling water so as to get myself in just the right mood for what's coming. Watching the little wavelets turn over along the edge, one after another, I feel my breath slow down. Then, from out of nowhere, the words "transparent eyeball" pop into my head. When I first read that phrase in Emerson's essay last fall, I couldn't make sense of it, but now, suddenly, I know what it means. It means feeling myself more transparent than glass and the wavelets and the little breeze and the pine trees and the bright blue sky passing through my transparency along with the air as I breathe more and more slowly, in and out. It means the currents of "Universal Being" flowing through me as I stand here looking out at the lake, putting myself in a state where tonight's performance hardly matters.

Finally, I turn away from the lake and head back towards the dorm, with a whole, long day still to get through. Back in our dorm room, I sit down and try to learn some French vocabulary, but notwithstanding the currents of Universal Being, I feel like I'm covered with ants, so I get up and clean out my closet and when that doesn't help I clean out Buffy Jean's closet too and take my laundry downstairs to put in the washers. Meanwhile, the question of whether I'm going to be nervous tonight is starting up in my head, and every now and then I hold out my bow hand to see if it's shaking. It isn't, but as the hours tick by I can feel my stomach tightening despite my best efforts to relax. It doesn't help that when we're warming up before the afternoon concert, a couple of fellow seconds come up and ask me if I'm nervous about tonight. They're just trying to be nice, but I wish they wouldn't have said that word, which by now is repeating itself in my head like a metronome: *nervous, nervous, nervous, nervous, nervous.*

The music on the afternoon concert is easy, only a Bach suite and the Barber *Adagio for Strings*, after which the Wind Ensemble plays the rest of the program. During the second half, I sit very still in my folding chair looking out over the balcony and let the liquid wind music flow through me, but every piece seems longer than the one before. All I want is for tonight to be over, but I tell myself not to be negative, not to think of my upcoming performance as an ordeal, just a chance to have fun making music, a chance to show everyone what I can do. Slow down, breathe, remember the transparent eyeball, let things flow . . .

At 4:30 the concert finally ends, at T minus four hours before I'm to go on stage. Slowly, I get up from my seat; slowly, I walk back to the dorm; slowly, I climb the stairs to our room. Lynn, our suitemate, comes in and says something to me, but her words seem far away as I sit breathing in and out. At five, I go downstairs for an early supper, though I don't eat much; by six-thirty, I'm downstairs warming up on slow scales and playing through my piece one last time; and by ten minutes to eight, I'm walking slowly over to C7A, walking and breathing. When I get there, Oliver has just started his cello concerto, and three other kids go on after him, each taking longer than the one before as I stand in the woods behind C7A with my fellow contestants, who are blowing on their hands and sighing loudly and giving each other backrubs to try to relax.

Finally, when Jennifer starts her flute solo, I take my violin out of its case and tighten my bow. My hands are sweating now but still steady. Is Jennifer's piece over yet? Maybe, but no, it goes on. Then again, it sounds almost over, and this time it is, and the clapping starts and Jennifer comes out looking happy and relieved.

A few moments later, I'm walking out with Mr. Pedersen to a subdued ocean of clapping that rises and falls away again as I move towards the piano and arrange myself in just the right spot, still calm and in control, breathing slowly in and out, not looking at the audience. I nod to Mr. Pedersen, and he gives me the A to tune to, but as I start to tune I suddenly catch a glimpse of Jeff sitting in the back with his brass-playing friends, and in front of them Suzy Smock and all the best string players, and Buffy Jean in the front row, and in front of that, all the faculty judges lined up behind a long table, and then all at once something goes down my backbone and when it gets to the bottom my heart begins to pound and my legs are shaking, my hands are shaking, my violin is shaking, my mind is a sea of white, and I can only think Get control, Get control. But meanwhile, the hard curve of my instrument is already pressed against my neck and the big, wet squarish frog of the bow is somehow being dragged along the string to make a weak, pathetic, trembly old lady little A. *She can't even tune right,* they must be thinking as those fingers, which are someone else's now, not mine, struggle at the big, slippery pegs, struggle slowly with the tuning to put off starting until I can calm myself down and be ready, the audience coughing and willing me to start as I go on tuning and stalling knowing I'm still not at all ready.

If I could just sit down and close my eyes for a minute or two, then I'd be ready. If I could just go back stage and lie down and breathe deeply until my heart slowed back down, I'd be ready then, but instead I have to start without being ready at all, the violin coming up under my chin and the bow setting itself on the string and all of it arranging itself to look on the outside perfectly ready to go but with no warm core of readiness inside to direct the nod that the head is giving Mr. Pedersen to start playing so now it's all gone off away from unready me, the hands the arms the violin the bow the piano, the whole contraption galloping miles off from where I've been left standing, silently shouting after it to come back and then I'll be ready, watching the raucous flopping of the bow and the iron vise of the left hand with its fingers strangely glued to the strings and hearing the grotesque parade of withered noises coming out of my f-holes in an outlandish caricature of the lovely round tones that came out when I practiced.

And along with the noises, a voice in my mind is pleading with the audience *Don't listen to this This has nothing to do with me It only sounds this way because I'm so nervous Let me start over and show you how I really sound* Now the triplets that I worked on until they flowed along like liquid silver are blurring by in streams of brown muddy water and every time the bow comes up to the frog it makes a walloping slap like the bottom of a boat hitting a wave Now the octave arpeggios at the bottom of the page are looming up ahead like Niagara Falls and I'm about to go over *Oh God Here they come* smudgy dead squawks all of them.

Now the tutti with the piano is going on without me while I grope frantically in the white sea of my mind for the words that will reconnect my hands and arms with these big crazy Frankenstein ones, the words that will finally grab them and hold them like two gloves for me to slide my own warm hands and arms up into and bring the warmth once again flowing out through the arms the hands the bow the violin the music.

Now the tutti is over and my sound fills out warmer for a few phrases It's almost good It's getting better It's going to be good *She's good* they'll say *She was a little nervous at the beginning but once she got ahold of herself she was great* but now something else is grabbing it all away again, the notes again coming out all rusty corkscrews wrenched from the f-holes and flung out every which way *Oh Jesus Here comes the high A* and now the little finger is going splat off the fingerboard like someone falling into a puddle and an awful wheeze like a broken bellows and then to the audience I'm silently crying *I can hit that note I must have hit it a thousand times Really I have* and the finger missing another leap The piano trilling insanely as I hurry on and on with something inside me still shouting *get control you can still get control* which is all a waste, of course The first line is what always decides it and if that's lost it's all lost and the rest is just one long miserable dying surrounded by relatives wishing you'd hurry up about it.

The voice in my head is still shouting *get control* even now but it doesn't matter nothing matters but getting it over with the last line coming up and now only the final chords are left to finish it off chop chop and it's over and from far off the sickly polite clapping and the heart slowing down under my violin and the hands coming back to being my own again and the voice in my head saying *Oh please, let me start over and play it again now that I can play it myself That wasn't me Please let me play it* but instead I'm bowing stiffly not smiling at all and stumbling out into the entryway and shoving my violin back in its case and grabbing it up and hurrying down the road to the dorm with Buffy Jean and Tim, her new oboist boyfriend, hurrying along behind me and Tim going "Cindy, come back, it wasn't that bad!" but the tears are starting to flow already and all I want is to get to my clean, white bed.

And then I'm there, crying and crying, pounding the pillow and hugging myself and moaning. Buffy Jean is saying comforting things but I can't hear them because all I can think about is the hours and hours I spent practicing those passages until they were note-perfect, all those hours flushed away that I can never get back. And about all the mean things Jeff and his friends and Suzy and her friends must be saying about me. And about the glorious career I dreamed of having, the performances in JVS and Kresge and Julliard, all of it going up in a puff of smoke because now I know this is what happens when I try to make my dreams come true. This is what will always happen, and no one will ever get to hear the beauty that's locked inside of me, the beauty I can make only in my practice room, and I only wish my mother were here to hold me and tell me it's all right, though I'm also glad she wasn't here to see me make such a total fool of myself as I just did.

Towards morning, I finally fall asleep for a few hours, only to wake up wishing it was all just a bad dream but it wasn't. I want to stay in bed and never have to see anyone again, but something makes me get up anyway. I dig through my top dresser drawer until I find a white elastic hair band, yank my hair back, and make myself look as ugly as possible. Then I put on some powder to cover a few blemishes, but no lipstick or rouge. Desolate, that's how I have to look, so desolate that anyone who sees me will know I know how horribly I played last night and not say anything to make me feel even worse than I already do. "Poor Cindy," they'll say, and shake their heads. "Ever since she bombed the Mendelssohn that time, she just hasn't been the same. Poor Cindy."

Buffy Jean is still sleeping, and after I'm dressed I tiptoe out of the dorm and down to the sun-decker, to the same bench I sat on just twenty-four hours ago feeling so hopeful gazing out at the sparkling wavelets and imagining myself a transparent eyeball. Today, I'm no transparent eyeball but a victim of dread—horrible, thick, brown dread sucking me down like quicksand. The thought of going to today's orchestra rehearsal is unbearable, and I'd rather die than go hear any of the other contestants tonight. Then, tomorrow morning, the competition will be over, and I'll have to go look at the list of winners knowing that my own name will not be on it, despite the teeny tiny hope that my performance was way better than I thought even though I know that's crazy. And after that, at my lesson on Tuesday, I'll have to face Mr. Chausow and tell him I'm sorry for making him look like a bad teacher and then, in a few weeks, I'll have to play in the orchestra accompanying all the winners and smile and congratulate them afterwards even though I'm dying inside. Horrible, horrible, horrible!

All of this makes me suddenly almost wish I never started playing the violin at all, never took lessons from Mrs. Sexton and came to Interlochen and got into the Academy, wish that I were back at home going to Roosevelt and planning to go to Iowa State and become a nurse and meet a handsome doctor and get married, which was what I thought I would do when I was in third grade reading Cherry Ames books. I could still do that, of course. Tell my parents I want to come home and forget about the violin and just be a normal person for a change. It would make them happy if I did that, thrilled to have me home again, in fact, but for some reason I can't, don't ask me why. For some crazy reason, I know that I have to make myself go back into the dorm and eat breakfast and after that go back to my room and get my violin and take it down to the basement and start practicing my scales. And I also know that I'll have to play my stupid Mendelssohn again for concertos next summer and next fall start auditioning for colleges and then play my senior recital no matter how nervous I get.

And if my auditions are all so bad that I don't get into any music schools, then I can finally quit the violin and become a nurse, which would be a huge relief, though to be perfectly honest, I don't think I'd make a very good nurse.

Chapter 34. Summer Interlude

Well, you could knock me over with the proverbial feather. Surprise, surprise, wonder of wonders—I just made first chair viola at the National Music Camp! Doing that at the Academy would have been something, but at the Camp it's even better, as there are a lot more good string players here in the summer.

Of course, it's not the same as if I'd made concertmistress—it's just viola, after all. Plus, I'm sure the only reason I beat Jane Cleveland was that she has a new boyfriend, this tall, movie-star-handsome fellow-violist named Rod. She probably didn't practice all week from having her head in clouds, and who can blame her for that? I'd probably be the same way if Jeff had loved me back, but Jeff's not here this summer and anyway, he spent the whole last month of school with this red-headed dancer named Carmen. So much for his not dating any girls so he could get into college!

But I just about dropped dead of surprise this morning when, after Jane and I both played the passage from Shostakovich 5th and closed our eyes, I heard Mr. Bundra say, "There is a change." For a moment I thought I hadn't heard him right, but then Jane got up to change places with me, and I knew I had.

Jane congratulated me, of course, but I could tell she was upset, probably mad at herself more than anything. Meanwhile, although getting first chair viola gave my ego a boost, it also put me in an awkward position, knowing that Jane, when she practices, is really way better than I am. Maybe it's just my inferiority complex, but I'm sure next week she'll practice like crazy and that will be the end of first chair for yours truly. But I can at least enjoy my place in the sun for a few days. After all, it's not as though I've never led a section before, thanks to TJ.

And God only knows, my ego needed this boost, after that Mendelssohn disaster at the Academy, which I don't think I'll ever quite live down. The first week or so after my tragic fall, I felt like wearing a paper bag over my head, but I went right back to practicing, which helped. And things weren't as terrible as I expected. In fact, some folks even tried to make me feel better. Miss Malocsay, who coaches the second violins, said just about everybody has trouble with nerves at one time or another and that I shouldn't let it discourage me but try to learn from the experience. And Mr. Chausow said that I just need to get more solo performance experience and should plan to play my Mendelssohn again this summer.

"If you fall off a horse, you have to get back on," he said, something I already knew from taking riding lessons back in Iowa.

When I looked at the list of concerto winners, I wasn't surprised that I didn't win, but I was surprised to see that Dawn Sommers, who sits second chair first, didn't win either, so I was in distinguished company. Instead, Suzy Smock won, of course, and Karen O'Donnell, who's never gotten higher than fifth chair but seems too dumb to get nervous, and a little eighth-grade prodigy named Cheng-han Lin.

TJ discovered Cheng-han in Taiwan when he was on one of his good-will missions for the State Department winning hearts and minds in the Far East and paid all Cheng-han's expenses so he could come over here to the Academy. When Cheng-han showed up in the middle of last year, he didn't even have a full-sized violin and had never played in an orchestra before. His sound wasn't much, but his left hand was perfect. He could play all the hardest passages and not miss a note. I think he'd probably been playing the violin since he was about three, so it was second nature. I wonder if they have the Suzuki method in Taiwan, which would explain this.

Mrs. Sexton hates the Suzuki method, which was started by a Japanese teacher who worked with very young children. His idea was that since children learn to talk before they can read, it's natural to teach them to play by ear before teaching them to read music. Whole armies of little kids have been taught this way who play the Bach double concerto en masse like perfect little wind-up toys, but Mrs. Sexton says they have trouble learning to read music and don't play with any expression. I wonder if that's true or if Mrs. Sexton just feels threatened by the competition between Suzuki teachers and regular teachers like herself.

When Cheng-han first came to Interlochen, he didn't speak any English yet, which must have been lonely for him, as I doubt that anyone here speaks much Chinese. TJ started him at the back of the second violin section and before long, he was my stand partner. How I managed to keep him from beating me week after week I'll never know. For concertos, he played Mozart G Major, a much easier concerto than Mendelssohn. It was pretty good, but I bet they only picked him instead of Dawn because he's so young and because they wanted to show off how international Interlochen is.

Last week, I played the Mendelssohn again in the summer concerto tryouts, and although it still wasn't perfect and I didn't win, it went well enough this time that I didn't feel like I needed to put a paper bag over my head afterwards. A couple of my cabin-mates took me out for a Melody Freeze and said nice things, and life went on with no big crisis this time. At least I got back on the horse, as Mr. Chausow said I should.

Part of why I've been practicing so hard this summer is that I have this fabulous violin teacher. Her name is Carol Glenn and she's a concert artist who studied with Ivan Galamian and teaches at Eastman and is married to Eugene Liszt, who teaches piano here and is a concert pianist. Miss Glenn has a southern accent and a lovely warm way about her that makes you feel like the most beautiful, gifted person in the world. For the first few weeks, we worked on exercises, and she completely overhauled my bow-arm. Then, after she got me through the Mendelssohn audition, she started giving me some really hard music. I have a new concerto now, the d minor by Henri Wieniawski, which Miss Glenn called a "show piece," and also some Paganini caprices, which are the hardest, most super-hard pieces in the whole violin repertoire. I can practice for hours on just one line and still not be able to play it, but if I ever get so I can play those caprices, I'll know I'm really good. Miss Glenn said that just working on them should improve my left hand. She also said I need to be more aggressive when I perform.

"You're a gentle person, Cynthia," she said, "but you can't be gentle with the violin. You have to pretend you're somebody else and put some fire into your playing." I love Miss Glenn so much that it makes me want to practice hours and hours, which is a good thing, with college auditions coming up in the fall. Come to think of it, maybe if I got first chair this week, it was also partly because of Miss Glen, not just because Jane got a boyfriend.

Meanwhile, Mr. Bundra, who coaches the quartet I play in with Karen McPherson on first violin, keeps trying to persuade me to switch to viola. Last week, our quartet played a couple of movements of Beethoven on a recital, and afterwards, he followed me out and told me to "throw that violin away." Then, at sectionals, he asked me to come by his studio and talk to him. When I got there he told me he was leaving the Academy, where he'd been teaching all last year, and would be joining the faculty at the University of Michigan in the fall, where he'd love to have me come study with him.

I thanked him but said I wanted to stick with the violin.

"Yes, well, we need to talk about that," he said. He proceeded to give me a big sales pitch for the viola. He said that yes, violins get to play the tune more in orchestra, but as you mature you start wanting to listen to the whole orchestra and not just your own line, to "experience the whole texture of the music." He said the career opportunities for viola are way better than they are for violin. He said that although the solo repertoire is more limited than the repertoire for violin, it's also more interesting.

To be polite, I told him I'd think about it and let him know what I decided, knowing perfectly well that I wouldn't think about it for more than five seconds. Because although a well-played viola can sound lovely, you can't make it soar the way a violin can, not the way Nancy Jaynes did singing the high A the day my parents told me I could go to the Academy. A violin can take you above the clouds, but a viola can't, not really. It's too bad, as I might even be able to win concertos on viola, and go to Julliard and all that, but then I'd have to spend the rest of my life playing viola when my heart was with the violin. It would be like marrying someone you don't love just because he makes a good living and you want to be married, okay for some people but not for me. I want real love when I get married, and I want to play the violin, not the viola.

Nevertheless, on Sunday night, I lead the viola section proudly in the concert and get to shake Mr. Roller's hand when he makes the rounds to thunderous applause, as Shostakovich 5th ends loud and is a huge crowd-pleaser. Then, on Monday, we get the music for the next Sunday's concert, on which my old friend Thor Johnson is here to conduct Vaughn Williams' *Job*, and I practice like mad all week. I can't help remembering, though, what Mrs. Sexton said about how Debbie stopped challenging because of bad feelings in her section. I ask another violist who's in Jane's cabin if Jane was upset after I beat her and she tells me Jane "cried a little." In orchestra rehearsals, every time I make a mistake I can just hear Jane thinking that she should still be first chair, not me, even though she never would say that out loud. Is that what Mrs. Sexton was talking about? Does it mean I should let Jane win and not try to beat her? I want to stay in first chair, but I also want to be like Debbie, someone who cares more about other people's feelings than about winning, and I don't know which want I'm going to give in to.

Finally, Friday comes, and Jane and I both play the first passage from *Job*, and I have to admit, Jane sounds better than I do. "There is a change," comes the verdict, just as I expected, and Jane and I switch places, which is kind of a relief. Then, after the rest of the section has gone through tryouts and challenges, Mr. Bundra asks me if I want to challenge Jane back, and instead of giving the usual nod, I hear myself tell him no.

I didn't know until that moment what I was going to do, but now I've gone and done it.

"No?!" Mr. Bundra repeats, looking at me like he thinks I'm crazy. In all the time I've been here, I've never heard anyone refuse to challenge back after losing a chair, so I guess I've made history.

"No," I say again. "I don't want to challenge." He nods okay, but still looks a little concerned, which immediately makes me wish I hadn't done what I just did, history or no history. I was trying to be like Debbie and put other people's feelings before winning, but Mr. Bundra and the rest of the section couldn't know that. They probably all think I'm either completely out of my tree or maybe just stuck up, acting like I think I'm too good to play the game the usual way, or maybe they think I'm a coward who doesn't want to risk getting beaten a second time.

And maybe they're right, but how can I know?

Chapter 35. The Project

"Do do sol sol la la sol. . . fa fa mi mi re re do," sixteen string players vocalize in bored voices, along with Waldie Anderson's operatic tenor. We're seated in rows holding various wind instruments in our laps, alternately singing and playing, while in the next room, the wind players—plus one percussionist--are doing the same with stringed instruments. We're all participants, that is to say, guinea pigs, in experimental classes for the Interlochen Honors Musicianship Project.

Thirty-three of us here at the Academy are enrolled in the Project—16 string-players, 16 wind-players, and 1 percussionist—all of us with full scholarships for a year, courtesy of the U.S. government. This is because Dr. Maddy got this huge grant, which he announced in a special meeting I went to last summer and must have been what he went to see "the folks over in the government" about when we went to Washington to play at the Watergate. He told us the Project would involve taking class lessons in all orchestral instruments in a program designed to prove that teachers could teach a lot of different instruments at the same time and that what you learned on one instrument carried over and put you ahead when you started the next one.

Enrolling in the Project would mean taking fewer academics, of course, but by the end of the year you'd have at least some familiarity with flute, clarinet, oboe, bassoon, trumpet, trombone, French horn, tuba, violin, viola, cello, string bass, harp, and percussion. This sounded like fun and would be ideal for those who wanted to become composers, conductors, or music educators. It would not be ideal for me, since all I wanted to be was a violinist, and I love academics and was looking forward to third-year French, but the thought of calling my parents and telling them they wouldn't have to pay a penny for my whole senior year was too much to resist, so I filled out the application form and here I am, in the basement of JVS, singing "Twinkle, Twinkle, Little Star" instead of reading Flaubert and doing physics experiments.

In addition to paying for our scholarships, the Project also pays the salaries for three teachers. Waldie Anderson, who managed the International Youth Symphony for my first two Interlochen summers and is an accomplished singer as well as a bassoonist and music educator, is the head Project teacher. Assisting him in the wind class is Byron Hanson, who recently graduated from Eastman and was a star accompanist in the summers, accompanying most of the concerto winners. Along with being a crack-shot pianist, Mr. Hanson also plays the trombone and baritone and has a master's degree in music history and theory, so he can help with all sorts of odds and ends. The string teacher is Miss Rosemary Malocsay, whom I knew last year as the second violin section coach at the Academy.

We string players get to play each wind instrument for four weeks. My first wind instrument is the oboe, on which you blow through a tiny reed that you have to keep trimmed just so with a little knife. Why anyone would want to play an instrument that required all this fussing with reeds is beyond me. It took me three days to get any sound at all to come out of my oboe, blowing and blowing, which meant that I spent the first three days sitting in the very back seat in my row. This is because the "Maddy method" involves constant challenges for the front seats, which is supposed to motivate you to learn faster.

We go through the same routine over and over in wind class. First, we sing the tune in solfege. In other words, using *do, re, mi,* etc., like in *The Sound of Music.* Then we play the tune together. Then we play it one by one, starting with one of the front corner players and working back through all the rows, while those who aren't playing are supposed to finger their notes on their instruments. Each time somebody messes up, he gets moved back a seat, just like in challenges. It all runs like clockwork and is about as much fun as working on an assembly line. Meanwhile, the teachers wander back and forth between the rows, hovering over us, adjusting positions, and making the occasional suggestion, like art teachers do when you draw.

After a week or so of wind class, those of us playing oboe meet with Mr. Jaeger, the oboe teacher, for a group private lesson. This helps a lot, and by the end of my four weeks on oboe, I'm almost starting to sound decent on "All through the Night." But then I have to start over on a new instrument, the flute. With the flute there are no silly reeds to mess with, but I have a different problem: dizziness. With the oboe, my breath went through the instrument in a tiny, tight stream, but with the flute, it goes rushing right out, after which everything starts going black in my head. During the first week, I spend a lot of time with my head between my knees, but after that it gets better, and eventually, I get to where I can also play a half-decent "All through the Night" on the flute. Then, it's on to the bassoon, on which I do pretty well until I leave my reed in my knickers pocket and it goes through the wash, which kind of spoils the sound.

The wind class is our second class of the morning. Before that is the string class, in which we string players learn those instruments we don't already play using the same methods, while the wind players do the same on the wind instruments. For me, this means only the cello and the string bass, since I already play the violin and viola, so I should get to be pretty good on the lower strings by the end.

During the third hour every morning, we're supposed to do all sorts of different things to broaden our musical experiences even more, theory and composition and percussion and harp and maybe some music history. Plus, along with orchestra and private lessons on our major instrument, we're also required to sing in the Academy choir. The whole point is, according to Mr. Anderson, "to immerse you in as many different aspects of music as possible."

Supervising the whole shebang is Dr. Maddy, who wanders between the rows along with the teachers, jerkily correcting people, growling out streams of words, and making sure everything is done according to his method, which is supposed to teach us as efficiently as possible. Which is why at the top of the blackboard are written the words, "Good teaching: every student is productively occupied every moment." It makes me think of that book, *Cheaper by the Dozen*, which is about an efficiency expert named Frank Bunker Gilbreth and his psychologist wife and their twelve children. The Gilbreths did "motion studies" to help workers in factories make more widgets faster, and they applied a lot of their methods to teaching their own kids things like typing and foreign languages. I wonder if Dr. Maddy ever read *Cheaper by the Dozen*.

Thus, our mornings go by, one after the other in the instrument-learning factory, while the other Academy kids are taking classes in calculus and chemistry, history and Spanish. But in the afternoon we have a couple hours of academics, then orchestra, then dinner, and after dinner, choir rehearsal.

The choir director is Mrs. Jewell's husband, Mr. Jewell. Along with directing the choir, he also works in the personnel office, and he has a ham radio in their dorm apartment where he tries to get stations in other countries for a hobby. He's big and bald and jolly and walks with a slight limp because he had polio as a child. Along with the Academy Choir, he also conducts a famous professional choir called the Kenneth Jewell Chorale. Mr. Jewell calls us altos "misplaced sopranos" and when it doesn't sound so good, he says, "That's coming—so's Christmas" and when it's better, he says, "that was almost beautiful." Choir is more fun than orchestra because you don't have to compete for chairs, and Dr. Jewell never yells at people the way TJ does, so you can just relax and enjoy the music.

One good thing about the Project is that the classes require almost no homework, leaving me with more time to practice than I had last year. Since I'm no longer on study table, I can practice all evening and do my homework at late study. This is a Godsend, as I'm getting ready for college auditions and my senior recital, and also because Dr. Johnson moved me into the first violins this year so I get to battle my way up and down like everybody else (at the moment, I'm fifth chair). And since I can't take many academics, I also have more time this year to study for the two classes I do have—American government and senior English. I even have time to do extra credit stuff, which feels great.

The government teacher here is Mr. Mendel, a quiet, little bald man with a German accent that makes him sound like one of the bad guys in a World War II movie, but he's from Austria, which he left to get away from the Nazis, so he's actually one of the good guys. I guess he appreciated American democracy so much that he decided he wanted to teach kids about it. Right now, he's got lots to teach us about current events, because ever since his landslide victory last November, President Johnson's been going to town, getting the Voting Rights Act passed by a huge majority. Burt Merrill, the viola student with whom I briefly shared a stand during my first camp summer, worked last summer as a page for Senator Everett Dirksen of Illinois and was in the Senate when the law was voted on, a huge moment in American history. Because of the new law, states can't keep Negroes from voting by making them pass really hard tests or playing other kinds of mean tricks on them. The assignment this week was to read about the War on Poverty, which is part of President Johnson's Great Society and involves all sorts of government programs with names like Medicare and Medicaid, Food Stamps, and Headstart, which Mr. Mendel mapped out on the board.

Government's okay, but I love my English class with Mrs. Stocking, the red-haired matron who teaches senior English. Mrs. Stocking is tall and plump and looks like she should have a British accent but doesn't. This whole year is British literature, and our textbook is a wonderful anthology of over 1300 extra-thin, densely-printed pages that starts with a long, creepy, very old poem called *Beowulf* and ends with modern writers like T.S. Eliot and Dylan Thomas. And the textbook isn't all of it—we'll also be reading a couple of Shakespeare plays and a bunch of novels, Mrs. Stocking says, and we have to do a lot of writing, including our "senior theme" next semester.

Our first writing assignment this year was to describe a personal experience that influenced us in some way. At first, I couldn't think what to write about. Then, one afternoon at lunch, I was sitting across from this ninth grader named Louis Feldman, a skinny, smart-alecky little kid with braces on his teeth. He was a loyal member of my second violin section all last year, and I've come to think of him as a kid brother.

"So what's it like being a snobby first violin? Louis asked, wolfing down a large forkful of spaghetti. All last year, we seconds joked about the firsts being snobs, but now I've gone over to the enemy, as my ex-fellow seconds frequently remind me.

"It's okay," I said. "I miss our section, though. The firsts are all such cutthroats." They aren't really, but I said that to be nice to poor Louis, who's still stuck in the seconds.

A couple of seniors from my English class had sat down at our table by then, and the subject of Mrs. Stocking's assignment came up. I'd wracked my brains, I tell my classmates, but I couldn't seem to come up with a topic.

"Nothing that important ever happened to me," I said. "I mean, no one in my family ever died or anything. I could write about my dog getting hit by a car, but that would be really trite…"

"Hey, I got it," Louis interrupted. "Why don't you write about that time last year when you got so nervous and bombed the Mendelssohn?" The other kids at the table looked away, probably afraid that Louis bringing up that awful experience would make me feel bad.

Which it might have, if it weren't for the fact that my English essay immediately started writing itself in my head. All I had to do now was put it down on paper. Sitting at my desk after dinner, I wrote the whole thing out in pencil, then copied it over with my blue Papermate cartridge pen. Only after I'd finished did I realize that the essay was only supposed to be three pages and this was four-and-a-half. Would Mrs. Stocking take off points for it being too long? I could probably cut some, but then I'd have to copy it over, and I needed to get downstairs to practice, so I didn't. Instead, I just sat there proofreading:

The Priceless Failure

During my first year at the Academy, I spent many a peaceful afternoon sitting by the lake daydreaming. It was my favorite pastime. One sparkling Sunday in May, having nothing else to do, I wandered down to the beach and sat down to think. Well, I thought, this is the big day. Today I am going to prove myself. I am going to show the others that I can play the violin too. I am going to win the concerto contest.

The essay went on to explain how frustrated I'd been by my situation as principal second violin forever and how I longed to show everyone what I could do. It told how I saw winning the concerto contest as my only chance to be somebody and how when I got up to play, I fell apart and made a total fool of myself in front of everyone I wanted to impress. But the essay didn't end there. It went on to tell how I dealt with my misery by going back to the drawing board:

Practicing became my greatest comfort. I could concentrate on music and forget what others thought. One evening as I was practicing, I suddenly thought, "Why, this is why I play the violin—not to impress others and attract attention, but simply because I love music. Now, I no longer cared what others thought, because the worst had happened, and I had survived. I discovered that one can live without constantly being praised and admired, and that such a life is the most wholesome and worthwhile.

After I've finished proofreading, I sit there for a while, trying to decide if the essay is good or bad. I can never tell. It seems like a lot of times when I think I've written something great, the next morning I read it and it's so awful I have to tear it up. I wonder if I'm in for a nasty surprise tomorrow morning, but when I reread it after I get up it still seems okay, and Mrs. Stocking gives me 48 points out of 50 on it, so I guess maybe it is.

When I get my paper back, all of a sudden I feel really good, and not just because of the grade. It's also because I realize that I couldn't have written this essay right after the Mendelssohn disaster happened. It would probably have been way too schmaltzy back then, no matter how many times I rewrote it. But now I've reached a point where I can write about my experience without my tears dripping all over the paper, and doing that makes me feel like it's finally over. It's what Dad, who has his own column now on the *Register* sports page, calls "getting distance" on things when you write.

Chapter 36. Saved by a Miracle

This fall, all the seniors are filling out college applications. I work on mine every Sunday morning. Sitting at my desk, I fill in blank after blank in blue ink, trying to produce the kind of small, neat, intelligent-looking handwriting that might impress the admissions officials, and praying that I won't make any smudges, which will almost certainly cause them to reject me. I'm especially careful with the Oberlin application because Oberlin is my first choice, less careful with my last choice, the University of Iowa, which I'm pretty sure will admit me, smudges or not.

All the applications require essays about your ambitions and why you want to go to their school. My ambitions are simple: I just want to have a brilliant career as a professional violinist. Except that's not all I want. I also want to take lots of liberal arts to make me a well-rounded human being. I'm not sure if these two ambitions are mutually exclusive or not, but that's what I want.

By October, I've applied to four schools: Oberlin Conservatory, the University of Michigan, Indiana University, and the University of Iowa. My parents would love for me to go to Iowa, since I'd be near home and it wouldn't cost them so much, but as far as I'm concerned, the Iowa application is just insurance against having to live at home and go to Drake University in Des Moines, God forbid. The reason my first choice is Oberlin is that it has both a great conservatory and a great liberal arts college—with a five-year program so you can get a degree in each—perfect for me.

Oberlin also has a reputation for its students' political activities, which bothers Dad a lot and me a little. It was the first co-ed college in the U.S. as well as the first racially integrated college, which I think is great. I also think it's great that after that Alabama Sunday school was bombed, killing those little girls, a bunch of Oberlin students went down to help rebuild the church. But I have to admit, I'm not that kind of saint. I want to focus on my violin and my studies, not do things that could get me killed.

And there's also Dad's paranoia about my marrying a Negro if I go to Oberlin. Before he'd let me apply there, he made me promise that I won't date a colored guy if I get in. I promised, just to get him to sign the forms, but I had my fingers crossed behind my back.

Of course, none of this will matter if I don't get admitted to Oberlin. It might help that the head violin teacher there is Stuart Canin, who used to be at the University of Iowa and is friends with Mrs. Sexton. But everything really depends on auditions. I already auditioned at Iowa last summer, thanks to Dad dragging me up to Iowa City. I didn't play that well, but the teachers said it was fine and I should be able to get a scholarship. The auditions for Indiana aren't until February, but Michigan's and Oberlin's are in December. My parents and I talk on the phone and make a plan for them to meet me in Ann Arbor and drive me to both auditions before the holidays.

Meanwhile, the cafeteria is buzzing with seniors discussing their applications. Kids are applying to all sorts of places, mostly music schools—Oberlin, Michigan, Indiana, New England Conservatory, Cincinnati Conservatory, Cleveland Institute of Music and, of course, Julliard. You may be wondering why I'm not applying to Julliard myself, given the number of times I've mentioned it, and the answer is, I don't know. Maybe I'm afraid my teachers will laugh if I tell them I want to apply there, or maybe it's that I want more liberal arts than I'd get there, or maybe it's Dad saying he doesn't want me running around New York City with "nothing but weirdos" for friends. I just know that something inside me says no, and I have no choice but to listen to it.

In October, we seniors spend big blocks of time in the cafeteria taking SAT tests and National Merit Scholarship tests and Advanced Placement tests. The tests are nerve-wracking, but also kind of fun. I think I did okay, probably better on the English stuff than on math, but what does a music major need math for anyway?

With the tests over, all I need to do now is practice for my auditions. These require not only a concerto movement but also a movement from a Bach unaccompanied sonata or partita, neither of which I've ever worked on before. Mr. Chausow helps me learn the Adagio of the g minor sonata, which isn't too hard once you've puzzled out all those fancy little thirty-second notes noodling around the main pitches. The good thing about Bach is that it never goes up that high, so you don't have to worry about missing leaps, though the double-stops can be hard to get in tune. For my concerto movement, I'm going back to good, old Mendelssohn one last time, after which I don't plan to play it again for a long, long time.

As my audition dates come closer, the thought of playing to determine the whole course of my future is almost too huge for me to think about. To bomb my upcoming auditions would be unthinkable, like bombing an audition in a concentration camp in which you'd be shot if you messed up. Well, maybe not quite that bad, but it would almost certainly mean I'd end up back in boring old Iowa.

That's not how it turns out, though, because just in the nick of time, Providence intervenes. I'm in my basement practice room one evening playing through my Bach for the umpteenth time, remembering how Mr. Chausow said that if you concentrate when you practice you won't get so nervous when you perform, and getting more and more frustrated because concentrating when I practice seems to be the one thing I can't do. Every time I go back and start again, I promise myself that this time I'll keep my mind on the music, but just a few lines into the piece, I wake up and realize that it's wandered off again, like the sheep going astray in Handel's *Messiah*. Finally, I give up and just sit there staring into space, feeling more and more hopeless.

To say you have to concentrate is all well and good if you're someone like Annie Kavafian, who probably came out of the womb concentrating, but for me, a natural-born daydreamer, it's like being told to climb Mount Everest. I don't want to mess up these auditions, but my bad concentration means I may be doomed to do just that. I feel like hitting myself in the head, but since that would just make my brain even worse, I don't. Instead, I take some Kleenexes out of my pocket and have a good cry, after which I just sit there, feeling my breath slow down and waiting for I-don't-know-what.

Then, out of the blue, a brand new idea pops into my head: Thoughts need to be trained just like fingers and muscles. That's it! In other words, I need to decide ahead of time what I'm going to think at every point in the music and practice thinking as well as playing. I don't remember any teacher ever saying that to me, but there it is, a whole new way of looking at things, filling me with excitement. I know now why Archimedes went rushing naked out into the street after he discovered specific gravity in the bathtub, shouting "Eureka!"

I set my violin down in its open case, snatch my Bach music down off the black metal stand, spread it across my lap, and start figuring out what I'm going to think during each phrase. Soon I have a whole sequence mapped out: breathe out on the split-chord down-bow, plenty of vibrato on the high G, save your bow on the up-bow, crescendo towards the frog, nice clear trill, etc., all the way through the piece. Then, for half an hour or so, I sit there with the music in my lap, not touching my violin, just going over and over my planned thoughts. Finally, I stand up and play through the piece, shutting out the world while the thoughts come into my head, one after another, like a lot of Berma Shave signs along the road, with total concentration. And as a bonus, I just happen to also be playing this Bach movement better than I've ever played anything in my life.

After thinking the last thought and playing the last note, I sit down, close my eyes, and thank God, my unconscious, or whoever it was who gave me this miraculous idea just in time to save me from spending the rest of my life back in Iowa. The next night I go through the same thought-training practice with my Mendelssohn, and when I play my pieces for Mr. Chausow using my new "Think System," to quote Harold Hill in *The Music Man*, he has nothing but praise.

In December, I fly down to Willow Run airport near Ann Arbor, for my Michigan audition. My parents, who drove there from Des Moines, meet me at the airport and take me to the U of M School of Music. When I walk into the audition room, I'm surprised to see only two men, one of whom is my old friend, Mr. Bundra. The other is a string bass teacher named Clyde Thompson, but apparently it doesn't matter that neither of them is a violin teacher. They ask me what I'm going to play, and I tell them. Now comes the test: Will my thought-training experiment work for me or not?

It works. On both my Bach and my Mendelssohn, the thoughts unroll one by one, my sound stays warm and solid, and I gather confidence as I play, ending when the professors stop me, and although they don't say much, I can hear approval in their voices and see it on their faces. Leaving, I'm filled with joy, not just because I think I probably passed the audition, but because for the first time in my life, I managed to stay completely in control during a performance.

The next morning, we drive down to Oberlin, Ohio. It's a little town that Mom says reminds her of Grinnell, where she went to college for a year in the 1930s. The landscape is totally flat, and there are millions of bicycles and hardly any cars. As soon as I see the Conservatory building, I know I have to go to Oberlin. Designed by a famous Japanese architect, it's huge and white, inside and out, with marble-like hallways, rows of tall, diamond-shaped windows, courtyards, and a Japanese garden out in front. The hallways connect clean white spaces for studios, classrooms, practice rooms, an auditorium, and a music library. It's the closest thing to heaven I've ever seen.

By 8:00 the next morning, I'm in a Conservatory practice room warming up. At the audition, I recognize Mr. Canin, who's joined by a couple of other violin teachers. I play through my pieces again using my new Berma Shave method and leave the studio feeling that I've done my best, though I couldn't tell what the teachers thought, who were all very serious.

If I don't get into Oberlin, I probably don't deserve to, I tell myself, as we head out of town and onto Interstate 80 under the blank December sky, but that's not what matters. All that really matters is that I played my best and gave myself a decent chance. Meanwhile, the song, "I Dreamt I Dwelt in Marble Halls" is playing over and over in my head while visions of that lovely Conservatory building refuse to leave. Don't get your hopes up, I tell myself. If you get your hopes up, you're sure to be disappointed. Remember what happened last year with concertos. Don't do that to yourself again.

But, oh, for those marble halls . . .

Chapter 37. Triumph

Yikes! What am I going to do? I spent the whole vacation polishing my Handel Sonata and Wieniawski concerto to play for my senior recital on January 25, expecting I'd be sharing the recital with Nancy, my old stand partner, but Mrs. Bert, who plans the concert schedules, just told me that Nancy isn't going to be ready in time and asked if I could add enough music to play the whole recital myself. And on top of that, Mr. Moore, the piano teacher who was supposed to accompany me and has had the music since Thanksgiving, just informed me he doesn't have time after all. Problems, problems.

I talk to Mr. Chausow and we decide to add the Bartok *Romanian Dances* to my program, which aren't too hard. All I have to do is memorize them, and I'm good at memorizing so that should be okay. Which just leaves the problem of finding a pianist. I ask a couple of other piano teachers, but they're all too busy, and I'm about to start with some of the better piano students when I remember that one of our project teachers, Byron Hanson, was a star accompanist in the summer. After class, I go up and tell Byron what happened and beg him to help a lady in distress and, bless his heart, he agrees.

Byron and I meet the next afternoon to play through the music. The Handel and Bartok aren't too bad, but I've never played the Wieniawski with the piano before, and Byron says it will "take some work," which is putting it nicely. The trouble is, there isn't much time. The Midwestern orchestra tour is from January 14 to January 20, and my recital is on January 25. That gives us just a few days before and after the tour to rehearse.

The tour is mostly in Michigan, except for a concert in Orchestra Hall in Chicago and another in Waukegan, Illinois. There's some free time in Chicago when the other kids go sight-seeing, but I stay in our hotel room practicing. January 25 is getting closer, and I still can't play the up-bow staccato in the Wieniawski. On the bus coming back to Interlochen from the Upper Peninsula of Michigan after our last concert, I sit with my recital music on my lap going over my planned thoughts, which is all I can do.

At my next lesson, Mr. Chausow advises me to play the up-bow staccato notes just plain staccato, which he says no one will notice, so there's one more problem solved. Meanwhile, Byron, bless his heart, rehearses with me in the Fine Arts Building at least once a day, and sometimes even twice.

Rehearsing with Byron isn't just rehearsing. It's more like having a lesson, as he constantly makes suggestions and sometimes tells little stories. He always says things in the kindest way, and I'm playing all my pieces nine times better because of his help. As the days go by, I begin to look forward to our rehearsals.

The three pieces are very different and need different kinds of work. The Handel, being baroque, has hardly any dynamics marked in the music, so we have to make those up ourselves. There are lots of passages of detaché, sawing back and forth, which can get boring if you don't do things with dynamics like echoing loud phrases with soft ones and crescendoing up to high points. There are also several repeats in this piece that I can easily forget to do.

The Bartok is a lot of short dances, each of which is different from the others. Some are schmaltzy Romantic, one of them has a whistly sound, and others sound more like I'm playing percussion than violin. While Handel is very formal-sounding, on the Bartok I have to try to play like a gypsy. This isn't easy for a shy blond girl from Iowa, but remembering what Miss Glenn said about pretending to be somebody else, I do my best.

My big piece is the Wieniawski Concerto, which has millions of notes, lots of fancy double stops, and some beautiful soaring melodies. What Byron and I have to practice most is the rubatos, since with Romantic music you don't just play along at the same speed all the time. Instead, you "rob Peter to pay Paul," as Mrs. Sexton used to say, speeding up in some parts and slowing down in others. Also, unlike in Handel, in Romantic music, it's considered good taste to slide—glissando, it's called—when you move from position to position, and of course, you have to vibrate like crazy. It's all in imitation of what Italian opera singers do.

My favorite part is the Romanza, the second movement, which is just a simple melody that gives you a break from all the fancy stuff. The more we work on this piece, the more I get to love it. Playing through the Romanza with Byron one Saturday evening under the yellow stage lights with the hall dark and empty, I feel something magical, as though I'm waltzing around some Russian ballroom in a beautiful gown with a handsome lieutenant for a partner, and I wish we could go on playing forever.

The hall isn't always empty, though. Mr. Chausow comes to some of our rehearsals and sits in the back, stopping us here and there, checking the balance, and reminding me to stand up straight when I play, which I have a bad habit of not doing. And one afternoon when we're playing through the Wieniawski, I glance out at the empty seats and see Dr. and Mrs. Maddy sitting side-by-side in their red sweaters. Before they leave, Dr. Maddy tells me my playing sounds good and that they're both looking forward to my recital.

By Sunday, I'm beginning to think that I'm actually going to get through my recital without making a complete fool of myself. On Monday, we rehearse all afternoon, and by the end, I think it might even be good. Byron, who by now has become my hero, compliments me on my progress and says he's sure it's going to be fine. It makes me sad to think that once the recital is over, I won't be rehearsing with him anymore.

Now that I think I can get through the music all right, my only problem is what to wear. Most girls wear simple woolen dresses for their recitals at Interlochen, not formals, and I don't have anything that feels right. I could wear my dress uniform, but I'm afraid the shoulder pads on the blazer will get in my way. Finally, I settle on a simple, navy blue wool dress that a friend offers to lend me—nice, but not too flashy, with nothing that could interfere with my playing.

On Tuesday evening, I sit in the little room at the back of the Fine Arts Building with Byron and go through all my planned thoughts, staring down at the music on my lap. Out of the corners of my eyes I can see students and faculty streaming in. I see most of the other violin students and Dr. Johnson and the Maddys and Paul Rolland, a violin teacher from the University of Illinois who's here giving master classes. I try not to think about any of these people but just keep going from one thought to another until it's time for Byron and me to walk up onto the stage.

After tuning, I nod to Byron and start the Handel, which goes fine until we reach the last movement, when I forget to do one of the repeats. Byron does a good job of covering for me, so I don't think most people noticed, but now the recital isn't going to be perfect, and I have to accept that and go on. Damn!

The Romanian dances go better, with no memory slips. With the audience there, I feel myself putting more fire into my playing than in the rehearsals, doing my gypsy act and getting some good applause when I've finished. Then, after a short intermission, comes the Wieniawski. By now, I'm completely warmed up and get through all three movements with just a few minor stumbles, hardly noticeable, and even try to say something with the music. It's amazing how much easier it is to perform when I get to play a lot than if I have to play just a little. If I play only one piece, it can be wrecked by nerves, but when I get to play piece after piece, I begin to run out of adrenaline, and the more I play, the calmer I feel.

I finish my concerto with a flourish, after which the applause is loud and long, with my friends in the audience all standing up and yelling "Bravo!" Then I'm at the back of the Fine Arts Building with Byron, thanking and thanking him, after which one person after another shakes my hand, including Mr. and Mrs. Chausow, the Maddys, Mr. Rolland, Miss Malocsay, Mr. Anderson, and, finally Dr. Johnson, who stands there talking and talking about how impressed he was with my performance. "Listening to you play," he says, "I just couldn't believe my ears. I couldn't believe that it was Cynthia playing like that." After he's gone, Buffy Jean comes up and gives me a huge hug and escorts me back to the dorm, where some friends have put a sign on our door that says "Congratulations, Cindy. You're a real star!" and Buffy Jean gives me a box of chocolates she bought for me in Traverse City as a surprise, and we eat the whole box to celebrate.

Then, suddenly, the hoopla is over. Buffy Jean goes off to wash her hair, and I don't quite know what to do with myself after my triumph. I feel too restless to sit down and study for the English test I have tomorrow, which is what I should do. I wish I could go outside and run through the woods, but it's below zero outside and the snow is way too deep. Instead, I pace back and forth, replaying all the compliments I just received in my mind and feeling a twinge of excitement with each, knowing that tomorrow there will be more, but also knowing that at some point the compliments will end and then the letdown will start, as it always does.

That's the way it is, I think. If a performance goes badly, you want to jump off a cliff afterwards, and if it goes well, your head gets swollen for a few hours, and after that you have to go back to plain old everyday life. For a moment, I wonder if all the work I did was really worth it, but then I remember all the times when I couldn't play the hardest passages in the Wieniawski and how good it felt when I finally got to where I *could* play them. I remember the times the lights came on in my head and something in the music suddenly made sense. And I remember playing through the Romanza with Byron in the Fine Arts Building on that magical Saturday evening. Yes, it was worth it, I tell myself, though not necessarily because of what happened tonight.

The next day, life goes on. More compliments come my way, of course, but they begin to thin out after a while, and by the time of orchestra rehearsal that afternoon, I'm starting to think about other things. Challenges are coming up on Friday, and next week are finals. In JVS, I sit down in fifth chair, where I've been stuck for a few weeks, and start practicing the hardest passages in Smetena's *Moldau*, which we're performing on Sunday, along with Beethoven's Fourth Symphony and some easy little pieces by Anton Webern that sound like something from outer space. I'm still sawing away when TJ comes up onto the podium and gestures for us to quiet down, then turns to speak to the orchestra.

"I went last night to what was the most extraordinary student recital I have ever heard," he starts out. What could he be talking about? I wonder, then suddenly realize that it's *my* recital! TJ tells the orchestra how I spent the last week under the "same grueling conditions" as the rest of the tour orchestra and still managed to play an entire recital from memory, including a concerto of "extreme technical difficulty" and a sonata as "musically difficult" as the Handel. Then he says that I'm the first student he's known who didn't ask to be excused from orchestra on the day of my recital.

"This is what Interlochen is for," he says. "It's this kind of thing we're working for. If nothing else happens while I'm here, this year will have been worth it." As TJ talks, I struggle to keep the silly smile from spreading across my face like it always wants to when I get compliments. I can't believe what I'm hearing. My recital wasn't perfect, after all. There was that memory slip in the Handel and I messed up a couple of runs in the Wieniawski. I'm sure Karen O'Donnell's recital will be better than mine was. Why is he saying all this? Is it because he feels guilty about having picked on me all last year and wants to make up for it?

"We need more Cynthias around here," TJ says. "Cynthia, we're proud of you." He comes down off the podium and shakes my hand and everyone claps, and I smile and thank him, but afterwards, as we start *The Moldau*, I'm thinking, he didn't really say that I played that great, he just said he was impressed at how hard I'd worked, so maybe that was just like praising a kid with cerebral palsy for trying hard and getting to where he could sort of walk. Besides, I bet all the seniors who haven't played recitals yet are going to hate me, since now they're going to have to memorize all their music and none of them can ask to be excused from orchestra on the day of their performance. By the time my mind gets through thinking those negative thoughts, which is what it does when you have an inferiority complex, I almost wish TJ hadn't said anything at all, but not quite.

And, to put the lid on things, there's what Louis Feldman says, coming up to me as I'm putting my violin away.

"Now, at last we know who our former fearless leader really is," he says. "Not only is she now one of those snobby first violinists—she's Dr. Johnson's pet!"

Chapter 38. Carnegie Hall

I'm on the stage of Carnegie Hall, warming up on the fast passages in Kodaly's *Concerto for Orchestra*. I'm sitting third chair, right out in front of the audience, and next to me a serious black-haired boy named Jake Levine is sawing away on some of the same passages. Jake is president of the student council this year and from a totally different planet than I am but as stand partners we make a pretty good team.

After a while I stop playing and look out at the five birthday-cake layers of seats as the people-frosting trickles in onto the lower two layers. I tell myself that I'm sitting on the same stage where nearly all the world's greatest concert artists have performed for the last seventy years, but it's hard for me to believe it, especially since this elegant building wasn't even supposed to be here by now. Some stupid real estate tycoon bought it and was going to tear it down and put up a horrible red high-rise, as shown in *Life* magazine, but violinist Isaac Stern had different ideas and started a campaign to save Carnegie Hall and the rest is history.

Thus, we all owe tonight to Mr. Stern, though apparently, he had some help from his friend Jack Benny. I remember seeing a program on TV a few years ago on which the two of them appeared together. It was called "Carnegie Hall salutes Jack Benny." It started out in Benny's dressing room, where he told his assistant that he wasn't nervous at all and then went off without his pants.

Then, on the stage (he had pants on by then), he played the first movement of the Bach Double Concerto with Isaac Stern and the Philadelphia Orchestra. When they tuned their violins, Benny sneaked a finger down onto his A-string so it sounded like it was a half-step sharp even though it wasn't really, and he kept coming in wrong until Stern went off and got Eugene Ormandy to come in and conduct. Benny didn't actually sound too bad, so it was hard to tell if that was the way he really played or he was still clowning around. After they'd finished, Stern presented Benny with an award for all the money he'd raised for symphony orchestras around the country, and I still remember him saying that although Jack had used his violin countless times as part of his comedy acts, he'd "never made fun of music, only of himself." It's weird to think that when he said that, Stern was standing right up there in the space next to the first violin stand.

More and more people are coming in the doors now and making their way to their seats, probably mostly either family members of kids in the orchestra or people who've gone to Interlochen themselves sometime between the 1930s and last summer. While we were dressing, I heard Miss Cadwell, one of the counselors, call out, "Skitch Henderson is here—with his beard." I have no idea who Skitch Henderson is, but I see a man with a Mitch Miller-like beard up in the balcony, so maybe that's him.

This is our third concert on this February tour. On Monday, we left Traverse City very early in the morning and flew to Washington, DC, where we played a concert at the State Department auditorium. It was just an ordinary auditorium, but there were lots of politicians and diplomats in the audience, the whole point being to get more countries to send kids to Interlochen and maybe even get the State Department to send the IAA orchestra abroad on a good will mission. The concert got a great review the next morning in the Washington Post, which called the string section a "disciplined, many-splendored thing."

That morning, we went on a special tour of the Capitol building that was just for our group. The tour guides told us about all the paintings in the rotunda and showed us where President Kennedy's coffin lay in state. After that, the guides took us to visit the House and Senate chambers. Neither was in session, and because my old violist stand-partner Burt Merrill had been a page in the Senate, they let him take us down onto the floor, where we even got to sit at the senators' desks. I don't know whose desk I was sitting at, but I heard one of the trumpet players say, "Hey, this is Daniel Webster's desk! I'm sitting at Daniel Webster's desk!"

In the afternoon, we went to the University of Maryland and played a concert there, and after that, we got onto some buses for the long, slow ride up to New York City. I spent most of the trip reading a modern translation of Chaucer's *Troilus and Criseyde*, which I'm going to compare with Shakespeare's version of the same story for my senior English theme, which is supposed to be ten to fifteen pages long, with footnotes and all that.

We didn't get to our hotel until after midnight, but we still had to get up at eight o'clock the next morning to have time for sightseeing. There were various choices, and I signed up to go to the United Nations, which I'd always wanted to see, ever since I was here in New York with my family when I was five years old and for the UN you had to be six, and Dad took me to the museum while Mom went with Davy, who got this great collection of little flags there, which made me jealous. Then, after lunch, we came here to rehearse, and everyone started getting excited. Some kid got ahold of a whole lot of buttons from Avis Rent-a-Car that said "We Try Harder" on them and handed them out and we all wore them to dinner, even TJ. Of course, we had to take them off when we dressed for the concert back stage, exchanging our usual dress uniforms for bright red blazers and navy-blue skirts or pants.

Now, here I am on the stage of Carnegie Hall, wearing my own red blazer, and the house lights just went down. Karen comes out on the stage and gestures for the oboe to give us the A to tune, after which the applause starts up as TJ comes out, looking like a giant penguin in his white tie and tails. He gives the audience a couple of quick bows, then climbs up onto the podium. Glancing around at the orchestra, he's all smiles, and you'd never know that he chewed out a couple of kids during the afternoon rehearsal. He takes a deep breath and raises his baton for the first piece, Mozart's Linz Symphony.

The notes of the symphony aren't difficult, but if you make any mistakes in Mozart, everyone is going to know, unlike in Richard Strauss, for example, where there are so many notes you can get away with faking. Playing the symphony in Carnegie Hall, I feel that we're all collectively on a tight-rope, but fortunately, no one falls. During the slow movement, I find myself wondering why I can't feel anything when I play this symphony, unlike Haydn's "Hen" Symphony, which we played last year and I loved. No matter how hard I try to listen and appreciate it, this piece leaves me cold. I know other people are playing and listening to the music and thinking how beautiful it is, which makes me feel lonely and defective, but I can't help it—I feel what I feel, which in this case, is nothing much. I guess pieces of music are like people—some are just better matches with you than others, and you can't expect to like them all.

I do like the Kodaly *Concerto for Orchestra*, which is what we play next, even though the violins don't have the greatest part. Maybe I've finally grown up enough to enjoy listening to the whole orchestra and not just my own line, as Mr. Bundra said I would the time he tried to talk me into switching to viola. The Kodaly is a modern piece with lots of accidental-ridden notes for the violins that were a real pain to learn but it doesn't have much in the way of melodies, at least not for us. The cellos have some lovely solo lines in one of the slow sections, but not the violins. For violins it's just saw, saw, saw, chop, chop, chop. But

I love listening to the brass and woodwinds in the fast parts, and the cello lines feel like a warm comforter on a cold night.

After the Kodaly, Dr. Maddy comes out, also in white tie and tails, to conduct Berlioz's *Roman Carnival* overture. The Berlioz is a show-piece that, unlike the Kodaly, does have some good melodies for the violins and lots of fireworks. It ends super-loud, to thunderous applause, of course. By now, I've learned that the kind of applause you get has as much to do with how a piece ends as how well it's played. Pieces which end softly rarely get much, but pieces that end with a lot of loud chords usually get a lot unless the performance is terrible.

Finally, after the intermission, we get to the piece I've been waiting for: Shostakovich's First Symphony. Dr. Johnson told us that Shostakovich wrote it before the Communists in Russia started cracking down and sending composers off to Siberia, which is why some people think it was his greatest symphony even though he was only nineteen when he wrote it. It has lots of solos that show off the first chairs and sometimes solo lines for other chairs as well. There's even a passage in the first movement with four separate solo lines for the first four violin chairs, including the one yours truly is sitting in. When we get to that part, I try to forget that it's a solo and just play through it as if I'm with a whole section and it goes all right, but afterwards, I think, Ha! I just played a solo in Carnegie Hall!

In this piece, there are oodles of Places that I wait for, including the whole last two movements. For some reason, during this symphony I see more visions in my head than during any piece I've ever played, and the more times we play through it, the clearer the visions become in a kind of mental screen-play, like in *Fantasia*.

The first movement starts with a lot of little tentative-sounding bits of tunes, mostly in the woodwinds, that make me see tiny puppets dancing on strings. Then the first clarinet starts a theme that sounds a little like "I Love a

Parade" and gets tossed around from clarinet to flute to violins to bassoon and eventually works up to a loud part, which is like the puppets all lining up and marching down the street in columns, then marching off to where the music ends all soft and tentative again.

Then comes the second movement, a Scherzo, which has only one beat per measure and a lot of very fast sixteenth-notes, a real dance of death. Almost from the beginning, I can see skeletons dancing, especially when the piano comes in, which sounds like rattling bones. But then, all of a sudden, a flute enters with a slow, second theme, and I spend a few moments in a Japanese garden with stone Buddhas and lily pads before the bassoon picks the first theme back up again and we're back to the dancing bones, which come crashing down in a big pile with some loud piano chords near the end.

Then, in the third movement, my visions really take off, from the opening haunting melody in the oboe to the gorgeous cello solo with the dangerous leap—I pray the first chair doesn't miss it and she doesn't, thank God—to the rhythmic patterns of Da dadaDaaaa da da! that starts with the trumpet and gets repeated over and over by one instrument after another, not just in this movement, but in the last movement as well. As we play, I imagine myself waking up in the girls' dorm back at Interlochen and going outside and discovering that everyone has mysteriously disappeared. I wander around all over the campus, peering in windows, checking cabins, and scanning the horizon for lights, but find no sign of life anywhere, and after a while I somehow know that I'm the only person left on earth. It's like that *Twilight Zone* episode about the bank clerk who wears glasses and loves to read and goes into this really thick safe during a nuclear attack and is the only person who survives. He finds a library, but then he breaks his glasses so he can't read any of the books and at the end he sits down and cries.

The third movement ends with a great snare-drum roll that crescendos up into the fourth movement, in which I go through all sorts of different feelings about my terrible aloneness every few measures, from total anguish, to resignation, to a beautiful feeling of peace on one lovely major string chord. It all leads up to this fantastic tympani solo on the same Da dada Daaaa da da motif, which is repeated three times while the whole rest of the orchestra stays silent and seems to get right to the heart of things. Watching our amazing Japanese tympani player, Koji Akiyama, as he crouches over each drum in turn, hammers out the motif, flings his stick dramatically back and then freezes as the vibrations die down, I feel myself transported back to some ancient time, long before symphony orchestras, back to the very beginnings of music.

Finally, the first chair cello comes back with another lush solo, and after that the music gradually gets happier. My spooky visions are overwhelmed by a new determination to survive and thrive, and I can feel the adrenaline rushing through all of us—strings, woodwinds, brass, percussion, piano, everyone—as we play ever more joyfully up to the very last page, where the words, "Oh, I want to *live*! Oh, I want to *live*!" repeat themselves over and over in my head with the trumpets as we finish off a performance which brings down the house and gets us a standing ovation.

Then, a few moments later, we're back in our dressing rooms, packing up our instruments and getting out of our red blazers, chattering excitedly and rushing out into the dazzling New York streets, free for the rest of the evening to go anywhere we want.

Chapter 39. What's Wrong with Me?

The pain jolts me awake just after midnight in early March. It's the same old pain that I've had off and on since fifth grade, a dull, throbbing ache all over my abdomen, not just on the lower right side where it's supposed to be if you have appendicitis. The first time this happened, my parents took me to the emergency room, where a nurse with a trayful of glass slides stuck a needle in my finger and a doctor informed us that my "blood count wasn't elevated," which it would be if I had appendicitis, and sent me home. By the next morning, I felt better, and that was that. Another time, in the seventh grade, I came home from school in the middle of the day with the same awful pain, but again it got better and no one did anything. Both times my dad, whose appendix ruptured when he was a kid, paced around saying "are you sure it's not her appendix?" and making me feel even worse with his worrying, but Mom said it was probably just pre-menstrual cramps and gave me lectures about how "we women have to learn to be tough."

This time, I'm sure it's not cramps, as I just finished my period last week and anyway, cramps are nothing compared to this. I turn over onto my stomach, but that doesn't help. It feels like I've swallowed a rolling pin that's flattening all my insides like pie-dough. I try taking some deep breaths, but that doesn't help either. Finally, I wake Buffy Jean up and she goes and gets Miss Wysong, and the two of them lead me, doubled over and clutching my stomach, down the stairs and through the dark cafeteria, into the Stone Student Center, and up the stairs to the infirmary.

The Academy infirmary is just a bunch of hotel rooms with gray cinder-block walls, in each of which are two or three narrow beds fitted with ironed white sheets and army blankets. Miss Dustin, the young night nurse, helps me into one of the beds and takes my temperature, which is up a little, 99.8.

By morning the pain is a little better, and my temperature's gone back down, but when Mrs. Pauley, the daytime nurse, comes on duty, she calls Dr. Johnston, the school physician, and he tells her to send me to the ER at Munson Hospital in Traverse City. Then she calls the girls' dorm and arranges for Miss Wysong to accompany me. Buffy Jean comes with her to the infirmary and brings me some clothes to wear.

"I'm sure by tonight you'll have had your appendix out, Wizzie," she says. I must have heard Buffy Jean's story of her own "emergency appendectomy" about six times, and she, like my dad, is sure that my appendix has to be the problem. She walks down with us to where a green van is waiting and hugs me extra hard before I climb aboard.

At the ER, a nurse takes a blood sample so they can find out, once again, that my blood count is normal, just as I knew they would. Then a doctor and three interns, all serious-looking men in white coats, come in and poke my stomach. I hate having my stomach poked, not only because it hurts, but also because my stomach isn't exactly the most attractive part of my body. The fat comes bulging up on both sides of each doctor's fingertips as he presses, and by the time they're done, I'm nothing but a big, saggy pile of white bread dough.

The doctor and the interns go off in a corner and confer, then leave me lying there with a sheet over my half-naked body. Finally, another doctor comes in, a surgeon who introduces himself as Dr. Stark. He wears black, horn-rimmed glasses and looks like Barry Goldwater. I know immediately that he dislikes me. Don't ask me how I know, but I do. Maybe it's the way he looks off into the distance as he presses down on my abdomen, but I think it's more just the tone of voice he uses as he fires question after question at me, like Mr. Burger cross-examining witnesses on *Perry Mason*. You'd think from Dr. Stark's tone that it's my fault that my stomach doesn't hurt in the right place. What does he want me to do—lie?

"So how long did you say you've had this pain?" he demands, poking me in the bread dough some more. "Does that hurt?" How about that?" His hands move up and down from place to place. "Have you ever had pain like this before? When was the last time you ate? What did you eat? When was your last menstrual period?"

I answer everything, but no matter what I say, I can tell that it's wrong and that he sees me as a lazy, nervous hypochondriac who's probably being overly dramatic so she can get out of going to classes.

"What are your periods like? How often? Do you have any discharge? Is it yellow or white? Have you ever douched? When was the last time you had intercourse? Is there any chance you could be pregnant?" These are not questions I want this Goldwater creep to ask me, but I'm stuck here on the table with only a white sheet over me and have no choice but to cooperate if I ever want to get back on my feet again.

After I'm dressed, Dr. Stark informs me that he doesn't think I have appendicitis or anything serious, that it's probably just indigestion, and that I can "go back and lie around that infirmary for a few days." The way he says "that infirmary" makes it sound like the kind of place where girls lounge around in black garter belts. He also informs me that he wants me to "douche out"—whatever that is—with vinegar every day and that the nurse at Interlochen will help me with this.

After I've spent a few more days in the infirmary, the pain has begun to subside, and I'm able to eat some broth and Jello for lunch and do a little reading for English. I'm halfway through "Elegy in a Country Churchyard" when Mrs. Pauley comes in and says she has something to show me. She leads me into one of the infirmary bathrooms, where she opens a small cardboard box and takes out a yellow rubber bag with a long tube dangling from it.

"Now, this," she says, "is something every woman should have. It's called a douche bag." She shows me how to measure vinegar from a bottle and dump it into the bag, fill the bag the rest of the way up with water, and hang it from a coat hanger she has suspended from a towel rack on the back of the door. Then she fits a nozzle onto the end of the tube, hands me some icky, biological-looking diagrams that explain how to insert it, and leaves me to experiment.

By the next morning, I'm well enough to leave the infirmary, though I still have a little dull pain in my abdomen. Mrs. Pauley helps me get my things together and reminds me I'm to come up every night after dinner to "do your little procedure." I go back to the dorm but don't tell anyone, even Buffy Jean, about the douching, which makes me feel like one of those unclean lepers in the Bible.

Except for this new nightly ritual and a slight residue of pain in my abdomen, things return to normal for the next few weeks. Normal at this point is pretty good, actually. In English class, we're reading Wordsworth and Coleridge, in wind class I'm playing the French horn, which I like better than the other brass instruments, and I'm learning the notes of the first movement of the Khachaturian violin concerto for my lessons. Plus, I'm getting to be friends with Byron, the hero of my senior recital, whom I see every day in

Project classes and also in the cafeteria, where he eats surrounded by a lot of silly, adoring senior girls like yours truly. Occasionally, I even get to eat alone with him, though almost always one of his other fans shows up to spoil it. Whether I'm alone with Byron or with a group, our conversation is mostly Byron teaching. One day I mention I'm supposed to read "The Rhyme of the Ancient Mariner," for example, and he spends the next half hour telling me the whole plot. I'm never sure if Byron does this just because he loves to teach or because he wants to keep me aware of the fact that he's a teacher and I'm a student so I won't get my hopes up for anything between us.

Like me, Byron isn't particularly good-looking in the Hollywood sense. He's taller than I am but very thin, with a triangular, fox-shaped face and pointy chin, and wears glasses. But he's so smart and nice that he's starting to look better and better to me. Mom always said that when you love someone, you start loving the way they look, and it's true. But, of course, he's a teacher, and anyway, it would still be impossible because Byron has so many other, prettier girl fans, some of whom I'm starting to hate, especially this violist named Violet who's always chasing after him.

On March 19, I fly home for three weeks of spring vacation. I've been home only a few days when the pain in my midsection suddenly comes back full force, this time accompanied by a temperature of 101. I also have my period at the time, and Mom diagnoses my condition as flu plus menstrual cramps and calls my Uncle Parker, my cousin Judy's obstetrician father. He comes over to the house and pokes my stomach, confirms that the pain isn't in the right place for appendicitis and prescribes some laxative suppositories.

That night, while my parents are in the other room watching a movie on TV, I lie in bed listening to Brahms First Symphony on FM radio and taking my temperature every half hour, which goes higher and higher. By the time my parents' movie is over, my temperature is 104, but then it goes back down to a little over 100, where it stays for about a week before it finally goes back to normal and the pain is once again tolerable. I stay in bed all week working on my *Troilus and Cressida* paper, sitting up with a pillow across my knees and a tray of note cards and books Mom gets for me at the Des Moines public library.

I'm still sick in bed when a big envelope arrives from Oberlin with a letter telling me that I've been accepted by the Conservatory. It's what I wanted, but it's hard for me to be that happy with a stomachache, and I can't help wondering if I'll live long enough to make it to Oberlin. I hope so, because right now I have a whole string of exciting things to look forward to: first, the concerto competition, which I might actually have a chance to win this time; then graduation, with parties, presents, and maybe even some awards; then a whole summer of playing in the University Symphony and studying with Miss Glenn and more conversations with Byron and then—maybe, if I'm lucky— the marble halls of Oberlin Conservatory and a whole new life.

With all that on the horizon, I have no choice but to get well and stay well and I would—if only I knew what was wrong with me!

Chapter 40. Death of a Pioneer

The moment I sit down at breakfast and hear Byron talking in a subdued voice to a group of Project students I know what must have happened. It's a Monday morning in April, and the previous Tuesday, Waldie informed us that Dr. Maddy had gone to the hospital in Traverse City after suffering a "coronary occlusion," which was probably a fancy way of saying he had a heart attack. Waldie said he was resting and seemed to be getting better, but still, a heart attack is a heart attack. So, I'm not surprised when I learn that early this morning, Dr. Maddy died.

Some of the girls are crying, and everyone seems stunned, but the main thing I feel myself after hearing the news is guilt. This is mostly because of something I said to Dr. Maddy just last week that I now really wish I hadn't. When we seniors signed on for the Project, we were told that next summer we could choose to come back in either the high school or the university division. But two weeks ago, Waldie announced that Dr. Maddy had decided we'd all have to come back as high school students. Needless to say, we weren't pleased. High school students live in cabins and can't go off campus or stay out late, whereas university students live in dorms and can go wherever they want and stay out until midnight. Not to mention the fact that university students get credits for their courses from the University of Michigan, which high school students don't, and high school kids have to deal with challenges and university students don't. An intense discussion ensued, in which we students presented our arguments, during which I opened my stupid big mouth and said what I now regret.

"The problem for me," I said, "is not so much playing in the high school symphony as the difference in living conditions between the two divisions." "Living conditions" was wrong, I thought, as soon as my words were out, not exactly the right phrase, but it was too late.

Dr. Maddy frowned over at me, his bushy eyebrows bunching up in the middle. "Well," he growled, "this place has been going since 1928 and this is the first time anyone ever complained about our accommodations." Obviously, he'd misunderstood "living conditions" as having something to do with buildings and taken the whole thing personally, when I just meant I wanted to be able to go off campus and stay out late, but I didn't know how to explain that to him now that the damage was done.

"They're getting to the age where they want more freedom to come and go," Waldie told Dr. Maddy, though whether he understood Waldie or not, I'll never know. The whole thing made me want to crawl down a hole in the ground.

The discussion went on, but now Dr. Maddy is dead, and I can't help feeling that my upsetting him that day was partly what killed him. That's ridiculous, of course, but I'd still give anything not to have said what I did, even though the next day Waldie announced that they'd worked things out so we could be in the university division after all and maybe my saying it helped make that happen.

The other reason I feel guilty is that although I truly appreciate all the things Dr. Maddy did for us in founding the camp and the academy and keeping things running all these years and getting the grant for the Project and even coming to my rehearsal and my senior recital and saying such nice things to me, he hasn't exactly been fun for us to work with in the Project, especially lately. He'd either be standing up at the front of the class growling at the teachers if they did anything that wasn't according to his wonderful, assembly-line, super-efficient "Maddy method" or he'd be looking over some kid's shoulder and making it impossible for him to concentrate, muttering incomprehensible things in his ear, or fumbling around with his music and trying clumsily to point to things. I know this was just because he was old and probably already sick, and I'm sure he was a wonderful teacher when he was young, but now that he's gone, he won't be involved with the Project anymore, and my relief about this makes me feel even more guilty as I sit listening to Byron talk about what may happen now to the academy and the camp.

He says the trustees will have to select a new president, and meanwhile Dr. Johnson will run the academy and Dr. Wilson will run the camp, which they mostly do anyway. The Project will go on as planned, with Waldie in charge. The biggest loss for Interlochen with Dr. Maddy's death is going to be in fund-raising, as he was still really brilliant at getting rich people to donate money, and there's probably no one who can take his place in that respect. And, of course, everyone will miss having him around to inspire us.

That morning in orchestra, Dr. Johnson starts the rehearsal by talking about Dr. Maddy's death and about our performance last night of Tchaikovsky's Sixth ("Pathetique") Symphony, which Dr. Maddy had planned to conduct. After he got sick, TJ took over, and all week he bawled people out for not playing their parts "better, better, better." Now he reminds us that Dr. Maddy had loved Tchaikovsky and says it almost seems like there was "something supernatural" going on during our performance because he couldn't believe how well we were playing and that we "did things that we had never done before." It was only a few hours after that, he says, that Dr. Maddy died.

Then comes the public funeral, the burial, and the memorial service for Academy faculty, staff, and students. The funeral is in JVS, the big gymnasium with a stage along one side. The trustees are there, and music educators from all over the country. There are prayers and speeches and music, and the orchestra plays the slow movement from Brahms' First Symphony. After the service, we students all march out in our blue and gray dress uniforms and line the sidewalk while Dr. Maddy's casket is carried past us and put into the hearse and driven away.

The Academy's own memorial service for Dr. Maddy takes place the following Sunday morning in the Fine Arts Building. The choir sings two anthems—Brahms' "How Lovely is Thy Dwelling Place" and "For All the Saints" by Ralph Vaughn Williams—with Dr. Jewell conducting us, and then Burt Merrill gets up to speak for the students. After a brief prayer, he starts out,

"When a man says, 'Yes, it will work, it will work. I know it will,' what do you do? You agree. When a man says, 'Of course you can do it, of course you can,' what can you say? You agree. When a man says, 'I have faith in you, in all of you,' what do you do? You thank him, for he has paid you the finest compliment which can be paid. A man who said all these things was our Dr. Maddy. He was a friend to all, companion to everyone. He took the interest in his fellow citizens to do something for their welfare. He devoted his entire life to us. That was our Dr. Maddy. He had a spirit, an indomitable will to go on living, and that will, yes that spirit, is with us today, here in this room. That is our Dr. Maddy now, and no one will ever take his spirit from us."

Burt talks about how Dr. Maddy devoted his entire life to young people and about how he himself kept growing younger and maintained a "boy's heart" for his whole life. He talks about Dr. Maddy as a "bridge builder" and quotes a couple of his favorite slogans that showed him to be a citizen of the world—"Dedicated to the promotion of world friendship through the universal language of the arts" (the words written over the Kresge stage) and "in the arts there are no enemies." And he talks about Dr. Maddy as a man with a dream who "did something about it," saying that he "never stopped reaching for the stars" and "kept living, thinking, planning, even to the very end" and what a wonderful example he set for us. Finally, he compares Dr. Maddy to the sun, the beauty of which we don't appreciate until after it sets, when it leaves behind all sorts of beautiful colors.

After the service, I go down to the lake and sit for a while, imagining that behind my bench there are no buildings and no people, just a lot of trees, which is all that would be here if it weren't for Dr. Maddy. I think about that first small group of kids who came to this place in 1928 and the talented, slightly crazy young man who greeted them. I think about how that young man pushed and begged and borrowed and practically sold his soul until the buildings got built and the teachers got hired and the trustees met and planned and more and more kids showed up to play and sing and act and dance and sculpt and paint. Then, in my mind, I can see Dr. Maddy and Mrs. Maddy sitting at the back of the Fine Arts Building in their red sweaters when Byron and I were rehearsing that day and I think about his always just being there, a part of the landscape in this place that he created. And I think about Burt's metaphor of the sunset and about how that's exactly how it's been for me, always just taking Dr. Maddy for granted and sometimes even being irritated by him so long as he was still around, and only now that he's not, being able to see the beautiful colors that he left behind.

I think about all this, and then I sit for a while longer, and then I start to cry, and my tears are unselfish ones for a change, and wash away at least a little of the guilt.

Chapter 41. Providence Intervenes

The blank page in the spiral notebook stares up at me, refusing to be filled. I jump up from my seat in the girls' dorm upstairs lounge and pace back and forth, but nothing comes into my empty head. I sit down and go back to staring at the notebook. Finally, I start to write, but when I read what I've written, it sounds so stupid I scratch it all out.

I wouldn't be in this mess if it weren't for the official-looking letter I found in my mailbox just before we were leaving to go play a concert down in Lansing, which I read sitting on the bus:

> *Dear Cynthia:*
>
> *The Interlochen Arts Academy, its faculty and administration are extremely proud to notify you that because of your truly superior record in both the performing arts and academic disciplines you have earned the title of Salutatorian (high honors) for the graduating class of 1966.*
>
> *Cherish this honor as one of distinction and may it be one of many distinguished records you will receive during your life. We are indeed fortunate to have a person of your proven ability as a member of our student body.*
>
> *With personal congratulations,*
>
> *Reginald Eldred, Principal*

Mr. Eldred's letter sent my spirits instantly soaring. I wanted to jump up and brag to everyone on the bus, but instead I just told Gloria, my seat mate, who congratulated me in a bored-sounding voice and went on reading her magazine. But when I got back and told Buffy Jean, she jumped up and down and hugged me and called me her "Wizzie," and when I called my parents they told me they were proud, and when I told Byron at breakfast, he said, "Well, is that so? Well, my goodness--Congratulations!" and reached to shake my hand. "My goodness" is Byron's favorite expression, and I've started to say it a lot myself.

Being chosen salutatorian came as a complete surprise to me. It wasn't like winning concertos or getting to be concertmistress, where you work and work and triumph only after a spectacular performance. This just sort of happened, as if God had suddenly decided to shine His spotlight down on me. I'm not even sure why the faculty picked me, as I got one B+ on my report card last year and I'm sure there were others with nothing but A's. I wonder if someone added up the points wrong. I suppose it must have been because of my senior recital and the *Troilus and Cressida* paper, which Mrs. Stocking loved. Anyway, an honor's an honor, and although it's not exactly winning concertos—I played all right at this year's auditions and everyone thought I'd win, but for some reason, I still didn't—it does mean performing in Kresge, since at the honors convocation, the salutatorian makes a speech.

Of course, it goes without saying that my salutatorian speech will not be just any speech. No, it's going to be the greatest speech anyone ever made at Interlochen, President Kennedy's inauguration speech and Lincoln's Gettysburg Address and that speech of Churchill's about fighting on the beaches all rolled into one, a speech to end all speeches. Which leaves me with only one problem: I have to write this wonderful speech, and right now, nothing is happening. Nothing.

The longer I stay stuck, the more scared thoughts go through my head, and the more scared thoughts go through my head, the longer I stay stuck. What if I stay blocked until the night of the convocation? What if my turn comes to stand up and talk, and I have nothing to say? Or what if the talk I end up with is just plain terrible? This could be like one of those nightmares where you're naked in public or have to sight-read a piece you've never seen before in front of a huge audience. With the blank page staring up at me, I'm starting to wish I never got that letter, which I probably didn't deserve to get anyway.

Calm down, something says then. If worse comes to worse, Mrs. Stocking will help you. Sure enough, in class the next day, she says she wants to meet with me and Arty Whittaker, the valedictorian, to talk about our speeches. I'm sure Arty will have no trouble at all writing his speech, being first in our class, unlike yours truly, who's only second, after all.

My job as salutatorian, Mrs. Stocking explains to us, is to greet the people, and Arty's job as valedictorian is to say goodbye, but that's not all we should do. We should each also try to come up with a central inspirational theme to focus on, and ideally our two themes should complement each other. After some discussion, we decide that I'll talk about humility and Arty will talk about confidence, and Mrs. Stocking gives me a copy of something she thinks I might want to quote. It's called, "Desiderata" and starts out,

Go placidly amid the noise and haste and learn what peace there may be in silence . . . Speak your truth quietly and clearly; and listen to others, even the dull and ignorant; they too have their story. If you compare yourself with others you may become vain and bitter; for always there will be greater and lesser persons than yourself.

This seems perfect for Interlochen, where competition is the name of the game. Mrs. Stocking's help gets me started so I'm able to write a good first paragraph greeting the people and to begin thinking about the rest, but that's as far as I get because the next day in orchestra rehearsal, in the middle of the first movement of Mahler's Second Symphony, my stupid abdominal pain suddenly starts up again. I make it through the rehearsal, telling myself I absolutely can't get sick the week before graduation, but by evening I'm back in the infirmary with a temperature of 101.

The next morning, Mrs. Pauley gets me an appointment to see Dr. Johnston at his office in Traverse City, so I don't have to go back to the ER. The pain is a little better by the time I get there, and I assume I'll be going back to the infirmary, where I can finish my speech and study for my English final. Dr. Johnston, however, has other ideas. He calls in my unfavorite person in the whole world, the surgeon Dr. Stark, who pokes my stomach some more, and I have to admit, the pain is settling into my lower right side this time.

"Her temperature's been up to 101, Ed," Dr. Johnston tells Dr. Stark. The two of them confer, then Dr. Stark comes back in and tells me he's decided to operate the next morning. He says he thinks there are two possibilities: either I have appendicitis, or I have something he calls "ileitis," which is inflammation of the ileum, which is part of the small intestine. He draws a picture to show me, though I already know what an ileum is, along with a duodenum and a jejunum, from learning the parts of the intestines in Miss Appelhof's biology class last year, which just goes to show that you never know what things you learn in school may come in handy. If my problem is appendicitis, Dr. Stark says, he'll take my appendix out and that will be that. If it's ileitis, on the other hand, he'll just close me up again and refer me to an internist for medicines and a special diet. Meanwhile, he'll call my parents, who will probably fly up here tomorrow, he says.

After Dr. Stark has left the room, the nurse comes in to help me dress. As she helps me into my shirt, it suddenly hits me that I'm going to be spending the next umpteen days flat on my back missing what was supposed to be one of the high points of my life, and I start bawling my head off. The nurse, a plump, motherly woman, pats me on the shoulder and tells me it's going to be all right even though we both know it isn't.

"But I'm going to miss my graduaaaaation!" I wail. "I was supposed to make a speeeeech! I want to diiiiie! Why don't they just let me die?!"

"Now, you just listen to me," says the nurse. "I bet somebody's going to do something real special for you on your graduation day. And you'll probably be the person everybody remembers more than anyone there. There's nothing like being missing to make you stick out. You'll be famous! People will be signing cards and sending you presents. I bet some of your friends will even come to see you."

On the way over to the hospital, I think about what the nurse said and try to cultivate some PMA. I imagine an entourage arriving from the Academy to play "Pomp and Circumstance" in my hospital room. Maybe Dr. Johnson will come and make one of his speeches. And, of course, Byron will have to come, along with Waldie and Miss Malocsay and maybe Mrs. Stocking. Maybe if I'm really, really brave and don't complain about anything and make wry jokes like those British heroes on their way to the gallows and even show kindness and concern for the other patients, I'll become famous among the nurses, who will tell my visitors what a wonderful, brave patient I was, and everyone at the Academy will hear about it, and maybe Byron will even see me as some kind of heroine and fall in love with me, which would be even better than getting to make my salutatorian speech, which I no longer have to worry about writing, which is the one good thing to come out of this, since I still have only the vaguest idea what I would have said. Who knows--maybe Providence just intervened to save me from making a fool of myself!

By the time I get to the hospital and am wheeled into a room upstairs, my biography is writing itself in my head, telling how brave I was while being admitted to the hospital and facing surgery all by myself and never complaining about anything. A nurse brings me a gown to put on and I climb up into the bed that's to be my home for the next umpteen days, and she shows me how to raise and lower the top half of the bed and use the little button-thing to call the nurses if I need something. I'm sure I won't use the button much, though, since we heroines never complain.

"You're not to have anything to eat or drink," the nurse says. "We don't want you throwing up during your surgery, do we?"

"That's okay," I say in my most heroic voice, even though my stomach is growling and my throat feels parched. "I didn't really want anything anyhow."

Lying in my hospital bed, I feel the pain in my lower right side lessening and wonder if I'm really sick enough to be here. Maybe I should tell them I feel fine now and see if they let me get up and go back to school. But no, they wouldn't do that. Anyway, I'm not sure I'd want to stop the surgery now even if I could. If I went back to school, I'd just be waiting for the pain to start up again. Now at least I'll finally find out what's been wrong with me all these years, which may be worth missing my graduation for. Maybe.

Having settled this, I start to think about what the surgery will be like. My biggest fear is that the ether will make me sick like it did after I had my tonsils out in the third grade. I haven't thought about that in years, but now the whole experience starts coming back. I remember a nurse putting a mask over my face with this red-and-white dishtowel soaked in some awful-smelling stuff and how when I breathed in, I saw this icky, maroon-colored target with light blue and yellow circles pulsing while a woman's voice screeched "Kiya, kiya, kiya!" faster and faster. Finally, I woke up in a big baby bed with bars in a room full of other kids in baby beds. My throat hurt, and unlike the other kids, who all ate their ice cream and went to sleep, I was awake all night throwing up from the ether. This does not bode well, but then I remember

Mom telling me they don't use ether anymore, now they use something called sodium pentothal, which is just a shot that knocks you out and doesn't make you dizzy or anything.

Relieved by this thought, I look around the room. The walls are institutional green, and it has two big windows along one side and two other beds besides mine. One is empty and in the other a little red-haired girl is sleeping. Her mother whispers hello and tells me her daughter, who's five years old, is to have her tonsils out in the morning and I tell her about my appendix and she wishes me luck.

Throughout the evening, people come in and out of the room: nurses to take temperatures and give pills, a woman with a tray of tubes who pokes my finger, doctors on their rounds, the little girl's father. Finally, the night nurse gives me a pill to make me sleep and turns out the light. In the dark, I listen to noises coming from the lighted hallway, footsteps and nurses' voices and carts and beds rolling by, until the noises begin to blur together like an orchestra warming up before a concert and suddenly the room is filled with light and it's morning and a nurse is standing over me with a basin of soapy water and a razor to start what she calls my "prep," which turns out to be a bunch of highly unpleasant things they do to you before surgery.

Finally, a couple of orderlies show up with a bed on wheels and lift me onto it even though I'm perfectly capable of moving myself. As the banks of fluorescent lights in the ceiling pass over me, I'm already starting to get drowsy from some medicine they gave me and I drift back into challenges in the basement of JVS and Mr. Bundra's voice going "there is a change" and then I'm back in the Youth Symphony with Dr. Maddy in his red sweater conducting *Death and Transfiguration* in my very first concert at Interlochen, the piece I planned to have them play for me on my deathbed to see if that's what it's really like, and all at once Dr. Maddy looks down at me and winks, and I somehow know that whatever happens it's going to be all right but then, with a bump, I'm back in my bed rolling under the lights with a nasty needle in the back of my hand and a tube going into it from a bottle dangling on a pole.

A cold breeze hits my face as the bed turns and goes through some double doors into a big room with a table in the middle. Two men lift me onto the table, which has a big, round light staring down at me like a giant eye, which makes me feel like the frog I dissected in Mr. Hood's class last year, and I think about the tiny spaghetti inside the frog's middle and how I picked it apart with a sharp little knife and I want to tell them if I'm going to die and go be with Dr. Maddy, I'd rather do it anywhere but here on this ugly steel table under this big, ugly light, but I'm too tired to say anything and then someone does something with the bottles on the pole and mumbles something about an anesthetic and my thoughts start to fuzz up again.

Sodium pentothal, I think, as I fall backwards into black nothing.

Chapter 42. Graduation Day

"Cindy, wake up," says the voice of Mrs. Neal a moment later. What is Mrs. Neal, my Hanawalt music teacher, doing here? I wonder. Is that really her? Where am I? What's going on?

"Wake up," the voice says again. "You're in the recovery room. You had surgery, Cindy. You had your appendix out."

I start to gag. Something hard is stuck in the back of my throat, and the lower part of my abdomen is a mess of pain, partly sharp, partly dull. I groan and open my eyes. The lights are too bright, and I close them again. Phrases from *Death and Transfiguration* float through my head.

"Am I going to die?" I ask. If she says yes, I'll ask for the music, but no, the woman with Mrs. Neal's voice, who doesn't look at all like Mrs. Neal but instead is fat and blond and wears a nurse's uniform, wouldn't know what I was talking about, I'd need someone from Interlochen for that, Byron or Waldie or Dr. Johnson or Mr. Chausow, but they're not here.

"No, of course not. But you need to lie still. The doctor doesn't want you to throw up because it could hurt your incision, which is why you have that tube going into your stomach. You won't need to eat or drink anything for a few days—the tube will be doing it for you, though you can have ice chips if your mouth is dry."

"It feels awful," I say. "I feel awful." I'm supposed to be heroic and not complain, I remember then, but I don't care about that anymore. All I care about is the thing in my throat, which I now realize is also in my nose, being gone so I can swallow and blow my nose, and about the pain in my abdomen letting up.

"Yes, I know, honey," says the nurse, "but this will help." She jabs a needle into my arm, and I already hurt so much I don't even feel the shot. Black clouds come pouring into my head and blot everything out, and when I wake up again, I'm back in my regular hospital room with no idea how I got there.

Again I'm hurting, and I press the button for the nurse to come, and she gives me another shot, and again the clouds come pouring in and when they pull apart again, I see Mom and Dad standing over me under the dim yellow lights, with the window shiny black behind them, and I suddenly remember that I had my appendix out and how my dad kept insisting all those times that I had appendicitis when everyone else said I didn't.

"You were right, Dad!" I croak out before they've even said hello.

They didn't fly here, they tell me, they drove. They figured they had to because they were going to have to take me and all my stuff home from Interlochen when I get out of here. They started this morning from Des Moines and drove straight through, stopping only to get gas and call the hospital. The first time they called, I was still in the OR, and Dr. Stark told someone to "tell them she's all right and it was her appendix."

"To keep from worrying, we listened to a White Socks game on the radio," Mom says.

"They beat the Yankees eight to seven," Dad says. "Just by the seat of their pants, too. It was a great game. Tommy Agee hit a double in the bottom of the ninth and got Robinson in from second base and that was it."

"I was so glad when they won," Mom say. "I knew if they won you'd be all right, darling, like it was a good omen or something."

The next morning, Dr. Stark comes in to check my incision and talk to us. He says I'm a very lucky girl, that my appendix had ruptured, probably several months ago, but instead of spreading through my body, the poison had gone into an abscess, which is why there is a rubber tube sticking out of my incision, to finish draining it out. I remember that night at home during spring vacation when I was listening to Brahms First Symphony and my temperature went up to 104 and I just know that's when the rupture happened and I guess that means I could have died that night, which makes it seem kind of unimportant that I'm missing my graduation, since if I'd died I would have missed a lot more than that, the whole, beautiful world, in fact. No Interlochen, no Oberlin, no violin, no Byron, no friends, no dating, no career, no getting married, no children, no grandchildren, just a lot of blackness followed by God-only-knows what. It ought to give me the creeps, thinking that, but somehow it doesn't seem very real, maybe because of the awful way I feel right now, so maybe it's a good thing I feel so awful.

I spend the next several days waiting for my next shot of pain medicine and for the nurse to bring me ice chips to wet my mouth even though I can't swallow. When the medicine starts to wear off, I start to hurt, but I learn by trial and error that if I breathe into the pain it hurts less than if I tighten up, which is like breathing out so your bow doesn't shake when you're nervous. To pass the time, I try to remember the Wordsworth poems I memorized for Mrs. Stocking's class, the one about the daffodils and the other one about the poet's heart leaping up when he beholds a rainbow in the sky. I visualize whole fields of daffodils even though I've never seen a field like that, and I think that if I ever get out of here, I'm going to go find a field of long, green grass and take my shoes off and lie on my back looking up into the blue and then I think the words "green pastures and blue skies" over and over, which is all I can think about so far. I can't think yet about going home, about coming back up here to Interlochen, about college in the fall or going anywhere else in the future, just green pastures and blue skies out there somewhere, waiting.

Meanwhile, people come in and out of the room all day and all night, doctors and nurses and visitors. Buffy Jean comes one evening with her parents and brings me a basket of flowers, and on Sunday Byron and Miss Malocsay, who are both Catholics, stop by together after mass and bring me a card that all the Project kids signed. They say it's getting hot outside, and the students back at Interlochen are swimming in the lake. They talk about the concerto winners' concert and I say it's a good thing I didn't win, since I wouldn't have gotten to play anyway. They tell me about W Clement Stone giving a speech at an assembly and asking for two minutes of silence and Byron says he looked at his watch and it was only a minute and a half, which is funny, but if I laughed it would hurt, so I don't. I don't want them to leave, but Byron says he'll try to stop back again, so at least I have that to look forward to.

Meanwhile, the other beds in my room are emptied and filled and emptied again. The little girl who had her tonsils out goes home and another little girl comes in who suddenly goes all rigid and funny and the nurse pulls the curtains between our beds and afterwards she tells me the girl had a "seizure." Then, in the middle of the night, they bring in a girl who's about my age, crying and swearing at the nurse, who's trying to get her to go to the bathroom on the bedpan. Later, she and I talk a little and she tells me she took a bunch of pills to try to kill herself but then got scared and had her friends bring her to the ER to have her stomach pumped, which she says was horrible. She says she goes to Traverse City High School and that the kids at TC High all think the Interlochen kids are a bunch of weirdos. In the evening, a whole gang of kids come in and pile onto her bed and sit there smoking until the nurse comes in and gets mad and chases them out, and I think about how some day, when I write my memoirs, this will make an interesting anecdote in the part about my adventures having my appendix out in Munson Hospital.

By the night of the honors convocation, they've taken my feeding tube out and I'm able to sit up and have Jello and water and clear soup for dinner. My mom goes to the honors convocation to get my awards while my dad sits with me and says things to try to comfort me. First, he quotes some French doctor I never heard of named Emile Coué, who used to look in the mirror every day and say, "Every day in every way, I'm getting better and better." Dad has lots of philosophical quotes like that which he loves to pull out at times like this, which is probably where I get my philosophical streak. Then, he starts telling me the same stories he told me when I was little, which always start out, "Once upon a time, there was a little girl who lived in a green house at the bottom of a hill," and when that isn't enough to get me crying he sings a little of the song we used to sing in two-part harmony that goes, "Show me the way to go home, I'm tired and I wanna go to bed, I had a little drink about an hour ago and it went right to my head," which does cause two tears to roll down my cheeks but I don't want him to see so I turn away and tell him I'm tired and I want to go to sleep and he leaves.

The next morning, my parents are both at my graduation, and I lie there imagining daffodils and green pastures and blue skies and kids marching up to get their diplomas and my mother going up when my name is called. For lunch, the food people bring me creamed chipped beef on mashed potatoes, which tastes wonderful, and I plan how I'll tell everyone that today I "graduated" to solid food so it really is my graduation day after all and maybe get a few laughs.

When my parents arrive, Mom gives me a play-by-play account of the two events that I missed. At the beginning of the convocation, she says, they announced that Cynthia Housh would not be able to give her Salutatorian address because she was in the hospital recovering from an appendectomy but that her mother would come up and receive her awards on her behalf. I got paper certificates for honors in English and violin and also a special little book with a blue leather cover for being salutatorian, and every time Mom went up to get one of these, the kids in the audience "went wild," she says, clapping more for me than for anyone who was there, so I guess that nurse in the doctor's office was right about at least one thing. Mom sets all my awards out on my bed tray and also my diploma, which has another blue leather cover, and she also hangs the gold tassel around my neck that I got for being salutatorian. I open the little blue salutatorian book and read, "Scholarship Award, presented to Cynthia Helen Housh in recognition of outstanding academic achievement and leadership by the administration and faculty of the Interlochen Arts Academy" and see that it's signed by Thor Johnson and Roscoe Bonisteel, who's one of the trustees, and dated 9 June, 1966 and that there's a little silver shield on it that says "Salutatorian" and another like it on my diploma.

Along with the certificates, my parents also bring me some yellow roses, a pretty pink nightgown they bought at Milliken's, a gold watch from Grandma and Grandpa Harter, and a whole pile of graduation cards from relatives, some of which have money in them. Then, a little while later, Byron and Waldie show up, and Byron gives me a little book called *Springs of Indian Wisdom*, inside of which he writes, "To Cynthia, on her Graduation Day, June, 1966, Byron." It's not exactly a love note, but I know that I'll keep it until the day I die, and when I open it and read the first quote, from someone named Bhartrhari, it seems like it was written just for me:

Even the severed branch grows again,
And the sunken moon returns:
Wise men who ponder this
Are not troubled in adversity.

This wasn't exactly the graduation day I imagined, but it was still better than just a plain day in the hospital. I can't help wondering, though, what I would have said in that speech I didn't get to give.

Chapter 43. University Woman

June 23, 1966

Dear Cindy,

Thanks so much for your interesting letter; it arrived yesterday and I'll reply that you may rest assured there will be no problem concerning your arrival on July 4. As we mentioned while you were confined, we can easily manage to accommodate your situation and have expected all along that this would be the outcome.

I will see to it that you are properly registered and I'll see Miss Glenn perhaps on Saturday. I understand that she is "bringing" several of her ESM students along, but I doubt that there will be any problem. I will assume that you want an hour per week and have this arranged accordingly. You may be interested to know that you will receive college credit (2 hrs) for the project classes this summer as well as for your other work here, so you will actually earn 6 credit hours for your total program. These will appear on the transcript you will receive, and will represent study at the U of M as a part of this summer session.

If you need something to do, try writing some beginning melodies, taking into account your knowledge of string instruments. As planned presently, each student will be responsible for writing a tune a day, so you can avoid being behind in this area, anyway!

I will speak also to Mr. Harsanyi on your behalf so that he will plan to use you to best advantage when you arrive. Someone (perhaps CG?) is scheduled to play the Brahms concerto on that first concert the week you arrive, incidentally!

I'm glad that you enjoy "Springs" and know that it will be meaningful to you always.

Your main job now is just to get a good, well-deserved rest so don't overdo as you regain your strength. In the long run you will come out on top if you rest while you can! I have no doubt that you will easily manage to handle your work here with your usual flair: never have I seen anyone who looked so remarkably "healthy" after an operation!

We're all anxious to see you real soon; I've relayed the news to your friends and they all join in wishing you the very best!

Regards,

Byron

Before I leave Des Moines for Interlochen on the Fourth of July, my parents make me promise that I'll lie down and rest some every day and that I won't push myself too much this summer but just try to have some fun. I take them at their word, which doesn't turn out to be too hard with only University Orchestra, Project classes, and violin lessons to worry about. I could, of course, audition for concertos, but to make things less stressful, I don't.

Playing in the University Orchestra is a lot different than playing in the World Youth Symphony or the Interlochen Arts Academy Orchestra. There are no challenges, and the conductor, Nicholas Harsanyi, is a soft-spoken little Hungarian who treats us like professionals and never gets mad at individuals the way Dr. Johnson did, which makes it easier to just enjoy the music. I have to admit, though, I don't practice orchestra music quite as hard as I did with challenges and the threat of TJ's wrath, but then I'm not supposed to be working so hard this summer, and I do practice some. Along with our regular concerts, one of our jobs is to accompany the Festival Choir in pieces for huge choir and orchestra. We accompany them on the Messiah, with Maynard Klein conducting, and again on a big modern piece called *Songs of Walt Whitman for Chorus and Orchestra*, written and conducted by Norman Dello Joio—I love that name! The Dello Joio piece, which sets four of Whitman's poems to music, was commissioned for the conference of the International Association of Music Educators, which takes place during the last week of camp. Interlochen during the conference is crawling with music educators speaking all sorts of different languages and popping in and out of rehearsals to observe, observe, observe. Some of them even come to our Project classes. Along with Dello Joio, two other composers, both Hungarians—Dmitri Kabalevsky and Zoltan Kodaly—whose *Concerto for Orchestra* the IAA orchestra played on tour last year—are here. Dello Joio and Kabalevsky are just regular-looking guys, but Kodaly has longish gray hair and a beard and reminds me a little of Walt Whitman, or maybe Buffalo Bill.

Meanwhile, the Project classes continue, also a little more relaxed now that Dr. Maddy's gone and the teachers are winding things up. Along with our usual assembly-line instrument learning, doing a second round with some instruments, we also get to star in a movie they're making of our classes. If you ever get to see it, I'm the tall girl in the back row with the trombone, glasses, and no chin. At the end of the summer, we have a recital in the Shed—a kind of mini-Bowl—to show off what the Project accomplished, in which we play solos on some of the instruments we learned. I play "Barcarolle" on the cello with Byron accompanying me, and it doesn't sound too bad. I didn't think anyone would come, but a few of the music educators from the conference do wander in and speak to our teachers afterwards.

And, of course, I still look forward to every lesson with Miss Glenn. She gives me more Paganini caprices to work on, along with the Beethoven violin concerto, which has a great cadenza by Fritz Kreisler. I can tell Miss Glenn still thinks I should have applied to Eastman, but she says that a friend of hers named David Montague is going to be teaching at Oberlin, on leave from Cornell, to fill the gap until they find someone to take the place of Stuart Canin, who left Oberlin at the end of last year to be concertmaster of the San Francisco Symphony, unfortunately. She tells me about her experiences as a concert artist and how when she played the Beethoven with the Philadelphia Orchestra, Eugene Ormandy was "just so mean to me" (she's obviously just joking) when he set the tempo for the last movement. She lists off all the concertos I'll need to learn in the course of my career and tells me which ones end soft, "so you don't get so much applause." And she still says things that make me feel good. One day, pausing from a session on the Beethoven, she says, "Cynthia, you're getting so pretty!"

If I'm any prettier, it's probably because as a University Woman, I have the privilege of wearing a blue corduroy skirt instead of knickers, which I do most of the time. My mom made me this great wrap-around with a zippered blue corduroy vest to match, and I do think I look pretty good in it, a lot better than in knickers. Also, I'm now wearing my hair in a bun on top of my head like a ballerina, a definite improvement on that old lady frizz I had last year, which is now all gone, finally, after a couple more haircuts.

In my new, more relaxed life at Interlochen, I do a lot of reading. I read Steinbeck's *The Grapes of Wrath*, *The Making of the President 1960* by Theodore H. White, and also three books Mom sent me from a list to be discussed in freshman seminars during orientation at Oberlin—a depressing novel about a schizophrenic girl called *I Never Promised You a Rose Garden,* a book on world religions called *The Faith of Other Men,* and a novel called *Nostromo* by

Joseph Conrad that I find impossible to get into and don't understand, though I make myself keep reading it. Sometimes I read lying in my lower bunk in the dorm, but most of the time I read on one of the green park benches in the main plaza, hoping that Byron will see me and sit down and chat, which he sometimes does. He says he thinks I'm doing that hoping "some guy" will come along and sit down and talk to me. When I admit that's true, he says, "Well, if you really want to attract people's attention, you should take the jacket off the book and put it on upside-down."

I spend a fair amount of time sitting on benches talking to Byron, actually, not only on my favorite bench on the plaza, but also on the sundecker looking out over the lake, where we spend an hour doing a crossword together one Sunday morning, and on Byron's favorite bench in Kresge, which is way at the back, which he says is where the acoustics are best because of the whispering gallery effect. If I go sit there before a concert, there's a good chance he'll wind up there too. We watch a whole concerto winners' concert together and critique the performances. A high school girl plays the Mendelssohn violin concerto like I once dreamed of doing, and Byron tells me how Mendelssohn was a boy genius who wrote most of his music when he was young and then just sort of pooped out and disappointed everyone who thought he'd be another Beethoven.

None of which is to say that Byron pays any more attention to me than he pays to his other Project fans, but I don't care. I just enjoy every minute I'm able to spend with him, listening to him talk about all sorts of interesting things.

And it's not just on campus that we Project kids spend time with Byron. The day I arrive back at Interlochen, which is July 4, he takes a bunch of us to Lake Michigan for a cookout, and this becomes a regular habit. Nearly every weekend, he drives some of us there, where we often stay until late at night, watching the sunset and looking at the stars, with Byron instructing us on the constellations and lecturing on anything and everything. We also climb up the sand dunes, go to the House of Flavors for ice cream and the Big Boy for hamburgers, visit the studio-store of an artist named Gwen Frostic, who designs stationery and calendars that are sold everywhere in northern Michigan, and one evening drive into Traverse City to see a hilarious movie called *The Russians are Coming, the Russians are Coming.*

My favorite times, though, are at Lake Michigan. I love sitting on the beach next to the charcoal fire at sunset, looking out at the broad expanse of silver-gray water and watching the colors begin to flair out as the sun slips down below the horizon. And I especially love those sunset times when Byron is quietly retelling Tolstoy's story of the three hermits or that scary story from Mark Twain about the golden arm. I want these times to last forever, and the fact that my Interlochen days are slipping away makes them all the more precious.

For already, I'm starting to think about Oberlin and wonder what my years there will be like. My mom forwards me a letter from a girl named Nancy who's to be my roommate in a place called Dascomb Hall. She's from Maryland and loves horseback riding, and I write her back and tell her about myself and Interlochen. And, of course, Mom is getting charged up to get my clothes and things together for college. She writes that she went to a white sale at Younkers and bought me towels and sheets and says Grandma has started knitting me another sweater. I just hope she doesn't offer to get me another permanent at Shinn and Lorenz!

A few days before camp ends, I invite Byron to go have dinner with my parents and me in Traverse City, and we make a reservation at a place called the Pinestead. Byron drives me there, so it feels almost like a date, but nothing romantic happens, of course. Later that night, he invites me to go with him

and another Project girl fan named Marty Wallace to take Marty's roommate
to where the train stops. Afterwards, the three of us go say good-bye to Lake
Michigan, and I wish like anything Marty wasn't there and I'm sure she wishes
the same thing about me. When we say good-night, I start to say good-bye,
since I don't know if I'll see Byron again before I leave, but he says he'll look
for me at breakfast in the morning, and when I get into the cafeteria, he's
there.

My parents are out in the car waiting for me, ready to go, and after we've
eaten, Byron walks me out to the car, draping his arm across my shoulder for
the first and only time, which helps a little, but it doesn't change the fact that
a few minutes later I'll be riding away from him and from Interlochen with
only my parents for company.

"Don't worry," Byron says. "You'll be back."

"You promise?" I ask.

"Sure," he says. "I promise."

Afterwards, I think that conversation made no sense. Why should I ask
Byron to promise that I'll come back to Interlochen when I'm the one who'll
decide if I do or not?

A few weeks after I get home, I write Byron a chatty, funny letter, but
somehow I know I'm not going to get an answer, and I don't. I know he got
the letter, though, because after I get to Oberlin, Violet, who's also a freshman
here in the Conservatory as a viola major, tells me that in a letter *she* got from
Byron, he told her to tell me hi and that he enjoyed my letter and laughed a
lot at the funny parts. It doesn't feel good that Byron wrote to Violet but not
to me, but by then I'm starting to get a crush on a boy named Danny in my
ear-training class, so I don't care all that much, really.

Walking across Tappan Square on moonlit nights, though, I sometimes
find myself thinking back. One afternoon, when Byron and a bunch of us

were lounging around on the Lake Michigan beach, relaxing after a big picnic lunch, I turned and said to him, "Someday I'm going to write a book about this place, about my years at Interlochen, I mean."

"Well, then, I'll sue you for whatever you say about me," Byron said. His tone was playful, but I can't help wondering if underneath it he was serious, as they say jokes can sometimes be. I don't know what I could say about Byron that was so bad he'd want to sue me, and he's never told me any deep, dark secrets, but I still can't help wondering.

I really hope he wasn't serious, though, because now that Interlochen is all in the past, that book is starting to write itself in my head, and I think I may actually have to put it down on paper someday. Maybe. Someday.

Part IV
Sound the Call

Chapter 44. The Book

All sorts of things happen in the years after I say good-bye to Byron on that August morning. Through all of it, though I don't return to the actual place for many years, Interlochen remains somewhere in the background, shaping my decisions, underlying my studies, and just being there, like a much-loved friend. And every now and then, its magical influence reaches out to shift my life onto a surprising new path.

At Oberlin, which consists of two institutions—Oberlin Conservatory and Oberlin College, I survive freshman year in the Conservatory, but the wondrous smorgasbord of liberal arts courses my College friends are studying are calling to me, and in the fall of my sophomore year, I switch to the College to major in English. In my junior year I start writing poetry, and in my senior year, a professor likes one of my short stories enough to publish it in a literary magazine he's putting together, and my writing career is launched, while my violin languishes in its case.

Meanwhile, there is also a war. A horrible, bloody machine of a war that grinds up human beings on the other side of the globe and refuses to end. At Oberlin, this war means battles over visiting Navy recruiters and marches and noon vigils and sit-ins and constant defiance towards The Establishment. Dorm hours, gender segregation, and grades have all gone out the window by my senior year. The protesters are all sure they're right, just as those pursuing the war are all sure they're right. But I, the English major daughter of a newspaperman, am never sure who's right about anything and remain on the sidelines, joining the noon vigils only after students are gunned down by National Guard troops at nearby Kent State a month before our graduation, when, to protest, we wear no caps and gowns.

In the meantime, I read Shakespeare and Hemingway and Henry James, do a stint on the college newspaper, join a co-op and bake bread and play volleyball, let my hair grow down to my waist, spend one glorious summer bicycling in Europe, survive half a dozen broken hearts, several loveless, shame-filled experiments, and a couple of pregnancy scares, and somehow wind up in Ann Arbor taking courses in the School of Education with the intention of becoming an English teacher.

This intention peters out after I meet an ex-sailor physics major named Jim Ferguson through an ad in the *Michigan Daily*, drop out of Ed School, spend a year working as a clerk typist at the University Hospital, get married, then rediscover the violin and, in January of 1973, enroll in the School of Music as a transfer student. By the winter of 1977, I have a second bachelor's degree in stringed instruments, a part-time job with the Toledo Symphony, a few private violin students, and an infant son, Matthew Leighton Ferguson, born July 25, 1976, an almost bicentennial baby. What I don't have, but covet, is a house—we're still living in a tiny upstairs apartment in an old house on Mary Street—or a car I'm allowed to drive—long story. What I also don't have, I'm beginning to realize, is a marriage to a monogamous, even-tempered husband who loves me just the way I am and shares my worldview and interests.

But I have faith that all that will be sorted out in due time and meanwhile, I manage. In the evenings when the symphony rehearses, Jim arrives home at 5:15, and I leave at 5:20 to catch a bus to take me to the UM School of Music, where another bus waits to take a bunch of us Ann Arbor musicians down to Toledo. Some weeks I do this every night, other weeks only once or not at all. The rest of the time, I stay in my upstairs nest with my beautiful baby boy, teach the odd violin student, practice my orchestra music, and read, read, read.

Much of what I read is novels, both popular and classic, but now I also, for the first time, devour lots of women's magazines, my favorite of which is *Redbook*, which I wait to receive each month. I love the essays by Margaret Mead and Judith Viorst and I love even more the short stories and novellas, which are all about young women like me, struggling to balance children and husbands and housekeeping and romances and careers. Inspired by them, I decide to try writing a short story of my own. In search of material, I sort through some old papers and come across the essay I wrote back at Interlochen for Mrs. Stocking's English class, "The Priceless Failure," with a big, red "48" at the top.

Reading through the essay, I'm fully aware of its bad title, bad ending, and stilted, pretentious tone. But I can see that there's a story there, and with a lot more showing and a lot less telling, I can make it into something. Sitting in our beanbag chair with a clipboard on my lap, I sketch out the plotline and begin to write. The result takes place not at Interlochen but at an unnamed conservatory and includes a long stream-of-consciousness during the character's disastrous performance of the Mendelssohn violin concerto. When I'm finished, having no idea whether it's good or bad, I send the story off, not to *Redbook*, but to *The Atlantic Monthly*, from which I get back an encouraging rejection letter.

At this point, Jim and I find the house of our dreams, complete with hardwood floors, fireplace, formal dining room, and porch swing, and I forget about writing and devote the next year to making curtains, shopping for a couch, and painting walls white. Then, one November afternoon, when I'm in our dining room sipping Lemongrass tea and looking out at the first snow of the year, I'm suddenly transported back to that other first snow long ago at Interlochen when, on a certain Sunday afternoon, I followed Jeff Higgenbottom's dark red ski jacket along the path next to the lake with "Misty" playing in my head.

I remember the story I wrote back on Mary Street from my English class essay, and it occurs to me now that I might expand it into a novel about my Interlochen years. As one scene after another comes back to me, stirring up longings, I ask myself what it was about those years that keeps drawing me back. Why have I always felt that no matter what craziness was swirling through my life, Interlochen was the still point at the center of it all? Was it the lake? Was it the freedom from bills and diapers and unhappy husbands? Was it the dreams of romance, more perfect for remaining unrealized? Was it the music, the literature, the ideas all being so beautiful and so new? Or was it the belief that anything was possible if I worked hard enough?

I dig out the story I sent to *The Atlantic Monthly* and reread it. If I'm going to do this, I decide, I'll need to start from scratch. That night, on the bus to Toledo, I begin free-writing about Interlochen in an old spiral notebook, promising myself that I'll fill two pages every night. By summer, I've filled two hundred pages and made up a chapter outline, and by fall I'm starting to write my first draft. But while re-reading James Joyce's *A Portrait of the Artist as a Young Man* for the umpteenth time, I start thinking about the fact that my character, like Stephen Daedalus, needs to have a childhood, and I spend more months free-writing about my own childhood. Before long, I have over a thousand pages of experiments, and although I don't wind up with a workable manuscript, the writing process serves as a form of self-therapy that leads me out of my first marriage, yellow house, music career, and narcissistic straight-jacket, through various fantasies, heartbreaks, journeys, jobs, academic programs, and, eventually, into a whole new life in an ever-expanding world.

All this happens because I got nervous and bombed the Mendelssohn violin concerto at Interlochen and wrote an essay about it for Mrs. Stocking. Which I wouldn't have done if Louis Feldman had sat at a different table that day.

Chapter 45. The Call

Another twenty-odd years unfold before I get the call that finally brings me back to Interlochen. I move out of the yellow house, start a stillborn PhD in English, get a divorce, spend a year writing fiction and overdosing on rejection letters, work as an editor for a UM research center, play chamber music, binge on psychotherapy and twelve-step groups, play three seasons in the Ann Arbor Symphony, survive more broken hearts, decide to become a therapist, volunteer at a crisis center, start taking psychology courses, and answer personal ads in the *Ann Arbor Observer*, one of which is for a "DWM, 46, psychologist, PhD, reflective, athletic, looking for female companion with similar temperament."

Ira, my Prince Charming, makes all the men who broke my heart look like frogs. A genius of a child psychologist with a thriving private practice in West Bloomfield, he grew up in a poor Jewish family in Brooklyn, played basketball, went to night school, married, taught in an inner-city school, came to Ann Arbor in 1973 to get his PhD, stayed on, worked at a hospital, started his practice, had a daughter the same year I had a son, spent some years in therapy preparing to leave his daughter's mother, and got divorced. The fact that both of us felt bullied by our ex-spouses gives us plenty to talk about, in addition to my budding interest in mental health, for which he serves as a superb mentor. We spend a year co-habiting before getting married in our living room in August, 1992.

I apply for social work school and get my MSW at UM, spend a couple of years seeing everything from infants to elderly at a clinic in a nearby factory town, join a Zen temple, pass my ACSW exam, start a private practice in Ann Arbor, begin building a specialty in adult ADD, read a lot of books about organizing and clutter, and become fascinated with the issues people have with the things in their lives, about which I will later write two books.

When I get the call that reunites me with Interlochen, it's 1998, I'm about to turn fifty, and I'm in Lenox, Massachusetts, where Ira and I go for an annual feast of Tanglewood concerts and summer stock theater. When I check my phone messages one afternoon, one of them is from someone named Fred Sanders. I don't recognize the voice, but I do recognize the name, that of a trumpet major from the class behind me, not a kid I ever got to know. Fred explains that he's been trying to track down other alums in preparation for a reunion of IAA sixties grads that's happening at Interlochen in October. He particularly wants to know how he can reach Buffy Jean Perkins, having remembered that we were roommates and wondering if I might be able to help.

I've long since lost touch with Buffy Jean and have no idea where she is, but I return Fred's call anyway. We schmooze for over an hour, reminiscing about our years at the Academy and exchanging news about the people we knew. I learn that Kenny Jacobs is now a big-name composer and critic, that Suzy Smock, Jake Levine, and Louis Feldman are all lawyers, and that Jeff Higgenbottom is teaching trombone at the University of Wisconsin. Annie and Ida Kavafian, my fellow Project-student David Shifrin, and various pianists are all concert artists and many others are in major symphonies or otherwise distinguishing themselves. A few classmates have died, including the "whole rest of the trumpet section," Fred tells me, and I wonder if this includes Ricky what's-his-name, the pimply little trumpet-player who told Buffy Jean I wasn't good enough for Jeff.

By the time I hang up, I've decided to go to the reunion in October, and Ira wants to go, too. But as the date approaches, I start to have second thoughts. This will be the first Interlochen reunion I've ever been to in over thirty years. Will Byron be there? Will Jeff? What will they think when they see me? I don't look the same, though without that French poodle hairdo, I think I may actually look better now. But I haven't become a concert artist or played with a major symphony or done anything else spectacular compared with some of my fellow-alums.

Then I have an idea. I call up a woman named Gretchen who runs the alumni program. I tell her I'm coming to the reunion in October and about the speech I didn't get to make as salutatorian of my IAA graduating class and how ever since then, I've been wondering what I would have said.

"Do you suppose there's any way I could make that speech at the reunion?" I ask.

She tells me that on the last night, they have a special banquet in which the alums are invited to share their experiences, which would be the perfect occasion for my belated salutatorian address.

After I hang up, I immediately start drafting my speech, which goes through various transformations as I pace around our living room, from recounting memories of romantic rejection and the Mendelssohn concerto disaster to trying to make my adult accomplishments sound as impressive as possible to letting all that go and thinking about my audience and what I might actually have to give them.

Then, one glorious October Friday afternoon, Ira and I are on our way up US 23 through the red-gold trees. Finally, we reach the spot where US-31 and MI-137 intersect and the "Interlochen corners" billboard used to stand—

replaced now by a green highway sign—and my heart speeds up. Gone are the old, tall Cracker Barrel bakery to which Cabin 16 hiked on Sunday morning and the crummy little motel that once enraged my parents by charging them for an extra night because they didn't check out by 10 am, but with delight I recognize the Hofbrau, a favorite faculty hang-out, after which we pass a lot of new triangular banners on posts saying "Art Lives Here." Then the familiar, old scholarship lodges start slipping by one after another, and suddenly I'm seventeen again, feeling the familiar old surge of excitement as we turn into the main entrance.

Coming in, I see that "Interlochen Center for the Arts" has replaced the old "National Music Camp and Interlochen Arts Academy" sign, the name having finally caught up with the institution it represents. After registering at the Stone Student Center, the knotty pine interior of which is exactly as I remember it, Ira and I head towards the scholarship lodge I reserved, rustic but serviceable. As we unpack, I feel nervous, but when we get to the opening cocktail party and I see only a lot of middle-aged men and women sipping drinks and nibbling at cheese cubes, I calm down. Not until I look at people's name tags do I discover who's actually inside these Halloween-costume bodies. Fred Sanders is here, and my old Academy stand partner, Jake Levine, and a number of other people I remember but barely knew, though I don't see any of the key characters in my own Interlochen story, alas. Buffy Jean isn't here, nor is Jeff Higgenbottom or Kenny Jacobs or Byron Hanson, who I'm told still teaches at Interlochen but is away at a reunion of his own at the Eastman School of Music. Missing too are Thor Johnson, Kenneth Jewell, and various other Academy faculty who've gone to join Dr. Maddy by now. But I do see our former housemother Mrs. Jewell; Miss Dustin, the young night nurse who took care of me when I was sick; and Don Jaeger, who gave us oboe lessons when we were in the Project. I feel a little burst of happiness each time I rec-ognize another familiar face.

The next morning, we're taken on a tour of the campus, where our guides show us the many new buildings that have gone up since we left Interlochen. These include a new drama center, an art museum and studios, a building filled with nothing but piano and organ studios, a jewel of a creative writing center built all out of pine logs, a chapel, a full-sized auditorium/ concert hall, and several new dormitories. Between these new buildings, the old ones are mostly still there, including Kresge, the Bowl, millions of cabins, and the Fine Arts building, where Mrs. Sexton taught her string teaching classes, I played my senior recital, and Burt gave his eulogy for Dr. Maddy. The round classroom buildings are all the same, and the long, glass-lined concourse that connects them, with all the glass cases now filled, but JVS, the gymnasium/ auditorium where we played our academy symphony concerts is now a well-stocked library, with the music library in one wing, occupying space where we once had string challenges and Project classes.

On our way from building to building, we encounter students here and there, still wearing blue and blue, but slacks instead of knickers, which are now worn only for special occasions, we learn. In the afternoon, we're free to drift in and out of classes. Ira and I go to the drama center and watch a play being blocked, sit in on some of a choir rehearsal, wander among the closed cabins in High School Girls, and end up sitting on the sundeck overlooking Lake Wahbekanetta, where I agonized over my academy admission and where Byron and I once worked a crossword puzzle on Sunday morning. Finally, it's time to go back to our cabin and get ready for the banquet.

I've brought along a dark red dress to wear and a scarf decorated with autumn leaves, and as I tie my hair back in its usual pony tail and read through my speech a couple of times, I feel the same knot in my stomach I used to feel before challenges. At least I don't have to worry about my bow shaking, I think. Anyway, I'm an adult now, and not just any adult, but an adult therapist who knows lots of good cognitive coping skills. Being here as an adolescent is making me regress a little to my insecure seventeen-year-old self, which is normal for people at high school reunions, but I'm not seventeen, I'm nearly fifty, and if no one likes what I say in my speech, I'll still have a great marriage and family, a nice home, an MSW, and work that I love. Nothing will have changed, however my speech goes. Self-talk, that's what this is now called, not much different from PMA.

The banquet is held in the Fine Arts Building, which has been set up with round tables and a platform along one side and decorated with fall colors and candles. The food is better than anything I remember eating here in the sixties—chicken in a rich sauce, rice, vegetables, salad, hot rolls, and a fancy chocolate dessert. After we've eaten, Jake Levine, now an alum honcho who's serving as master of ceremonies, gets up and announces that it's time for us all to share what we've been up to since last we met.

As the sixties alums begin to talk, I'm surprised to discover that my own circuitous career path is not unique. I'm also surprised at how many alums have ended up with careers outside the arts, though often still enjoying them on the side, and how the arts they're now pursuing are often not the same ones they majored in here at Interlochen. Actors have become visual artists, musicians have become writers, dancers have become musicians. The talks progress around each table, with each person getting up to speak, one after another, and our table goes last. Finally, after all the other alums at my table have spoken, Gretchen seizes the microphone and announces "a special surprise." After Gretchen gives me a brief introduction, she comes over to our table and places a graduation cap on my head. Then I climb onto the platform to a recording of "Pomp and Circumstance," set my papers down on the lectern, and start to speak:

"Good evening," I start out, "I'm Cindy Glovinsky, Cynthia Housh in my Interlochen days, Class of 1966. I currently live in Ann Arbor with my husband, Ira, who is here with me tonight, and have a son, Matthew Ferguson, whom you may have heard on MPR or even NPR – he's a public radio whiz who's about to graduate from Michigan State – and a stepdaughter, Marni, who lives across the street from us. I'm on my third of three careers – first I was a part-time professional violinist and homemaker, then an editor at the University of Michigan, and am now a clinical social worker with a private psychotherapy practice. For reasons that will become apparent, I asked permission for a little extra time tonight to give a short speech, which is entitled "Closing the Circle: My Salutatorian Speech 32 Years Late." Before I give this speech, however, I need to tell you about the non-speech that is the reason why I asked to give the speech.

I tell them about the Salutatorian letter and my writer's block and how Providence intervened in the form of a ruptured appendix and how I've spent the last thirty-two years wondering what I would have said in my speech, which is why I've asked to give my speech tonight, "to resolve the issue once and for all." Having said this, I continue:

"So here we are in 1998, and having read the purple prose from my diary, I don't think I want to inflict the speech I would have actually given at age seventeen on you. What I think will work a lot better is to try to give the speech I would have given in 1966 if I had known what I know now, in 1998.

"So let's imagine. It's 1966, we're in Kresge Auditorium, the orchestra is spread out across the stage, the spotlight is on the podium, and I'm standing before you, looking just as I did then, but knowing everything I know now. Of course, I'm not going to tell you I know everything I know now or you would cart me away – I have to be kind of subtle – so . . .

"Fellow students, faculty, staff, trustees, parents, and friends: I come before you this evening to talk about our future, about where we, the Gifted Youth of America, are going to be at the dawn of the 21st century. What will have become of us by then? Well, first the bad news: take a good look around you. Some of the people you see, possibly even you, will no longer be here at all by then, anywhere except in the memories of those who are left, the lucky ones. Of the rest of us, some will be sitting on mountaintops, having spent our lives so far in one long climb to the very pinnacle of our chosen profession. Others will still be wandering over the broad plain of life, trying this and trying that, never becoming a Somebody but having a lot of fun. Most of us will be making our way up one hill and down another, sometimes pausing to admire the view or take a short side-trip. Many of us will have careers in the arts; some will not. All of us will use a thousand things we learned at Interlochen in ways that we can't even imagine now, and some of the most seemingly irrelevant things may turn out, in fact, to be the most important. Who knows, maybe even the stuff we learned in Mr. Mendel's government class, the one we had to take to graduate, all that trivia about grand juries and congressional committees and impeachment proceedings – maybe we'll even find a use for that someday. Who knows.

"And someday, class of 66 and 67 and 60-whatever, as the new millennium approaches, we will come back. We will circle courageously back from our many paths to Interlochen, to each other and to ourselves at ages 15, 16, 17, finding in those past selves measuring sticks for what we have become. And we will ask ourselves, What have we learned since we left this place? Has it just been facts, or have we learned the really important lessons that life has tried to teach us? Have we come to terms with the way we look, the way we talk, the way we love, and all the kinks and curly-cues of our own unique brain chemistry? Have we learned to speak up for ourselves and voice our feelings? Have we learned to keep our mouths shut and listen? Have we learned to take risks? Have we learned to think before we act? Have we learned to make mistakes ourselves and to let others make mistakes? Have we learned to balance having a relationship and having a self? Have we learned to help others without controlling them? Have we learned to take care of ourselves? Have we learned that we need other people? Have we learned to get angry or to get vulnerable? Have we learned to face facts, all of the facts without leaving any out, either the facts that make us unhappy or the facts that make us happy? Have we learned to laugh and to play, to cry and to grieve? Have we learned to quiet ourselves? Have we learned to be where we are? Have we learned that we don't run the universe? Have we learned, finally, that even at age 40 or 50-something, we still have a lot to learn?

"If we have learned any of these things, whatever our bank accounts, our orchestra chairs or our curriculum vitae, whatever we may see in the mirror, we can count ourselves as among Interlochen's successful alumni. And we can be grateful. For we will circle back also to say thank you. Thank you, Interlochen, for giving us so very much of all that we are."

When I'm finished, I'm greeted with a standing ovation and fall into my husband's arms. Then we all get up and troop down to the stage of Kresge, where the students are dancing to the popular music of their day, and the women throw down their purses and the men loosen their ties and we make our way out among the 15- and 16- and 17-year-olds and dance and dance and dance.

Chapter 46. Old Friends You'll Meet

After that, Ira and I revisit Interlochen almost every year, mostly in the summers, going to World Youth Symphony concerts and high school dramas and using our cabin as a home base for excursions to Lake Michigan, the Sleeping Bear Sand Dunes, and the Horizon Bookstore in Traverse City. These trips help keep me sane through my fifties as one of the 99%, years of struggling to get a small private practice going in a town with too many other therapists, skyrocketing private health insurance bills, two years of community college teaching that fail to lead to the salary and benefits we desperately need, and the hard decision to give up work that I love and, in 2006, take a nine-to-five university admin job with great benefits in order to keep us solvent. Depressed over career disappointments and seeing nothing on the horizon but ten years of office drudgery, I survive by making notes for a book on office workplace issues, listening to classical music on WRCJ, and joining an Episcopal church.

When Ira and I arrive at Interlochen for a brief visit in 2007, we learn that a reunion of camp alums is happening that weekend. The possible attendees include everyone who's ever been to Interlochen, and there's not much chance I'll see anyone I know, but I decide to sign up anyway. I pay my $20 at the registration table and am given a free T-shirt and a schedule that includes a tour, a meeting with the current president, a group photo, an ice cream so-cial, a bonfire, and an alumni choir rehearsal for the Sunday service in Kresge. The alumni choir event immediately catches my eye. I haven't got a vi-olin with me, but I can still sing, sort of. I find my way to the rehearsal hall, sit down on one of the folding chairs in the alto section and am soon happily rehearsing Mendelssohn's anthem, "How Beautiful are the Feet." My voice is hoarse at first, but the more we sing, the better it feels. I'm making music at Interlochen again! The next morning, I'm on the stage of Kresge with other aging alumni in white shirts and blue pants, hearing the same chimes, singing the same "The Lord is in his holy temple," and listening to the same "Camper's Prayer" I remember from Sundays long ago.

Singing at the Interlochen service inspires me, after I get back to Ann Arbor, to call up the music director of St. Andrew's Episcopal Church, Debo-rah Friauff, a fellow IAA graduate, class of 1980. Deborah says she'd be happy to have me in the choir, and I ask her to recommend a voice teacher. She rec-ommends Wendy Bloom, and I have my first lesson a few weeks later. Wendy is a radiant, black-haired forty-something with a love of laughter and birds—her studio window overlooks an assortment of diversely attended feeders—and a voice like vanilla ice cream.

Working with Wendy and singing in the St. Andrew's Choir does won-ders for my post-menopausal, over-the-hill, failed career blues. Now, I want to sing and sing, everywhere and anywhere: in the bathtub, over the ironing board, in the car, walking through the woods. My soprano isn't exactly Nancy Jayne's on that high A that brought tears to my eyes back at Interlochen, but it does give me some of the silvery voice feeling I discovered with "Shall We Dance" at the age of eight, only this time the silvery voice is my own!

Taking up singing opens up whole new musical vistas for me to explore. I sing art songs with Wendy, choral music with the St. Andrew's choir and the University of Michigan Choral Union, Broadway tunes in musical theater performances, opera choruses in a local performance of Verdi's *La Traviata*, and the Mozart Requiem in a performance at Carnegie Hall under UM conductor Jerry Blackstone. All this happens because I sang in the alumni choir at Interlochen, another instance of the place reaching out to steer me onto an exciting new path when all seemed bleak.

The summer after I first sang in the alumni choir, Ira and I are sitting on the wall outside Kresge during a World Youth Symphony (WYSO) rehearsal, when I notice a familiar, wiry figure hurrying up the aisle to speak to the conductor, then retreating back up towards the rear of the auditorium, then moving off to one side, as though trying to observe the orchestra from different vantage points. Looking again, I'm almost sure from the hurried walk that the figure is my old friend and hero, Byron Hanson, whom I haven't seen since 1971, when I ran into him at a performance by the Canadian Opera Theater in Ann Arbor's Hill Auditorium.

After the rehearsal ends and we head out of Kresge, I see this possible Byron sitting at a picnic table hunched over some scores, and I walk over to the table, hesitating.

"Byron?" I say. He looks up. Yes, it's him all right. His hair is gray, but he still has the same, fox-shaped face and intelligent eyes. I tell him who I am and his face lights up. As we exchange sound-bite versions of our life stories over the last 36 years, I notice that Byron's movements are a little jerky and wonder if something neurological could be going on. Has he had a stroke or is this just old age? He tells me he's now the band director at the Academy and that Ann, his wife, runs the human resources department. Waldie's also here for the summer, he says, but spends his winters in Florida, having taught at Florida State after leaving Interlochen.

The next afternoon, during a rehearsal with WYSO and the Festival Choir for a performance of Mahler's second symphony, in which we alums have been invited to participate, I catch a glimpse of Byron back where we used to sit during my last summer at Interlochen, though the seats are now beige-and-orange theater seats, not green park benches. When the rehearsal's over, I go out to greet him again and he introduces me to Anne and some friends.

We chat some more and I tell Byron that I've been thinking about writing a book about my Interlochen days. This is the absolute truth, a result of reading Julia Cameron's *The Artist's Way* and doing "morning pages," discovering in the process that the Interlochen story I abandoned years ago needs to be a memoir, not a novel.

"A great idea," says Byron. "If you need any help, let me know." We exchange email addresses, and I write to him as soon as I get home. In September, Ira and I spend a long weekend at the Stone Hotel, where Byron meets me in the lobby for a two-hour chat, during which he pours out all sorts of information, ideas, and opinions. I scribble like a madwoman in my big spiral notebook, knowing I probably won't use one-tenth of what Byron's telling me, but since I can't tell which tenth that will be, I try to write down everything.

We talk about when the theater seats went into Kresge and when the present-day Interlochen store was built. We talk about the politics of Interlochen, the tension between the camp people and the Academy, and the crisis and power struggle that followed Dr. Maddy's death. We talk about Dr. Maddy and Thor Johnson and other people we both knew, and Byron tells me where I can find some of them, including Dr. Maddy, whose headstone in a Traverse City cemetery is marked with the Interlochen logo.

We talk about the Project and I ask Byron what he really thought of the "Maddy Method." He calls it "old-fashioned" but also "efficient." Byron remembers Dr. Maddy scolding him one morning because he forgot to put the day's plan on the wall under the motto that was inscribed at the top of every classroom blackboard, "Good teaching: every student is productively occupied every moment." If I really want to understand Dr. Maddy, Byron says, I should take a look at Dale Carnegie's success books.

By the time we've finished talking, I have ten large pages of detailed notes plus various documents Byron found to give me. When I get home, I email Byron to thank him for his extraordinary help, and this leads to six years of intermittent correspondence during the times when I'm working on the book, which I have to put on hold a few times because of other commitments. In the summer of 2009, I learn that Byron has Parkinson's Disease. No longer able to conduct, he retires from his band director job and instead becomes Interlochen's first archivist, with an office in the library, from which he organizes information on Interlochen's history and writes a monthly column for *Crescendo*, Interlochen's newsletter. As I draft one chapter after another, every time I have a question, I email Byron and get a lengthy response filled with interesting tidbits.

Meanwhile, I start doing some interviews with alums and former faculty and reading those few books that are relevant to my subject. I read Norma Lee Browning's *Joe Maddy of Interlochen: Profile of a Legend*, a book of loving testimonials about Dr. Maddy. I read *Interlochen: A Home for the Arts*, a fact-rich history written by one of Interlochen's former presidents, Dean Boal. I read Louis Nicholas's biography, *Thor Johnson, American Conductor*. And yes, I finally read *Success through a Positive Mental Attitude* by Napoleon Hill and W. Clement Stone. Because both Stone and Maddy won Horatio Alger awards, I read several rags-to-riches stories by Horatio Alger, Jr. And because Stone's PMA dogma was derived from that of Emile Coué, whose words, "Every day in every way, I'm getting better and better," my dad quoted to me when I was in Munson Hospital, I read Coué's little book, *Self Mastery through Conscious Autosuggestion*, and because Stone refers to the novel, *Magnificent Obsession* by Lloyd C. Douglas, which I read in junior high, I reread that book. At which point, I realize that I'm starting to use reading ever more esoteric books as a way of putting off writing and decide I'd better stop and get to work.

From these books, I learn all sorts of things that I either didn't know in my own Interlochen days or only half knew. I learn, for example, that founding and presiding over Interlochen was only one of Joseph E. Maddy's major accomplishments, that although he never went to college, he was a pioneer in at least two other fields—public music education and radio—and taught at the University of Michigan School of Music. I also learn what a brilliant persuader Maddy was, that he could talk anyone into anything, at least where donating money and services to Interlochen was concerned, and what a colorful personality he had in his younger days. I learn that he always talked, walked, and drove fast, that he once buzzed Kresge in his private plane, that his extreme financial risks drove his business advisors crazy, and that he was perpetually having holes dug for buildings he had no money to construct, though sooner or later he always seemed to magically come up with the cash. I learn too, how close the Academy came to not happening at all and how Maddy's persuasiveness and Stone's generosity converged just in time for the school to open in the fall of 1962. In other words, I learn what a benevolent genius the elderly man I remember really was.

Along with learning more about Dr. Maddy, I also learn new things about the founding of Interlochen and its philosophy. I learn that Maddy's endeavors in public music education, radio, and the creation of Interlochen were part of a movement to democratize music that could be traced back to the Andrew Jackson era and beyond, at a time when American public education was evolving from one-room schoolhouses to large, multi-grade, bureaucratized school systems. I learn that Maddy and his equally colorful co-founder, Thaddeus P. Giddings, whose belief in competition as a motivator led to the Interlochen challenge system and who died before I arrived on the scene, didn't just make up all their ideas and methods but inherited many of them from their predecessors and predecessors' predecessors in the rapidly growing field of music education, which both men did a great deal to advance.

I learn about the battles surrounding the founding of the Academy, which many of the trustees opposed, the chaos resulting from Maddy's death during my senior year, the challenges faced by his successors, and the events that took place after I left Interlochen as the institution continued to grow and change in response to social and economic pressures. Administratively, the battles after Maddy's death could be summarized as traditionalists vs progressives. Fortunately, neither side seems to have prevailed, so that when we alums visit Interlochen, we find that the theme is still played, though not so often; the kids still wear blue and blue, though mostly not knickers and cords; *Les Préludes* continues to end the camp season from the Bowl, though two weeks earlier than when we were campers; and competition is still used for motivation, though instead of weekly challenges, students play auditions for faculty every few weeks and collaboration is also emphasized.

From Nichols' biography, I learn what a musical giant Thor Johnson was, and how lucky my Academy friends and I were to get to work with him for a few years. I learn that he was one of the few American-born conductors of his generation to make the big leagues, with a Horatio Alger biography like those of Joseph E. Maddy and W. Clement Stone. Johnson began his music education in the public schools in Winston-Salem, North Carolina, attended the University of North Carolina and University of Michigan, and was one of a handful of promising young conductors—Leonard Bernstein was another— whom Serge Koussevitsky chose to work with at Tanglewood. He studied with famous European conductors in Salzburg and Leipzig, conducted the Cincinnati Symphony for eleven years, taught at Northwestern University, organized

Moravian music festivals, toured with the Chicago Little Symphony, and was appointed by the U.S. State Department to serve as a cultural ambassador in the Far East and elsewhere during the Cold War, an era in which musicians occupied a special role as both peacemakers and propagandists. With such a resume, I can imagine that Johnson must have found working with a bunch of kids for a few years in the north woods awfully tame, which might account for some of his more impatient moments with us during orchestra rehearsals.

The books I read shed light on some of my own Interlochen experiences, yet from a twenty-first century standpoint, I can't help feeling that they don't tell the whole story. What jumps out at me now is that Interlochen was created by two white American males, with the help of various other white American males and females, whose cultural background shaped their artistic choices as well as their approaches to music education. The music played at Interlochen in the mid-sixties was almost entirely European classical, with only an occasional foray into jazz or non-Western music, and the other arts were probably similarly limited. Furthermore, as white male Americans, Interlochen's founders were raised on large doses of what Max Weber called "the Protestant ethic." According to this ideology, it was not possible to work too hard or be too responsible for one's own individual success or failure. Work was everything, stopping to smell the roses a waste of time, empathy was weakness, and if anyone failed at anything, it was not because of bad luck or lack of talent or social injustice but because he or she hadn't worked hard enough.

What I don't yet know, as I continue to read and interview, is that my memory is about to be given a far bigger boost than I ever dreamed possible. In the fall of 2009, my son Matt introduces me to a new computer plaything called "Facebook." At first I use this only to reconnect with extended family and watch videos of grandchildren, but friend requests soon start coming in from Interlochen classmates, even people I barely knew there, and I connect up with Facebook groups for Sixties Academy alums as well as Interlochen alums at large. Now, whenever my memories are hazy on a subject, I put up a post asking for help and get a whole slew of gap-filling comments.

Finally, one Sunday night in November, 2011, my phone rings, and I hear a low-pitched female voice with a Southern accent that sounds remarkably like . . . Can it really be? Yes it can, it is, after nearly fifty years—the missing Buffy Jean! She saw my contact information on a social network site called Classmates, she says, and thought she'd give me a call.

We spend the next two hours telling each other our whole adult life stories and reminiscing about the days when we shared the room with the powder blue door. Buffy Jean now lives in Kingsport, Tennessee and is the single mother of twin boys, now grown men with families of their own.

When I last heard from Buffy Jean, she was selling pianos and organs in a music store, and in sales, she now says, she found her calling. As she speaks, I think about how Buffy Jean's attractiveness and networking skills must have served her well in business. Thus, while we musicians and artists struggled to make ends meet, Buffy Jean won prizes for her sales skills and ended up managing a big piano and organ store, buying her own home, and purchasing first-rate instruments for herself while raising her sons.

Then the bottom dropped out of her success story. Buffy Jean developed severe gastric problems that led to surgery that took many hours. "I flat-lined several times before it was over," she tells me. "I'm lucky to be alive." Part of her colon had to be removed, which left her disabled and unable to work, though she still lives a full life, enjoying her grandchildren, going out for lunch with friends, exercising, and even traveling when she can.

"Are you going to the reunion?" Buffy Jean asks.

"Absolutely," I say. "How about you?" The upcoming reunion is to be held during graduation week the following June to celebrate the Academy's fiftieth anniversary. While most other reunions are only for alums from certain years, this one is for everybody who's ever gone to the Academy as well as those who taught and worked there. Buffy Jean says she's not sure she can make it, but she eventually decides to fly to Detroit and ride up to Interlochen with me from Ann Arbor. Meanwhile, Ira, who had planned to come to the reunion with me, discovers a conference he has to attend, so I invite Buffy Jean to share my room at a nearby Marriott, all the cabins on campus being full.

"Will that be okay with you?" I ask her.

"Cindy, I lived with you for two years," says Buffy Jean. "I think we can get along for a few days."

On the day of Buffy Jean's flight, I drive to the Detroit airport where, standing next to the luggage carousel, I see a face I recognize on a stout, busty woman with wavy hair. The face lights up when its owner recognizes me, and a moment later, I'm enfolded in a familiar, Texas-sized hug.

Back at our house, when Buffy Jean opens her suitcase, she presents me with two big yellow envelopes filled with papers from Interlochen that she's kept through her various moves, invaluable for my book research. "I kept every piece of paper that was ever put in my mailbox," she tells me. "I don't know why I kept them all these years, but I did. I always knew they'd come in handy if I kept them long enough."

The next morning, we pile everything into the car and head up US-23 towards Interlochen while listening to a CD of the Johnny Mathis songs we played during our years together and belting out the lyrics of "Chances Are." By mid-afternoon, we're at the Marriot unpacking, after which we drive on up MI-31 to Interlochen Corners.

The reunion begins with a cook-out on what's now called Osmond Plaza, the big main area where the green park benches have been replaced with circles of wire seats that remind me of the rollers we used to wear in our hair. Alums spanning six decades are arriving and greeting and we soon begin to connect with some old 60s friends. Burt Merrill is there, and Frances Fagan, a red-haired woman violist I knew who now plays in the Detroit Symphony, and Nina Cohen, a suitemate of ours who was an art major, and Jim Westlake, a clarinetist who's now an accountant, and Gloria Payne, a singer who was one of the few African American students when I was here.

Finally, a distinguished-looking man comes up and joins the group, and I wonder who this could be. I lean forward to look at his name-tag and feel my heart skip a beat: It's my old crush, Jeffrey Higgenbottom! Fortunately, this gentleman doesn't look at all like the Jeff I remember, so I can talk to him like he's somebody else. Maybe it's time I laid my cards on the table, I think. Make a joke of it and clear the air.

"Oh, if it isn't the great love of my life!" I blurt out, expecting laughter but not getting any.

"I'm sorry," I say, "it's just that I had the biggest crush on you back in the day. All in the past, of course. The far distant past. Like I say, it was the biggest crush, but then Buffy Jean spilled the beans to you and you told your friends and they all made fun of me . . ." I'm talking faster but still getting no laughter. Instead, the distinguished man looks at me like I'm from another planet.

"I'm sorry," he says, "I just don't remember anything about that." He turns away to talk to Francis, with whom I remember he used to be friends.

"Well, that went over like a lead balloon," I say to Buffy Jean as we walk on, giggling like sixteen-year-olds.

"I told you he was stuck-up," says Buffy Jean, "I knew that even back when we were kids. I always told you that."

"Oh, I still think he's shy," I said. "I probably embarrassed him."

"Huh," says Buffy Jean.

The days and nights that follow are filled with concerts by alum soloists and groups, a collage-concert in which some of us perform, a reading at the Writing House, financial presentations and administrative updates, cocktails and banquets in a big white tent, late-night bar-gatherings, and a dance with a live band on the last night.

At night, in our twin beds in the dark, Buffy Jean and I remember how we used to talk after lights out, and I remind her about the time she talked in her sleep about me playing football with a pink rose on my helmet. I tell her I've always wondered if that really happened or if she was just messing with me, but she says she can't remember, so I guess I'll never know.

"It's too bad your old flame Kenny Jacobs didn't make it to the reunion," I say. "I wonder if he still tells that story about Mrs. Duderstadt reciting the poem about the tree."

"I think that I shall never seeee, a poem lovely as a treeee," says Buffy Jean in a shaky, old lady voice, just as Kenny once did. "He later came out as gay, you know."

"I bet half the boys we knew here later came out," I say. "I think back then, most of them were just trying to figure themselves out."

"And half the faculty. I heard there was a purge in the seventies and some of them got fired. I wonder what happened."

"I heard that too," I say, turning over my foam rubber pillow, struggling to make it fit my neck. "But of course, it's all different now. I saw a sign in the concourse about a support group for LGBT students—not something you would have seen back in our day, that's for sure. I'm not sure Dr. Maddy even knew what homosexuality was, or maybe he just didn't want to know, with Van Cliburn and everything. Even sex between boys and girls wasn't talked about much, except in biology class. I remember Miss Appelhof being quite explicit and Bobbi Leibowitz asking the most embarrassing questions ..."

"Remember NBC?" Buffy Jean giggles.

"Of course," I say. "No Bodily Contact. Not that it was always observed. Remember date gate? Kids smooching right in front of the counselors, who were supposed to intervene if things got out of hand."

"And the breezeway," said Buffy Jean, "with girls pushed up against the wall. And there were other places .... "

"What amazes me," I say, "is that none of us went home pregnant, at least as far as I know. The grown-ups really did have a job on their hands, now that I think about it, with no Planned Parenthood or anything. But how did we all keep from going nuts? I mean, I guess there were a few suicide attempts, but not that many, considering all the pressure. The counselors were just a bunch of senior citizens. And I don't think they even had a psychologist on staff back then. There wasn't any good medication you could take if you were depressed, which most of us were, being adolescents. Nobody'd ever heard of ADHD or dysfunctional families, and meditation was something only Indian gurus did. We didn't even know that aerobic exercise made you less depressed. We didn't even know what aerobic exercise was. All I knew myself was what my dad told me, which was that I had an inferiority complex. How did I survive?"

"How did any of us?" says Buffy Jean.

***

In August, 2013, I spend a week at Interlochen attending a workshop in memoir-writing given by Katey Schultz. While I'm there, Byron and I watch a video together of the movie that was made of us during the final summer of the Project. There I am, in the back row, playing a trombone and looking very serious, and there's Byron, younger than my son, wandering back and forth between the rows. I really don't look that bad, I think when I see myself—why did I always feel so ugly? While I'm there that summer, I give Byron a draft of the chapter "Interlochen Preview" from this book, the first chapter I've written that actually takes place at Interlochen, and ask him to go over it for me.

In September, Byron sends me an email with helpful feedback on the chapter. He also tells me that Ann is seriously ill, just had surgery, and may need more. I send him my best wishes and several more emails but receive none back. Then, in June, 2015, I learn, somewhat belatedly, of Ann's passing, from the IAA Sixties Facebook group, which I believe explains Byron's silence.

When I attend Jerry Blackstone's Adult Choir Camp at Interlochen the following summer, Byron, in his last month as archivist, gives an excellent history presentation to the group, and afterwards I chat with him briefly and express my sympathy. I can tell that losing Anne and his own illness have taken their toll, and I'm not surprised when a few months later I learn that Byron's moved into a retirement facility in Traverse City.

Meanwhile, I struggle to find the time to finish a presentable draft of my book, hoping that when it's done I can visit Byron and show it to him, not because I expect him to read it, but just so he can know that all the wonderful help he gave me wasn't wasted.

Finally, during an alumni weekend in October, 2017, Ira and I visit Byron and I hand him my draft, which he promises to read, though I'm not sure he's up to it. His speech is difficult to understand, and at times the Parkinson's overwhelms him, but he's still Byron and does his best to make us comfortable. Finally, it's time to say good-bye.

"I love you," I hear myself say as we clasp hands. Then, all at once, I realize that love is what it always was, the only kind that matters, though it never really dawned on me until now.

Not a crush—just love, even back in the day.

Postlude

Sometimes, when I travel back to inhabit the mind of that teenage violinist in blue corduroy knickers, I wonder what she would have said if I'd been able to tell her what's happened since last we met and perhaps transport her here for a glimpse of her future and that of her world.

"You've got to be kidding," I imagine her saying. "You say you work at home typing things into a plastic box and that the person you work with is in China and you talk to her on your computer every day and can even see her on a screen if you want to? How can you expect me to believe that? Last I heard, we weren't talking to *anyone* in China, much less on some kind of plastic box. And what are those funny little things I see people holding up to their ears as they walk, talking as if no one around them can hear anything? Has everybody gone crazy or what? Well, at least we're not all going to be blown to smithereens—that's a relief.

"But how are things in the arts? And what about Interlochen? It's still there, you say, a little bigger with some lovely new buildings, and there are still symphonies and museums and things. But some politicians are trying to get rid of the National Endowment for the Arts? What's the matter with these people? And a lot of public schools don't even have art and music classes any more—that's terrible. Dr. Maddy's probably rolling in his grave.

"And what about me? Where am I going to end up? Sounds like I'm not exactly going to stick to my plan of having a big music career, then running into Jeff Higgenbottom at a reunion and us getting married and having four kids, all musical. I knew my life might turn out a little different from that, but a social worker?! You've got to be kidding. I'm supposed to be shy—remember? I have an inferiority complex. How could I possibly wind up being a social worker, of all things?

"Well, I guess life must have a few surprises in store for me, and maybe it's better not to know too much. So, I'm off to practice for challenges now. Thanks for the preview, which I'll do my best to forget, and I'll see you again in about fifty years!"

Acknowledgments

Although this is my own personal Interlochen story, I received a tremendous amount of help in researching the book from former and current Interlochen students, faculty, and staff. Two individuals merit special mention. The first is Byron Hanson, a long-time friend and former teacher of mine and a distinguished Interlochen faculty and staff member, now retired, whose last job was as Interlochen's first archivist. Byron not only assisted me in pinning down all sorts of important details but also encouraged me to start this project and supported my efforts at every stage. The second person who provided a wealth of information and support to me was Interlochen Arts Academy alumna Muffet Hopkins Holloway, who had a habit of saving every piece of paper we received in our mailboxes, from which I benefited immeasurably, as she lent me this goldmine of information to copy and peruse, along with photographs and clippings. In addition, I want to thank the following individuals who provided support, information, and/or editorial help through interviews, informal conversations, Facebook posts, emails, and face-to-face meetings: Waldie Anderson, Harold Cruthirds, Kaye Curren, Rohn Federbush, Cheri Ferrari, Ken Giles, Leo Gillis, Jim Glenn, Sue Harwood, Paul Jackson, Don Jaeger, Jane Lenoir, Paul McGlothin, Judy Miller, Claudia Polley, Andrea Pedolsky, Sue Vreeland Sander, Katey Schultz, Deborah Shepherd, Wendy Van Vechten, Brian Wenk, Donna Wessel Walker, Jennifer Wesling, and members of the Interlochen Arts Academy 1960s alums Facebook group. I apologize to any helper I missed—there were so many! Special thanks to Jerry Dennis for his excellent editorial suggestions and for helping me to find the right publisher. Thanks to my editor, Laurie Rose, for her enthusiastic embrace of this book and her excellent work throughout the production process, for which I also thank the entire staff at Thunder Bay Press. And the biggest thanks of all to my husband, Ira, for his loving support throughout this journey and for patiently listening to me read the whole thing aloud on long winter evenings.

About the Author

Music, Lakes and Blue Corduroy: A Memoir of Interlochen is Cindy Housh Glovinsky's fourth published book. In her past career as a social worker, she published three non-fiction books with St. Martin's Press, and her poetry and fiction have appeared in various literary magazines. Born in Des Moines, Iowa, she attended the National Music Camp and Interlochen Arts Academy, from 1964 to 1966, and has degrees in music, English, and social work from Oberlin College and the University of Michigan. In addition, Ms. Glovinsky, who lives in Ann Arbor, Michigan, has played in the Flint, Toledo, and Ann Arbor Symphonies, sung in the University of Michigan Choral Union, attended the Bear River Writers' Conference, and returned to Interlochen many times for reunions, concerts, and workshops.